Who Do You
Think You Are...
Anyway?

Who Do You Think You Are... Anyway?

How Your Personality Style Acts... Reacts... and Interacts with Others

by Robert A. Rohm, Ph.D.
and E. Chris Carey

Atlanta, GA

Published by Personality Insights, Inc.
Post Office Box 28592
Atlanta, GA 30358-0592, USA
Telephone: (770) 509-7113
E-mail: info@personality-insights.com
http://www.personality-insights.com

ISBN 0-9641080-3-8

First Edition: February, 1997
Second Edition: May, 1997
Third Edition: January, 1998
Fourth Edition: August, 2001

Printed in the United States of America

Table of Contents

Foreword: Dexter Yager vii

Acknowledgments and Dedication viii

Authors' Preface ix

Introduction xiii

1. Understanding Personality Styles 1
2. "Blends" of Styles 25
3. "Combinations" of Styles 47
4. Traits of Different Styles 79
5. Recognizing Tell-Tale Traits 95
6. The Truth About You 109
7. 25 Great Insights About Personalities 121
8. DISCover Your Child's Design 135
9. DISCover Your Spouse's Design 177
10. DISCover Your Work Design 211

Appendix
   A. How to Read Graphs 251
   B. Understanding the Seven "D" Blends 256
   C. Understanding the Seven "I" Blends 272
   D. Understanding the Seven "S" Blends 288
   E. Understanding the Seven "C" Blends 304
   F. Understanding the "Even" or "Level" Pattern 320

Foreword

They say that inside every fat book there is a thin book trying to get out. You are holding in your hands a book that is big because of its muscle, not its fat.

Years ago, as I began my career in business, I searched for books that would help me to work more successfully with others. I still recommend that anyone who wants to succeed in life spend at least fifteen minutes every day reading a positive, uplifting book.

Robert Rohm's books are worth reading because he has a way of making new things seem familiar and familiar things seem new. So, if you are new to studying temperaments and personalities, he will relate these ideas in ways you can understand and apply in your life. If you are already familiar with the basic concept, he will show you "twists" and "angles" that may be new to you.

Mostly I appreciate Robert's special approach because he says we are not "stuck" where we are — our "labels" are not our limits. Each of us has been born with certain gifts, and we have acquired other skills to help us through life. But no one has it all. The good news is that we can learn whatever skills we are lacking for success with others. *Who Do You Think You Are Anyway?* will show you how you can grow to become all you were meant to be, how to adapt and adjust your personality style to become a more effective servant and leader.

By investing in this book, you have invested in yourself. You are going to see a tremendous profit in your relationships as you take this information and invest yourself in others.

— *Dexter R. Yager, Sr.*
Charlotte, North Carolina

Acknowledgments

No book is ever the product of one person's thoughts, experiences or discoveries. Rather, it is a compilation of the contributions of many people — some directly, some indirectly.

Much of my practical knowledge about the "DISC System" has come through association with Carlson Learning Company, Performax Systems International, and Target Training International, Ltd. (TTI), which have done much to advance the understanding and application of this model of human behavior. Particularly helpful has been TTI's textbook, *The Universal Language DISC, A Reference Manual,* by Bill Bonnstetter, Judy Suiter and Randy Widrick. In addition to thoroughly documenting the validity and reliability of the Assessment Profile Process, I have appreciated its practical applications of this information.

My good friend Charles F. Boyd produced much of the information contained in Carlson's family-oriented applications and has been a valuable sounding board for many of the concepts presented in this volume.

My co-author is Chris Carey, director of product development for Personality Insights. He worked with me closely on *Positive Personality Profiles,* visualizing our unique DISC symbols, designing and editing that book, and helping me to clarify the concepts. In this book, he has coordinated our research and contributed much to its contents from his experiences and insights.

My true friend Rick Herceg is director of customer service for Personality Insights. He has kept our company afloat over the months that Chris and I have worked on this book, and has been a valued counselor as I seek to apply these truths in my own life.

Lastly, thanks to those who may find their stories revealed in these pages. Some have been examples for inspiration, and some for caution. All have been examples of our need for understanding.

Authors' Preface

As we start this book together, I feel it is important to put a few things in perspective.

First, I want to express my delight at the reception given my first book on personality styles, *Positive Personality Profiles.* It was a labor of love to put those thoughts and ideas on paper that I have presented so often in seminars.

As that book's editor read my initial manuscript, he commented that I must have dictated my actual seminar into a pocket recorder for my secretary to transcribe — the book read the same way I speak! Well... I had! So we worked together on taking some of the "Southern" out of it and clarifying some of the ideas I presented. It appears our efforts were successful, as almost 100,000 copies are now in print — and even "Yankees" have written to tell us how helpful the information has been.

Fearfully and Wonderfully Made

It is also important to comment on the "flavor" of that book. When I wrote *Positive Personality Profiles,* I had my "pastor" hat on. By this I mean that my arena for speaking and teaching about personality styles was churches, Christian schools, colleges, and conferences. In fact, I was serving in a large Atlanta church as Minister of Adult Education during its writing and I presented my seminars in my off-time.

So, that book was written for my audience, people who shared many of my theological views and wanted to understand more about their own amazing and complex design — "I praise you because I am fearfully and wonderfully made; your works are wonderful, I know that full well" (Psalm 139:14).

Of course, I am not making an apology for writing in that style. I simply want to acknowledge the audience for which it was intended and explain some differences you may observe in reading *this* book.

Since that time, my audience has *changed;* rather, it has *enlarged.* I have spoken to nearly one million people outside of churches since *Positive Personality Profiles* was published. Readers who have never heard me speak "live and in-person" have written to say they are sharing this information in a variety of nonreligious settings. Some companies are even using *Positive Personality Profiles* as a corporate training manual. The "secular" reach of that book has been amazing.

A Cultural Perspective

While that is exciting (and flattering!) news to receive, *this* book has been written with less "evangelical flair," so that individuals who do not share my faith *can* share a broader frame of reference in understanding and applying this information.

Of course, it would be impossible to remove all references to God or the Bible from what I write — they inspire me and are a part of my daily environment. In fact, I believe it is impossible to understand our time and culture without reference to the Judeo-Christian truths that have influenced them.

Theodore Roosevelt wrote, "Every thinking man, when he thinks, realizes that the teachings of the Bible are so interwoven with our civic and social life that it would be literally impossible for us to figure what life would be if those teachings were removed."

Herbert Hoover said, "The whole inspiration of our civilization springs from the teachings of Christ and the lessons of the prophets. To read the Bible for these fundamentals is a necessity of American life."

Horace Greeley observed, "The principles of the Bible are the groundwork of human freedom."

Wernher Von Braun noted, "In this age of space flight, when we use the modern tools of science to advance into new regions of human activity, the Bible — this grandiose, stirring history of the gradual revelation and unfolding of the moral law — remains in every way an up-to-date book."

George W. Crane wrote, "I have gleaned more practical psychology and psychiatry from the Bible than from all other books."

So, whether you prefer to approach its contents as a basis for inspiration or as a source for literacy, understand that biblical references do enjoy an appropriate place outside theology. When you come across them in this book, I hope you will see that I have tried to apply them while considering that your perspective on religion may differ from mine.

A Basis for Understanding

Just so you know at the outset, and so you will understand that my efforts are not focused on "preaching" at you through the printed page, let me explain what we have had in mind as we put together this book. There are several core beliefs that give the information in *Who Do You Think You Are Anyway?* a meaning beyond their words:

1. *You are special and you are worth understanding.* As the creation of a loving God, I believe your *worth* exceeds your *work,* and that you deserve to understand yourself and to be understood by others. Of course, I also believe you owe that same debt to others — and that the information in this book can empower you to understand yourself and others in ways you never thought possible.

2. *You are different by design.* I will never meet anyone else who is exactly like you, and I understand that it is no accident that you are who you are. God's love of diversity is seen in all his creation — he distinguishes between every snowflake, butterfly's wings, and fingerprint, when he could have saved a moment's thought by making each of them identical. (I discovered recently that here are over 600 kinds of beetles. This is either an incredible waste of cosmic energy... or God truly delights in diversity within His creation.)

3. *You are capable of growth and change.* None of us is "stuck" with our personality's character flaws and weaknesses — God loves *balance* in our diversity and has given each of us the ability to become more than we are now.

If you and I can agree on the three basic statements I have put in **bold** type (even if we do not agree on the "plain text" that expands on the concept), then we have formed a solid basis for communicating and understanding the valuable information in this book.

Whatever your belief system, I know your personal and professional relationships will benefit as you gain a better understanding of yourself and others by reading *Who Do You Think You Are Anyway?*

Introduction

What this book is all about...

In my first book on personality styles, *Positive Personality Profiles,* we covered a broad overview of human behavioral traits. I explained the different styles of behavior and tried, by means of many stories and illustrations, to paint a picture of each personality type for the reader. We looked at the different personality styles and talked about "D-I-S-C" types.

We also touched briefly on the *blends* of personality styles, referring to the fact that no one is purely a "D," "I," "S," or "C," but a *blend* of each of these four, to a greater or lesser degree.

And we spoke briefly about *combinations* of personalities. In our use of this term, a *combination* refers to how people relate or interact with each other. You and I each have a distinctive, individual *blend* of personality traits that forms our own style, but when we begin to interact together, *we* become a *combination*. As we work together, we produce a *combination* that is unique to our relationship. So, in reality, *this* book becomes the next step, because it expands on the theme of *blends* and *combinations*. We will be taking your "personality insights" skills to a new level.

The first step is understanding a broad overview of personality styles. We will accomplish this in Chapter 1, as we review the "Theory and Model of Human Behavior." We will explain what we mean when we talk about your "personality style," and we will show you how to apply the easily-learned "D-I-S-C" concept to what you are learning about yourself.

In Chapter 2, we will begin to demonstrate how all of this works together within an individual person (*your* "blend"), and then we will see how it works in conjunction with another person (*our* "combination") in Chapter 3.

This is the focus of *Who Do You Think You Are Anyway?* — understanding your own unique *blend* and how it interacts in *combination* with others. As we continue, you will understand which styles are most compatible — and why. (Although relationships are not built solely on compatibility, we have less stress and are more productive when we learn to "get along" with one another. After all, isn't that what friendships and relationships are all about?)

The goal of this book is showing you how to *become* all you wish to be, rather than planting a label that simply says "this is what you *are.*" Labeling can be disabling — our purpose is to be enabling!

By the time you finish reading this book, you should be able to practice seeing life through the perspective of others. You should know what to look for in order to understand another person's style. You should begin to see an individual's potentially negative response to a work or social environment *before* it becomes a problem. And you should be able to find ways of adapting your own style to mesh more effectively with others.

Someone once said, "A problem well defined is a problem half-solved." It has also been said, "Half of any job is having the right tools." Well, here goes! I am about to give you *both* halves:

1.) Define the problem
2.) Give you the right tools

Two *halves* make a *whole*, don't they? So, keep reading. We won't define the problem without giving you the necessary tools. It will not be long before you should be well equipped!

Because of my background (school principal, teacher, speaker, father of four), I have learned that people most appreciate information when they receive it in a practical form and can apply it immediately — and this is our goal at Personality Insights. We strive constantly to present our material better and more clearly in each attempt.

Certainly, we are not "bragging" that we are *better* than anyone else in communicating these concepts. It is simply our desire to be extremely clear and practical in their application. We have received many letters from people stating that, although they had heard or read about personality types in the past, our materials have "turned their lights on," and really caused them to grasp this information. After all, we understand that we would be of no service to our customers and clients, nor would we keep an edge in such a competitive market, without this focus. Besides, as Babe Ruth once said, "It ain't braggin' if you can do it!"

So, let us know how we do in this trip to the batter's box — we hope it hits a home run for you!

Robert A. Rohm

Robert A. Rohm, Ph.D.
Atlanta, GA

PS: In the Appendix, we have placed a great deal of information relating to assessment tools and graphs that allow you to "see" yourself according to your own, unique preferences and behaviors. This information should not be neglected, but we felt it would be better to allow you to peruse it at your own speed and according to your own interest level. In this way, we will avoid utilizing a lot of "C" type data that might confuse the issue for readers just beginning their study of personalities and behavior styles.

 **WHO DO YOU THINK YOU ARE ANYWAY?**

Chapter 1
Understanding "Personality Styles"

What is "Personality"?

I remember one of my daughters showing me *five pages* of sermon notes she had taken in church one Sunday morning. The pastor had spoken on "Overcoming Adversity." As I marveled at the thoroughness of her notes, she said, "Dad, what *is* adversity? The pastor never *told* us, but it sounds pretty bad to me!"

I thought to myself, *Isn't that interesting?* In the field of communication, we should not take too much for granted, especially when listeners may not know what we are talking about or an audience might not be familiar with all of our terms.

So, in order to get the total picture as we discuss personality styles, we should begin by understanding what a "personality" actually is. *Merriam Webster's Collegiate® Dictionary* defines "personality" as: "³the complex of characteristics that distinguishes an individual or a nation or group; esp: the totality of an individual's behavioral and emotional characteristics." Another source cites "habitual patterns and qualities of behavior of any individual as expressed by physical or mental activities and attitudes; distinctive individual qualities."

Knowing what we mean (and *don't* mean) is important in our discussion of "personalities" and "styles." Therefore... *What is human personality?* How does it work and what characteristics does it possess?

Personality Components

An individual's personality style is made up of several different components. A personality is not simply a behavioral style, an attitude, or an outlook on life — it is much more complex than that! Our true personality encompasses nearly every known area of life.

Because more than anything else, our "temperament" (that is, the way we are "wired") tends to color or influence the way we view things, we often look at what we call a "personality style" (a style of "behavior") as the most predominant force in an individual's life.

But in order to understand a person's *complete* personality, we need to take some other factors into consideration, such as:
- (a) their environment,
- (b) home life,
- (c) family,
- (d) position in birth order,
- (e) where they go (or went) to school,
- (f) the education they received,
- (g) the level of education they achieved,
- (h) their particular vocation and,
- (i) how it fits into their everyday life.
- (j) gender — male or female plays an important role in their overall personality. (Males and females have characteristics that are distinctive to their unique physiology. It would be foolish to think that a man could ever understand what a woman feels and experiences when pregnant or after giving birth. Our gender, indeed, plays an important role in our total makeup.)

Then, we also must remember to factor in:
- (k) culture — where we grew up, in what part of the country (North, South, East or West),
- (l) nationality or ethnic origin,
- (m) present age and level of maturity — since "you can be sixteen only once, but you can be immature forever!", growing older should help us to develop wisdom, maturity and additional insights into how life works best.
- (n) intelligence quotient (I.Q.), which reflects genetic factors and measures learning ability within the dominant culture.

Each of us learns at a different rate of speed — and we are sensitive to various media and instructional methods.

And finally...

(o) life experiences, which play a large role in developing our personality. Someone who experiences some very positive events in life perhaps will look more on the brighter side than someone who has experienced great tragedy.

None of these fifteen characteristics, in and of themselves, makes a person who he is. Rather, *all* of these things combine to give a person his true personality overview. All of these factors contribute to what others think of as your personality — the expression of who you are.

You Are "Wired," Not "Weird"

Our focus in this book is your personality *style* — your *wiring*, your *behavioral style,* your *temperament.* This is the actual, measurable frame of reference in which you develop a "style of life." It is your outlook on life. You need this in order to function as a human being. It is how you are "wired," what gives you energy. We are different, and "different" does not mean "weird" when we begin to understand.

For example, some individuals enjoy being in charge and making things happen. For reasons we will explain in just a few moments, this "frame of reference" or "style" is called a "D" type personality. Others, known as "I" types, like being around people, talking, telling stories and having fun. Still others are satisfied simply being part of the team, willing to take on a supportive role. We call these "S" types. And others are more systematic in their life style and are very predictable in their behavior. This style of behavior is known as a "C" type.

We demonstrate and, to some degree, even develop our personality by the way we "behave" in various situations. Our "behaviors" are a clue to who we really are, because whether we are aware of it or not, we fall into very predictable patterns of behavior according to our environment's stresses and tensions.

Our individual *temperament* or *behavior* style plays a major role in *how* the other fifteen aspects are viewed, categorized and prioritized in our life experience. It is rather like a foundation, on which all the others are built. One must remember, all of these are a composite of one unique personality — namely, *you!*

What is a "Personality Style"?

As we have said, most people have predictable patterns of behavior — very distinctive ways of thinking and feeling and acting. Because of these patterns, we respond to incidents in our life in certain ways; we view life through certain "filters." Strictly speaking, the ways in which these thoughts, feelings, actions, viewpoints, patterns, responses and filters impact us has been classified as our *"behavioral style,"* but in general, we tend to refer to it as our own *"personality style."*

There are ways to analyze, chart and understand your own unique personality style, so that you will be better prepared to deal with changing situations and different people in your life. The "art of understanding yourself and others" is the aim of this book, which will help you to develop better relationships with other people, build better teams, and have a more productive life.

This is not a new concept. Hundreds of years before the birth of Christ, Hippocrates developed his "Four Behavior-Style" approach to understanding people. He recognized that some people demonstrated highly assertive behaviors while others were low in assertiveness; that some exhibited very responsive attitudes while others were less responsive. Hippocrates theorized that the predominance of bodily fluids determined these styles, or "temperaments," and he named these styles after the bodily fluids he thought influenced them.

While we know today that the balance of bile and phlegm (pronounced *flem)* does not determine our disposition, the terms coined by Hippocrates are still in use — you may have heard the terms *choleric, sanguine, phlegmatic* and *melancholy* used to describe someone's personality style. You may have read books such as Tim LaHaye's *Spirit-Controlled Temperament* or Florence Littauer's *Personality Plus*. Both of these bestselling books adhere to this "Hippocratic" or "Medieval" model.

The Model of Human Behavior

In our experience, the most easily understood teachings regarding human behavior are based on the "DISC" model, a theory devised by Dr. William Marston, a Columbia University psychologist during the 1920s and 30s. Marston identified four major patterns of behavior that are present in everyone, to a greater or lesser degree. In 1928, he published this "breakthrough" information in his book, *Emotions of Normal People*.

Since that time, exhaustive studies have been conducted by university education and psychology departments, involving hundreds of thousands of subjects, with the aim of validating, refining and improving upon Marston's initial concepts. Research continues to validate this theory that, as individuals, our drives are "powered" either by our **outgoing** or our **reserved** approach to life, and that our direction is "steered" either toward **tasks** or toward **people**.

A number of other, highly sophisticated evaluation surveys, analysis tools and profiling instruments have been developed over the years. Perhaps you have taken some of these "tests," including the Minnesota Multiphasic Personality Inventory (MMPI), the Meyers-Briggs Type Indicator (MBTI), the Taylor-Johnson Temperament Analysis, and others. While these are designed to aid psychologists and human behaviorists, they are often so technical or diagnostic in nature that they offer little in the way of insights that most "average" people can apply easily, to enrich their personal lives, their business pursuits and their developing relationships.

Again, the "DISC" method of applying these personality concepts meets the needs of "average" people with information that most individuals can understand quickly, apply readily and communicate to others. At Personality Insights, we offer a variety of nontechnical assessments and reports aimed at helping you to understand your own personality style blend. This, in turn, allows you to develop a plan of action for greater success in your business and personal relationships.

If you have already completed our *"Style Analysis,"* you know the details of your individual style — and as you read this book, you will be able to see specific ways the information applies to you. If you have not yet completed a *"Style Analysis,"* you will probably want to do so when you have finished this book. (Information about Personality Insights' various assessments is available in our current catalog.) Then you can apply this information specifically and intelligently in your own life and situation.

As we begin to look at personality styles, we will "DISCover" three things:

1) **In your style, one trait is most predominant; it is your primary trait.**

2) **In each behavioral style, secondary trait(s) serve the primary trait.**

3) **In each behavioral style, there are varying levels of intensity in the primary trait and the secondary traits.**

1) The first statement **concerning your primary trait** means there is one *main style* or "driving force" behind your behavior patterns. Each of us possesses a *"motor"* that drives us at a "faster" or "slower" pace. Our *motor* determines how *outgoing* or *reserved* we are in dealing with life in general.

The diagram at the right shows strength or intensity in either the trait of being *outgoing* or the trait of being *reserved*. Lighter shading indicates less "intensity" in your style (closer to the neutral midline, or "average" in that trait), while darker shading indicates more intensity in this trait (away from the neutral midline, less "average").

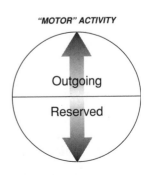

"MOTOR" ACTIVITY

Outgoing

Reserved

For instance, a very, very outgoing person could be pictured at the tip of the top arrow — "saturated" with an outgoing orientation and far removed from the neutral midline. Someone who is very, very reserved would be pictured at the tip of the other arrow — the extreme opposite of an outgoing personality style. In this illustration, the darker and the further from our midline, the stronger the trait.

Just as we have a *motor* that drives us, we also have a ***compass*** that "steers" us in the direction we feel we ought to take regarding *tasks* or *people.*

In the second diagram, we see strength or intensity in either the trait of being ***task-oriented*** or the trait of being ***people-oriented***. Again, lighter shading indicates less intensity in an individual's personality style (closer to the neutral midline, or "average" in this trait), while darker shading indicates more intensity in this trait (away from the neutral midline, less "average").

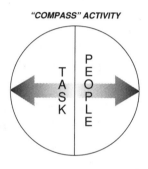

"COMPASS" ACTIVITY

For instance, a very, very task-oriented person would be pictured out at the darker tip of the left arrow — "saturated" with a task orientation and far removed from the neutral midline. Someone else who is very, very people-oriented could be pictured at the tip of the right arrow — the extreme opposite of a task-oriented behavioral style.

You can observe how these traits (outgoing versus reserved, task-oriented versus people-oriented) vary in intensity in yourself and in your friends or co-workers. You can also understand why an individual could not be *both* 100% task-oriented *and* 100% people-oriented, or 100% outgoing *and* 100% reserved at the same time.

When we put both of these illustrations together (on the following page), we will see our four quadrant Model of Human Behavior. As a ***predominant style*** — that is, the way you tend to be most of the time — this model shows how people tend to fall into four basic categories, which involve both their "motor" and their "compass."

Outgoing motor and *Task-oriented* compass, *or*

Outgoing motor and *People-oriented* compass, *or*

Reserved motor and *People-oriented* compass, *or*

Reserved motor and *Task-oriented* compass.

Applying "DISC" to the Model

Here is how the descriptive "D-I-S-C" letters fit in:

The "D" Type — the dominant, determined, doer

Outgoing – likes to be with the "movers and shakers" (faster motor)

Task-Oriented – looking for opportunities for advancement (task compass)

The "I" Type — the inspirational, impressive, influencer

Outgoing – likes to be "on the go!" (faster motor)

People-Oriented – looking for opportunities to be with friends (people compass)

The "S" Type — the steady, stable, supporter

Reserved – prefers taking things at a slower pace (slower motor)

People-Oriented – likes to associate with friendly people (people compass)

The "C" Type — the cautious, competent, calculator

Reserved – prefers to be careful when making progress (slower motor)

Task-Oriented – looking for projects and ways to be more efficient (task compass)

How can *you* make personal application of this information? You should start by understanding your one most predominate trait — as we said before, it is the driving force behind your behavioral style, making you a "D," "I," "S," or "C."

However, the shading in our diagrams on page 8 imply that your *most predominate* trait *is not your **only** trait* — you must have *some* percentages of the other traits as well! And if you have completed a *"Style Assessment,"* you can look at your own personality style graphs and see that more than just one set of traits make up your individual style. You probably show some of the other three traits in your graphs as well.

About 80% of the general population has a **blend** in which *two* or even *three* of the four behavior types appear as predominant — *above the midline* — if their styles were put on a graph. Remember, Marston said we are each a **blend** of all four behavior traits, to a greater or lesser degree.

2) So, our second statement from page 6 is: **In each behavioral style, there are secondary trait(s) that serve the primary trait.** While one trait can be described as *most predominate*, other traits may also be above the midline, and these "secondary traits" will serve by helping the most predominate (or "primary trait") to achieve its aim.

For example, if you are primarily a "D" with a secondary trait of "I," then you will: want to get the job done (a "D" trait) but you will accomplish it by focusing on or including and inspiring other people ("I" traits). If you are primarily a "D" with a secondary trait of "C," then you will want to get the job done (again a "D" trait) but you will accomplish it by focusing on the details of the task at hand and relying on data for support ("C" characteristics). This is how your secondary trait helps **support** or **serve** the primary trait.

3) Third, we said: **Varying levels of intensity can be seen in the primary trait and the secondary traits.** As suggested earlier, an individual who has a faster "motor" is said to be **outgoing**. However, still other individuals who are *more* outgoing may "run their motors" more "pedal to the metal" than the first outgoing individual.

In other words, someone who is predominantly outgoing does not have to be 100% outgoing. Most of us have some of the "opposite" trait, as well. A person could be 95% outgoing with 5% reserved. Another could be 87% outgoing with 13% reserved. Still another could be 64% outgoing with 36% reserved — but we would still say that all of them are *predominantly outgoing* individuals. (These percentages are used simply to illustrate the point. There is no tool that can perfectly categorize an individual by percentages.)

The same is true regarding our "compass" traits — people can vary tremendously in the forcefulness of their **task-oriented** or their **people-oriented** tendencies but still be thought of as **predominantly task-oriented** or **predominantly people-oriented**. Even an individual who is 54% task-oriented with 46% people-orientation would still be considered primarily **task-oriented**, even if only slightly so. Therefore, the definition of having a "D-type" behavioral style is simply that your highest-scoring traits are "D" type — you are primarily **outgoing** and **task-oriented.**

Introducing Personality Graphs

Since we have been referring to *"Style Assessments"* and "midlines," you understand that there are ways to *quantify* your personality traits into graphs that can be read and understood easily. This method of presenting the information is very straightforward, and once you understand how each of the four basic types deals with life, you can interpret a person pretty accurately just by seeing his or her graphs.

As an example, Personality Insights has worked for several years with InterNET Services Corporation, beginning with assessments that have helped their management people increase teamwork and efficiency. Steve Yager, a key player in the businesses, told me that since he has learned to read their graphs, he knows what to expect in dealing with employees. He knows how to build productive teams, how to help them approach a new project, and how to communicate effectively.

Since we will be referring to "high," "low," "midline," and "average" at various times, let's take a few moments to demystify the *"Style Assessment"* graphs. And remember, even if you have never seen a graph, you still will be able to understand what we mean. All of us learn more easily with visual examples, and this graph concept will help to "paint a picture" for you, enabling you to better understand personality styles.

The purpose of graphs is to provide an accurate, visual representation of the amounts of "D," "I," "S" and "C" traits that make up your personality style. The responses you select in completing your *"Style Analysis"* questionnaire have a numerical value — the more "D" type responses you choose, the higher your "D" score; the fewer "D" type responses you choose, the lower your "D" score. You transfer your score totals to a set of graphs, circling on the graphs those numbers that correspond to your "D – I – S – C" scores. Then you simply "connect the dots" from left to right, creating a graph that shows the "highs" and "lows" of your style.

Our purpose in teaching you how to think about personality styles in terms of graphs is to help you *see* areas in which adjustments need to occur in your life or in another person. When I first began learning the "DISC" system, I was not surprised to discover that I have a high "I" type personality. But I was shocked as I began to understand what a high "C" type personality is like. Then I recognized how I had created numerous problems for myself in the past: I had failed to exercise *careful, cautious,* "C" type traits in my life. When I finally *understood,* I *saw* — and then, I was able to begin a lifelong process of *adjusting* my style, rather than trying to change my entire life.

The following graphs typify the "look" of the graphs that are created in completing a *"Style Analysis."* The details have been simplified, but you can see the highs, lows and midline averages. By looking at each graph, you can see how much "D," "I," "S" and "C" are present. While a real report would show *two* detailed graphs, these examples use just one graph for each style. **(See *Appendix A* at the back of this book for information showing how to read a pair of graphs in depth.)**

Each of these graphs represents a "D-only" type of personality — that is, the "D" traits are above average (represented by the midline on the graph) and the "I," "S," and "C" traits are below average (they fall beneath the graph's midline). As you will discover, fewer people have this style, but it is a good place to begin, to illustrate our point.

 This graph shows a profile that is completely lacking in "I," "S," and "C" traits; "D" makes up 100% of the graph. This uncommon style displays no supporting traits that are associated with the other behavioral styles. More typically, we would expect to see a high-scoring "D" and varying amounts of "I," "S," and "C," as shown on the next page.

Target Training International reports that 1.2% of the general population have a style in which **only** their "D" appears above the midline on their graph. But even among this percentage, there are many possible variations. As shown in the following three "D-only" examples, it is more usual to find some influences from "I," "S," and "C" in a "D-only" type personality style.

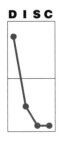 This graph shows a lot of "D" above the midline, with a bit of "I" below the midline, but no measurable "S" and "C" traits.

 This graph shows somewhat less "D," with some "I" and "S" below the midline, but no measurable "C" traits.

D I S C

This graph shows less "D," with more "I" and less "C" below the midline, but no measurable "S" traits.

Yet, even though there are variations in their graphs, all four are classified as predominate "D-only" type individuals (to a greater or lesser degree)!

It is unnecessary for us to demonstrate every little variable of a "D-only" type graph in print, and impossible to write an interpretation of each potential graph. *Just keep this definition in mind:* For an individual to be characterized as having a *"D-only"* type personality style, the *one trait above the midline* on the graph would be "D." For someone to be classified simply as a *"D type,"* the highest-scoring, most predominate trait still would have to be "D" (outgoing and task-oriented preferences and behavior), but *one or more of "I," "S," and "C" could appear above the midline*, as well (see below).

In addition to behaving according to our predominate or primary style, we also "borrow" from other traits that serve our primary trait. So, a "D" also could have an above-average "C" and utilize some of those traits in support of his "D." Of course, we can "borrow" only what we already have — but borrowing gives us some balance, so that we are not "one-dimensional."

Such blendings of styles are shown in the following examples using "D with C" blends. They represent individuals who have "D" as their predominate (strongest, most influential) trait — but their "C" traits are also above average. According to Target Training International, 2.6% of the general population has this "D with C" blend.

D I S C

This graph shows a lot of "D" with a good amount of "C" above the midline, and a bit of "I" below the midline. There are no measurable "S" traits

 This graph shows a little less "D" with less "C" above the midline, and more "I" and a little more "S" below the midline

 This graph shows a much lower "D with C" above the midline and with a bit more "S" than "I" below the midline

Yet, all of these graphs show "D" type individuals having "D with C" blends and varying levels of intensity!

Again, no one is *purely* a "D," "I," "S," or "C." We are each a unique "mix" of "D," "I," "S," *and* "C" traits. We refer to this mixture — what is happening in your behavioral makeup — as your individual personality *"blend."*

Keep in mind that there are no "right," "wrong," or "preferred" traits. We are simply "different" from each other, and "D-I-S-C" provides us with a language that honors and values the differences we see in people.

If you are extremely detail-oriented — in other words, if you are a very high "C" — you may be enjoying all of this chart information. But if you are not a "C," you may find it too involved, boring or confusing. *Cheer up!* We are almost finished with this technical part. When we finish this chapter, we will get into some practical application. (We have tried to provide something for each "D–I–S–C" style in writing this material!)

Just to make sure we are clear on our terms... Your *primary* trait is whichever of the "D," "I," "S," or "C" traits is *most predominate* in your own behavioral style — on a graph, it is the one highest above the midline. This primary trait determines your focus. **(See *Appendix B* in the back of this book for a complete showing of all possible style blends.)**

Whatever *secondary* traits you possess *complement* your primary trait — these traits are less predominate than your primary trait, but they are still above-average in strength. On a *"Style Analysis"* graph, they would also be above the midline — although not as high as your primary trait. These traits *support* your primary trait in achieving its focus and meeting its needs.

Remember, our earlier statement: **"In each behavioral style, there are *varying* levels of intensity among the predominant** (primary) **and the less predominant** (secondary) **traits."**

An Overview of DISC Characteristics

It is true that "all general statements are false... including this one!" But the next eight pages include some generally true statements about the four basic personality types, to help you get a handle on their basic focus, needs and outlook.

These pages will provide you with a broad overview of each type's behavioral characteristics. Again, since *no one is purely a "D," "I," "S," or "C,"* you may recognize some characteristics from each of the four types in your own behavior. Some of them actually are a part of your own natural style, while others may be adapted skills that you have learned to employ for success in your environment. Check them out...

The "D" Style

The **Dominant - Driving – Doer** Type

Symbol: Exclamation point — they are emphatic in everything they do

Focus: Get the job done — just do it! Overcome opposition and achieve your goals! Winners never quit… quitters never win!

Basic Need: Challenge – Control – Choices

Outlook on Life: To lead or to be in charge

Overview:

Someone has said, "When the going gets tough, the tough get going!" "D" type people are self-starters who know how to make things happen and get things done. It does not bother them to "take the bull by the horns," exert control, be in charge, and start the ball rolling in a straightforward manner.

"D" types, perhaps more than any others, know how to keep short accounts. They may seem harsh in speaking bluntly, but they simply want to get to the bottom line as quickly as possible. They don't hold grudges as long as progress is being made. They may go through several jobs before they find the right challenge that "rings their bell."

A "D" type individual is not afraid of a tough assignment, likes competition, handles pressure well and seeks individual accomplishment. They become very uncomfortable when things remain the same too long.

"D" types demand a lot from themselves and others. They know how to focus on end results, relying strongly on themselves and their ability to stick with the job until their desired outcome is achieved. They are very self-sufficient. They would rather lead than follow. It does not bother them to face a task alone — being individualists at heart allows them the determination to move ahead successfully until victory is achieved.

The "D" Type Is Good At...

- Overcoming obstacles

- Seeing the big picture

- Pushing the group ahead

- Accepting challenges without fear

- Maintaining focus on goals

- Getting results

- Providing leadership

- Handling several jobs at the same time

The "I" Style

The **Inspirational - Influencing – Impulsive** Type

Symbol: Star — they love to be the center of attention and recognition

Focus: I am for you! If we all pull in the same direction and stay motivated, there is no end to the success... and fun... we can have!

Basic Need: Recognition – Approval – Popularity

Outlook on Life: To persuade others to their way of thinking

Overview:

The "I" type of personality style loves social contact. People are their life! Whether with one person or a large crowd, they enjoy constantly being with others. They are not very good with details and tend to seek freedom from control. However, healthy accountability is the very key to their future success. They are friendly, carefree and outgoing, often exhibiting more confidence than ability.

An "I" type can meet total strangers and in just a few minutes make them feel right at home. They usually have a wide range of friends, young and old, crossing all socioeconomic levels. Their optimistic spirit makes them fun to be with and their happy disposition helps them get along with almost everyone. They exemplify Will Rogers' statement: "I never met a person I didn't like...!"

The "I" style likes to be in the center of a lot of activity. They are involved in many organizations, clubs or groups — wherever prestige or personal recognition is offered. They tend to identify with Peter Pan, not wanting to grow up and enjoying every adventure to the fullest.

The "I" Type Is Good At...

- Speaking persuasively

- Responding well to surprises

- Expressing ideas

- Accepting new people

- Creating enthusiasm

- Working well with others

- Having a sense of humor

- Keeping a positive attitude

The "S" Style

The **Steady - Stable – Supportive** Type

Symbol: Plus and Minus Sign — they bring a balance to the "people equation"

Focus: All for one and one for all. If we all work together, we can make a great team. Working together we can do it!

Basic Need: Appreciation – Security – Approval

Outlook on Life: To provide necessary support to bring harmony and help get the job completed

Overview:

The "S" type individual likes a calm, easygoing environment, where there is a predictable routine and things remain pretty much the same. They do not handle a lot of pressure very well. They prefer stability, security and credit for good work. They are highly adaptable because they seek to fit in and meet needs.

Perhaps more than any of the other styles, "S" types shy away from the spotlight. They are warmhearted, home-loving and easygoing. Because they sometimes "stuff" things inside, others may not know how they truly feel. They may hold a grudge — but not say anything about it.

The "S" type tends to be the most even-tempered and very predictable. They have a difficult time saying "no" and struggle with being forceful when necessary.

"S" types are not self-centered but they are territorial when it comes to their security. They do not like change. They prefer to work at their own pace without a lot of outside interference or deadlines. They may seem possessive at times, but that is simply because they know what they like — and like what they know. Without "S" type individuals, many things would go unfinished.

The "S" Type Is Good At...

- Showing sincerity

- Being even-tempered

- Emphasizing loyalty

- Building relationships

- Seeing an easier way to do things

- Providing dependability

- Being a team player

- Making others feel accepted

The "C" Style

The **Competent - Cautious – Careful** Type

Symbol: Question mark — they want to know the "why" behind what they do

Focus: Make sure things are done in a correct manner. Goods and services provided with quality ensure long-standing relationships.

Basic Need: Quality Answers – Excellence – Value

Outlook on Life: To be conscientious and consistent

Overview:

"C" type individuals need opportunity for careful planning. Their motto might be "Measure twice… and cut once!" They do not like mistakes or sudden unplanned changes.

When working with people who possess this "C" style, it is good to remember that they like to document everything they do. By paying close attention to details, they usually produce quality work with precise results. They seem to enjoy "detail" work and crave orderliness and organization. "Flow charts" were invented by this type of individual.

Sometimes others think "C" types are too cautious or overly concerned with their attention to details. It is difficult for them to take a "leap of faith" until they have mentally processed all their options. They like for things to "make sense."

When "C" type people finally make up their minds, they usually want to draft a plan and then see that plan through to completion. It bothers them to see unnecessary changes made without solid reasons. They tend to be "improvers" rather than "originators." Their cognitive skills help them see a better idea, but their cautious nature often prevents them from "coloring" too far outside the lines!

The "C" Type Is Good At...

- Working systematically

- Being conscientious

- Maintaining their focus

- Analyzing obstacles

- Striving for logical results

- Organizing material

- Thinking logically

- Evaluating situations

WHO DO YOU THINK YOU ARE ANYWAY?

Subjective Perceptions

We want you to feel that you are "part of the process" as you read this material. So, now that you understand the concept of personality styles, complete the graph at the bottom of this page by choosing plotting points that reflect how you see your own "D," "I," "S," and "C" traits. Admittedly, this graph will be subjective and unscientific, but it will provide an entry point for you to begin interacting with and personalizing the information in this book.

You have five segment choices in each category: high, above average, average, below average, and low. Simply choose one point for "D," one point for "I," one point for "S," and one point for "C." Then connect the dots, as shown in the example at the right.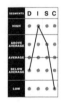

Again, this is purely subjective, and the choices you make on this page are not "locked in for life." We are simply allowing you the opportunity to experiment with the graph concept we are utilizing throughout this book. Review the descriptions on pages 16–23, then choose which segment you feel you fall into for each of the "D," "I," "S," and "C" traits. Ask yourself, "Of the descriptions of different styles I have read, which seem to describe me most closely?"

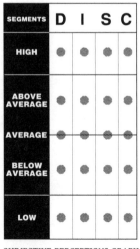

SUBJECTIVE PERCEPTIONS GRAPH

Please feel free to photocopy this page. Then you can ask your spouse or a friend who has read this book to complete a "subjective perceptions" graph on you. Also, after you have completed your assignment on pages 32 and 33, count the number of traits you have "checked off" that describe your style in *each* "D," "I," "S," and "C" category. Which of the four categories has the most check marks? Which has the least? Using these additional insights to provide another subjective view of your blend, where would you draw your graph's plotting points?

Chapter 2

"Blends" of Styles

As you worked with the information in Chapter 1, you have become convinced that you have some of each style in you. Of course you do — as we say often, *no one is purely a "D," "I," "S," or "C."* Before we finish this book, you will read that statement several more times. When I finish speaking at a seminar and someone says to me, "I feel like I have some of all of those styles in me... is that possible?", I realize we cannot say it too often.

Here it is in other language: *No one fits neatly and nicely into just one personality style. Each of us is a "blend" of behavior styles — different traits work together to create your own, unique personality style.* A "D" type person can also have some fairly strong "I," "S," or "C" qualities. An "I" can have fairly strong "D," "S," or "C" traits. "S's" and "C's" can also share strengths from the other types.

We will always find ourselves identifying with *some* of the behaviors and preferences of each personality type. In order to survive in our personal and business relationships, we have learned to adapt and adjust our own style to a variety of situations. We "pull to the surface" traits that are more appropriate for a situation, and we "squash" the traits that are less appropriate. Often, we have become so skilled at doing this that we find it difficult to identify and separate our *acquired, environmental* traits from our *natural, basic* traits.

For this reason, it really is very helpful to complete a *Style Assessment* so we can understand what *drives* us, what our true *passion* is, rather than what we have learned to do each day to get by. Also, beyond identifying our driving (or most predominate) trait, we can identify our special *blend* — the "toolbox" of secondary traits that helps your predominate trait accomplish its goals.

The Goal Is Balance

Our goal in understanding our blended style of behavior is to look at our strengths and weaknesses and make adjustments accordingly. In other words, if we are strong in our "D" trait, we need to understand that we probably want to be in charge of things and tend to be action-oriented. People who are strong "D's" often have more difficulty sitting around, relaxing and taking it easy. Conversely, a person who scores extremely low in their "D" characteristics has more difficulty in being the "make it happen now!" kind of individual. Certainly they can be leaders, but they are not naturally forceful. It just isn't a comfortable role for them if someone else can do it. The same is true of the other styles as well:

The higher the "I," the more talkative, outgoing and friendly the individual will be. The lower the "I," the more likely the individual will be withdrawn and less spontaneous.

The higher the "S," the more cooperative and supportive the person will be. The lower the "S," the less the individual will be interested in going out of his way to rescue you.

The higher the "C," the more the person will exhibit calculating and careful characteristics in daily living. The lower the "C," the less the person will be a "stickler" for details and exactness.

Regardless of our style, please understand that our goal is not to become a neutral, "nothing" style. Many times, people have told me they should try to get all of their traits and characteristics to fall in the middle of their graphs, so they could be perfectly balanced — not having any strong "D," "I," "S" or "C" traits. It is very commendable to want a perfect balance. After all, balance is our ultimate goal, demonstrating the appropriate behavior at the appropriate time (which, by the way, is our definition of maturity and responsibility). However, it is not necessary to try to become a "nothing" personality style. In other words, if we looked at your graph and all of your plotting points were dead center, we might think balance had been achieved. Such a pattern is known as "Level" or "Even" (more on that in the *Appendix)*. This type tends to be very the primary trait will be the *driving* force, but the secondary trait will *serve* the primary trait in order to bring about the desired end.

As an example, a "D" only type who wants *achievement* and *results* will probably rely on power and control to reach his target. However, if his secondary trait is "I," he will also be comfortable using tools of "emotional persuasion" to enlist others. On the other hand, if his secondary trait is "C," he will be more comfortable using tools of "factual persuasion" to gain support.

Abraham Maslow observed, "If the only tool you have is a hammer, you tend to treat every problem as a nail." In other words, we use the tools we have and the tools we understand. The advantage to understanding our own style is that we can monitor this process — and even modify it when appropriate. We can "borrow" more efficiently from our secondary traits. And when we need tools that did not come in our own toolbox (traits that are not "native" to our style), we can learn to "synthesize" them and "raise" our "D," "I," "S," or "C" at appropriate times. And we can learn to use our "native" tools more appropriately, too — we need not use a sledge hammer to swat a fly!

The following diagram shows how this process occurs, picturing a "connection" or "bridge" between *adjacent* styles. It is how your own particular style may "bleed over into," or "borrow from" its "neighbors," consciously or not, compensating for a lack in our most predominate style.

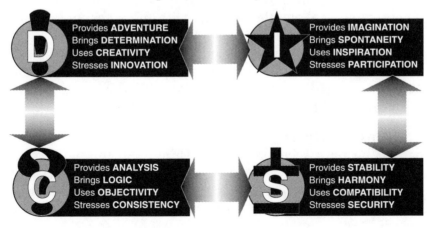

D
Provides **ADVENTURE**
Brings **DETERMINATION**
Uses **CREATIVITY**
Stresses **INNOVATION**

I
Provides **IMAGINATION**
Brings **SPONTANEITY**
Uses **INSPIRATION**
Stresses **PARTICIPATION**

C
Provides **ANALYSIS**
Brings **LOGIC**
Uses **OBJECTIVITY**
Stresses **CONSISTENCY**

S
Provides **STABILITY**
Brings **HARMONY**
Uses **COMPATIBILITY**
Stresses **SECURITY**

flexible in making decisions. This is a positive trait. However, in being too flexible, such an individual may sometimes have difficulty making focused decisions — and this is a negative trait. This type can struggle trying to "raise" the strengths that occur automatically in strong "D," "I," "S," and "C" types. To be very decisive or inducing or supportive or critical-thinking can be a "stretch."

A person who is high in any "D-I-S-C" area is more predominate in that area, and thus will struggle when trying to "lower" their strong traits appropriately. Someone who is "average" in that same area will have difficulty "raising" those same traits appropriately. So, again, no style is good or bad, right or wrong. They are simply different. It is perfectly appropriate that personality styles have extremes. This is what brings diversity and enjoyment to the human race. It is also one way we find enjoyment and fulfillment in working with others. Our goal is to keep our style in check, staying balanced and demonstrating the dynamic our personality style is able to deliver at appropriate times. When you understand your own style and the styles of others, you can begin to work in harmony, producing better results.

Using Appropriate Tools

The majority of people will show two plotting points *above the midline* and two plotting points *below the midline* on their Style Analysis graphs. It is also possible to have only one very dominant style above the midline, with the other three styles falling below the midline. And some people have three styles above the midline, with only one below the midline. (All of these variables are shown in graphs on pages 256, 272, 288, and 304.) If they seem confusing, imagine that each style will vary in strength and intensity from person to person!

Most commonly, people have one very dominant style, backed up by a secondary style. Think of it this way: Your *primary* trait ("D," "I," "S," or "C") is your *core* trait — it is your **passion.** Your *secondary* trait *serves* the primary trait; it supports and assists you in thinking, feeling and acting as you do. Again,

"Borrowing" from your other, less predominate traits is part of fitting in and working with others. For instance, the "D" type is defined as *outgoing* and *task-oriented*. What it has in common with the "I" type is that both are *outgoing*. What it has in common with the "C" type is that both are *task-oriented*. What they have in common may serve as a bridge, allowing the "D" to access some "I" and "C" tools (or traits), as well as what he can find in his own toolbox.

At times, circumstances may force you to use a particular style with which you are not comfortable. It may feel as if someone has just handed you a jackhammer! (If you see a major difference when you compare the plotting points on your *Environment Style* graph with the plotting points on your *Basic Style* graph, you have experienced this kind of "forced" adaptation.) The good news is that adapting yourself to these circumstances has probably caused you to grow and gain skill in using new tools that you would not have employed otherwise. "Bleeding over" helps you to do this successfully.

Our *Personality Insights Style Analysis* produces *two* graphs. *Graph I* shows how you behave in order to succeed in your environment. In fact, it is called your "Environment Graph." This graph tends to shift according to the role you must play in your environment. Our goal is learning how to adjust our "Environmental Style," so we will "fit in" and our behavior will be appropriate according to our situation. *We can learn to choose and use the tools we need for success.* Our second graph, *Graph II*, shows how you are "wired" in your "Basic Style." It is the "real you" — how you respond when you are relaxed and on "autopilot" will be revealed here. All those good qualities with which you seem to have been born, or acquired easily along the way, spring from here. And, as we will see, many of the troublesome character issues that each of us faces in life grow happily in the rich soil of our "Basic Style."

You probably have noted that the style which is *diagonally opposite* your primary trait ("D" and "S" are opposites, as are "I" and "C") is the one you *struggle with most* and *understand least*. While it may feel like using a hammer left-handed, you *can* learn to do it — and in some cases, you already have. Again, most people have no "natural" bridge between their opposite traits (3.1 % of the population are "D/S" or "S/D" while 2.1% are "I/C" or "C/I.") But we may be able to access our opposite trait through its link to our secondary traits.

This is fantastic news! Because of our "borrowing" ability, we are not completely lacking and unskilled in using other "D," "I," "S," and "C" tools. We can *grow... learn...* and *develop* new ways of becoming all we were meant to be!

To restate the concept, arrows connect adjacent styles in the diagram, but no arrows connect the "D" to the "S" or the "I" to the "C." They are not "naturally" *complementary* styles — they are *contrasting* styles. The "D" is outgoing and task-oriented, while the "S" is more reserved and people-oriented. One likes to be in charge, while the other is more comfortable in a support role. The "I" is outgoing and people-oriented, and the "C" is more reserved and task-oriented. One is verbal and likes activity while the other is thoughtful and prefers calm.

Although it is statistically unusual to have a "cross personality style" ("D-S" or "I-C"), it certainly is not impossible. This dynamic can create somewhat more tension, producing a somewhat "paradoxical" individual. The "D-S" will want to be in charge one minute ("D") and then will want to help you in your situation the next ("S").

One of my heroes is Dexter Yager. On one hand, he is the most determined person I have ever met. He sets his goals, dream by dream, and he never quits (his "D" traits). Then again, he is one of the most gentle individuals I have ever met. He gives and gives and gives of himself to others — the best example of a serving, supportive "S" type you could ever meet. (By way of explanation, if you are not acquainted with Dexter, you may wonder how he "rates" such frequent mention in this book. He is a proven master at developing leadership in others, and he shares his relationship-building concepts with business leaders who find them highly duplicatible.)

My good friend, researcher-analyst-motivator Ron Ball, seems to display an "I-C" style. He is one of the most dynamic speakers you could ever hear. On one hand, he can hold an audience's attention for hours — he is informative in his presentation and inspiring in his delivery (the "I" traits). At the same time, you can always tell that he has done his homework, is very well read, knows statistical information, validated by tons of data, and is extremely practical in his applications (the "C" traits). His talks are often organized into 20 or 30 major points, and many of these have sub-points, and their sub-points have sub-points. And — get this —he can deliver all of this information without any notes! What a mind! (It drives me crazy!)

Without understanding how they are "wired," people like Dexter might not know why they may feel uneasy at times when they are leading and "out in front," because they also want to provide support and allow you to be "out in front." People like Ron might wonder why they want to play when they are working and work when they are playing. But when they can understand and use their "cross-personality" style tools, they can do some amazing things!

Remember, as with *all* personality styles... we *should* and *can* learn to utilize all of the different "D-I-S-C" characteristics when necessary and appropriate.

The next two pages contain lists of common personality traits for each behavioral style. You will see words that seem positive and others that express room for growth. Knowing yourself as you do, put a check mark next to any of the words you feel accurately and honestly describe you in each category — there are no "right" or "wrong" answers. In doing so, you will see how you tend to "blend" and "borrow" in your own life.

Following these pages, you will find an overview of the characteristics of the four major blends: the outgoing "D's" and "I's," the reserved "S's" and "C's," the task-oriented "D's" and "C's," and the people-oriented "I's" and "S's." If your blend involves one predominate trait and one supportive trait above the midline on your graph, you can read about yourself in the corresponding overview. If your blend involves one predominate trait and two supportive traits above the midline, then you will want to look at the two different overviews that contain information relating to your blend. (We will get to that later.)

WHO DO YOU THINK YOU ARE ANYWAY?

____ Arrogant	____ Logical
____ Abrasive	____ Offensive
____ Ambitious	____ Optimistic
____ Angry	____ Persistent
____ Competitive	____ Pioneering
____ Conceited	____ Practical
____ Confident	____ Productive
____ Courageous	____ Proud
____ Crafty	____ Pushy
____ Cruel	____ Reckless
____ Decisive	____ Responsible
____ Deliberate	____ Responsive
____ Demanding	____ Results oriented
____ Determined	____ Rude
____ Dictatorial	____ Sarcastic
____ Direct	____ Self-confident
____ Domineering	____ Self-reliant
____ Driving	____ Self-sufficient
____ Goal oriented	____ Skeptical
____ Impatient	____ Straightforward
____ Inconsiderate	____ Strong willed
____ Independent	____ Stubborn
____ Leader	____ Unemotional

____ Accurate	____ Moody
____ Aesthetic	____ Negative
____ Analytical	____ Neat
____ Calculating	____ Nosy
____ Cautious	____ Orderly
____ Conscientious	____ Perfectionist
____ Conservative	____ Picky
____ Correct	____ Precise
____ Critical	____ Questioning
____ Curious	____ Rigid
____ Dependable	____ Self-centered
____ Doubtful	____ Self-sacrificing
____ Easily offended	____ Sensitive
____ Fearful	____ Stable
____ Fretful	____ Systematic
____ Gifted	____ Teachable
____ Idealistic	____ Theoretical
____ Impractical	____ Thorough
____ Inflexible	____ Traditional
____ Intense	____ Truthful
____ Logical	____ Unsociable
____ Low-keyed	____ Vengeful
____ Loyal	____ Worrisome

____ Carefree
____ Communicative
____ Compassionate
____ Daydreamer
____ Directionless
____ Egocentric
____ Emotional
____ Enthusiastic
____ Exaggerated
____ Excitable
____ Fearful
____ Fervent
____ Friendly
____ Fun
____ Gossipy
____ Happy
____ Imaginative
____ Impulsive
____ Independent
____ Involved
____ Lacking purpose
____ Loud
____ Manipulative

____ Mobile
____ Optimistic
____ Outgoing
____ Personable
____ Persuasive
____ Poised
____ Polished
____ Popular
____ Restless
____ Sarcastic
____ Self-centered
____ Sociable
____ Spontaneous
____ Talkative
____ Trusting
____ Undependable
____ Undisciplined
____ Unfocused
____ Unrealistic
____ Unstable
____ Verbal
____ Warm
____ Weak-willed

____ Amiable
____ Calm
____ Cooperative
____ Dependable
____ Dependent
____ Conservative
____ Consistent
____ Deliberate
____ Diplomatic
____ Easily manipulated
____ Easygoing
____ Efficient
____ Fearful
____ Good listener
____ Gullible
____ Humorous
____ Indecisive
____ Inflexible
____ Lacking initiative
____ Loyal
____ Passive
____ Patient
____ Possessive

____ Practical
____ Predictable
____ Relaxed
____ Reliable
____ Resentful
____ Resistant to change
____ Selfish
____ Self-protective
____ Shy
____ Single-minded
____ Slow
____ Softhearted
____ Spectator
____ Stable
____ Steadfast
____ Steady
____ Stingy
____ Systematic
____ Tactful
____ Timid
____ Trustworthy
____ Uncommunicative
____ Unmotivated

Twenty Characteristics of the Outgoing Style Blend

"D's" and "I's"

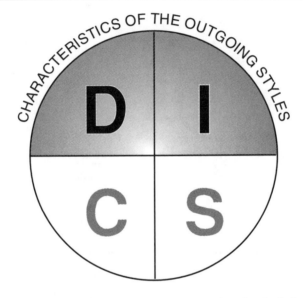

Both the "D" and "I" types are **Outgoing** in their behavioral style. They enjoy a lot of activity, excitement and change. They both tend to have short attention spans because they become bored easily. It is difficult for them to stay with a project over the long term. They tend to be great starters... but not-so-great finishers! Again, it has nothing to do with their level of skill or ability. Although they start with great vigor, once the "glitz and glitter" are gone, they lose interest quickly. They prefer chasing new ideas in other directions. If they recognize this tendency and bring it under control, there is no limit to their potential productivity.

The **Outgoing** Style tends to be *fast paced.* Their internal "motor" is constantly running at high speed. They are *optimistic,* often displaying more confidence than ability! They are almost always *energetic* and are usually the last ones wanting to go to bed at night (and sometimes the last ones getting up in the morning!).

They like to be *involved* in many varied activities — to them, "variety is the spice of life." They usually develop an attitude toward life that is *positive.* It bothers them to be around critical people, so they try to avoid as much negative as possible. (But when *they* sometimes get negative... it gushes out!) And they tend to be *enthusiastic,* trying to bring out the good, the better and the best in every situation. They figure it takes more energy to be pessimistic than optimistic — even more facial muscles to frown than to smile — so why not go for it?!

Following are 20 basic characteristics of "D's" and "I's"... the **Outgoing** Style:

1. They cannot understand life until they have lived it.

2. Their attitude is one of confidence and boldness.

3. They apply ingenuity to problems.

4. They enjoy learning new skills more than using them.

5. They like to read billboard signs (big pictures!).

6. They work in "bursts" of energy.

7. They are future-oriented.

8. They tend to reach conclusions quickly.

9. They are high on enthusiasm — low on patience.

10. They usually follow their inspirations — whether good or bad.

11. They frequently make errors in stating facts.

12. They move at a faster pace — dislike complicated statements.

13. Routine is boring — they get impatient and restless with long, slow tasks.

14. They are interested in results.

15. They like variety and action.

16. They act before thinking.

17. They prefer variety and change.

18. They are people of action.

19. They are solution conscious.

20. They look for new possibilities.

Twenty Characteristics of the Reserved Style Blend

"S's" and "C's"

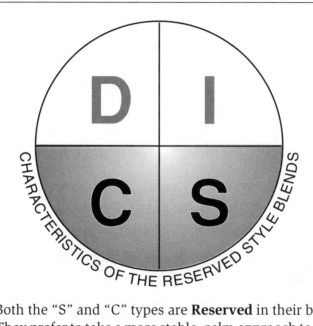

Both the "S" and "C" types are **Reserved** in their behavioral style. They prefer to take a more stable, calm approach to life. They are able to stick with a project longer because they tend to be "long term" people. They may not be quick to attack a new problem or opportunity, but when they do join in, their commitment is for the long haul. In other words, if we compare them to runners, they are more "marathon minded" than a 100-yard dash kind of person! Usually, they focus on the task at hand rather than chasing "rabbit trails." Often overlooked because of their low-key approach, this type is usually the glue holding a family or business together. Without them, the rest of us would be sunk!

The **Reserved** Style tends to be a little *slower paced.* Their internal motor runs at a consistent, steady speed without a lot of highs and lows. They don't work in "bursts of energy," but follow more of a "daily routine" or schedule. They prefer to be *cautious* in their approach to almost everything they do. When making decisions, you can almost always see that they are a little more *concerned* with the long term effects of a decision, rather than simply the decision itself. Speaking of decisions, they tend to be more reluctant in even *making* a decision, because they really do want to make a perfect one. They worry before, during and after the process! (They would do well to remember this wisdom from Charles "Tremendous" Jones: "God never made a person who knew how to make a right decision. The key to life is not making *right* decisions. The key to life is to learn how to make the *best* decision possible... then make *it* right!" Ahhhh! Great advice!) This type displays *critical thinking* skills when looking at a problem. Usually they can find what is wrong more quickly than they can see what is right. In certain professions (medicine, law, architecture... umpiring!) this is a great skill to possess. Finally, this type is *discerning,* often able to see through a situation faster and more accurately than other people. They have a sense of others' honesty and integrity, and can often quickly spot fakes and con artists.

Following are 20 basic characteristics of "S's" and "C's ... the **Reserved** Style:

1. They cannot live life until they understand it.

2. Their attitude is questioning and reserved.

3. They apply experience to problems.

4. They enjoy using skills already learned more than learning new ones.

5. They like to read fine print (little pictures!).

6. They tend to work steadily with even-paced energy.

7. They are present-oriented.

8. They tend to reach conclusions systematically, step-by-step.

9. They are high on patience — low on enthusiasm.

10. They rarely trust inspiration — whether good or bad.

11. They very seldom make errors in stating facts.

12. They move at a slower pace — dislike general statements.

13. Routine is okay — they can work on one project for a long time.

14. They are interested in ideas.

15. They like peace and quiet so they can concentrate.

16. They think before acting.

17. They prefer consistency and little change.

18. They are people of ideas.

19. They are problem conscious.

20. They look for data related to past successes.

Twenty Characteristics of the Task-Oriented Style Blend

"D's" and "C's"

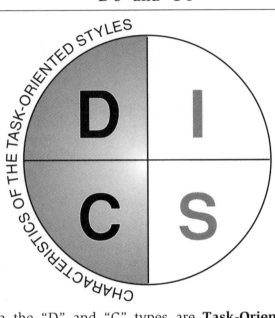

Both the "D" and "C" types are **Task-Oriented** in their behavioral style. They like to see their goals accomplished and progress achieved in all they do. When working as a team with others, they can sometimes seem difficult to work with. This is not because they are unkind; it is due more to their general outlook on life. The "D" type usually expects to be "right" about almost everything, and the "C" type expects to be even more right! Often, that creates tension within a group.

When "D" types are in charge of a task, their attitude is conveyed as, "I want this job done right and I want you to do it. And if you don't do it right, you will do it over — I'll see to that!" Think of their approach to tasks as "D" for "delegate." The "C" types, on the other hand, have a different approach: "I want this job done right... so I'll do it myself!" They figure they are better off doing it alone than having to count on someone else and things not working out correctly. They know they will catch the blame *and* have to do it over! They think all of this can be avoided simply by doing it correctly themselves. (This is often good advice, but it is a difficult way to grow leadership in an organization!)

The **Task-Oriented** Style belongs to "high-tech" individuals who are really into *form* and *function*. To them, there is nothing better than a well-oiled, finely tuned, high performance machine. Things ought to work the way they were meant to work! They also love *programs* — that means when you "plan your work and work your plan," things ought to fall into place the way they are supposed to. They love to make *plans*. Usually they are thinking about what may happen next or as a direct result of their plans. They seem to know instinctively that "if you keep doing what you have been doing, you will keep getting what you have been getting!" They plan to make things change... and things usually do. They love *projects*. They thrive on checking off their itemized and prioritized "To Do" lists as they accomplish each item, goal or project. Finally, they are into the *process*. They can see the necessary steps to get from Point A to Point B. They realize things do not simply "happen" successfully without undertaking a systematic process that will lead toward that goal. They line up their targets and knock them down one by one.

Following are 20 basic characteristics of "D's" and "C's"... the **Task-Oriented** Style:

1. They value logic over sentimental traditions.

2. They are truthful rather than tactful.

3. They have strong executive/administrative abilities.

4. They question conclusions.

5. They are brief, to-the-point, businesslike.

6. They hurt others' feelings without knowing it.

7. They can live without harmony.

8. They make decisions impersonally.

9. They ignore feelings; they like facts.

10. They are able to reprimand, and can fire when necessary.

11. They are firm-minded and exacting.

12. They are comfortable with ideas.

13. They guard their emotions.

14. They live according to plan — with a purpose.

15. They are more decisive than curious.

16. They like to have matters decided (settled).

17. They take pleasure in finishing projects.

18. They like the joy of enterprise and achievement.

19. They need to be treated fairly.

20. They structure their lives according to facts.

Twenty Characteristics of the People-Oriented Style Blend

"I's" and "S's"

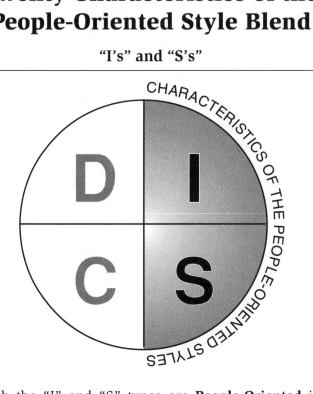

Both the "I" and "S" types are **People-Oriented** in their behavioral style. They love being with their friends. Their social life is their life! When you meet individuals of this type, you soon feel you have known them all your life. They warm up to strangers quickly, especially those who are nice to them or show them some recognition or approval. They usually smile a lot and speak to everyone they see. They tend to have hurt feelings more quickly because how they are treated really affects the way they feel. Their outlook on life is influenced largely by others.

When "I" types walk into a room, it is almost as if the room's temperature changes. Typically, "I's" walk right up, pat people on the shoulder or give a hug, and then... they start talking! They do this even with people who do not know them — they are not being fresh, just friendly. If they could wag a tail and jump up in your lap, they might remind you of a happy, friendly cocker spaniel! "S" types are friendly, too, but not as demonstrative. They show affection inwardly, rather than outwardly. "S" types want to visit with everyone when they walk into a room, but they would prefer for people to come to them, rather than their going to others. At all costs, they want to avoid seeming "pushy" or appearing obnoxious. The "I" worries very little about that possibility — "If someone has to be obnoxious, why not me?!" And if it commands a little more attention, then why not?

The **People-Oriented** Style belongs to "high touch" individuals who are into *relationships*. They really want you to like them, so they often "bend over backwards" to please you. They are not "pushovers," but they do want you to be happy — so they tend to give in easily. They tend to think everyone else sees life as they do. Unfortunately, this view often causes them to suffer emotional hurts. They like the approach of *caring* and *sharing*. Remember the slogan of the Three Musketeers: "All for one and one for all!" They work far better in teams rather than individually. They feel strong emotions about most things, and they *feel with their hearts* rather than thinking with their minds. Because they are more subjective than objective, they often chase unnecessary "rabbit trails," or expect to find gold at the end of their rainbow. Most of all, they are into *friendships*, wanting as many friends as possible. They have a "best friend" at school… at work… at church… on the elevator — you get the picture!

Following are 20 basic characteristics of "I's" and "S's"… the **People-Oriented** Style:

1. They value sentimental traditions above logic.

2. They are tactful rather than truthful.

3. They have strong social/relational abilities.

4. They accept conclusions.

5. They are not very brief; they ramble, are friendly.

6. They do not intentionally hurt others' feelings and feel badly when they do.

7. They desire harmony and are disturbed by conflict.

8. They make decisions based on others' influence.

9. They ignore facts; they like feelings.

10. They dislike having to reprimand, avoid unpleasantness.

11. They are sympathetic and flexible.

12. They are comfortable with people.

13. They "unload" their emotions.

14. They live according to the moment.

15. They are more curious than decisive.

16. They like leaving decisions open-ended.

17. They take pleasure in starting projects.

18. They like the joy of living in the present regardless of achievement.

19. They need to be appreciated and praised.

20. They structure their lives according to feelings.

Percentages of Blends

"D" Blends		"I" Blends		"S" Blends		"C" Blends	
1. D only	1.2%	1. I only	1.0%	1. S only	0.9%	1. C only	0.3%
2. D/I	12.8%	2. I/D	12.8%*	2. S/D	3.1%*	2. C/D	2.6%*
3. D/S	3.1%	3. I/S	12.1%	3. S/I	12.1%*	3. C/I	2.1%*
4. D/C	2.6%	4. I/C	2.1%	4. S/C	17.2%	4. C/S	17.2%*
5. D/I/S	7.3%	5. I/D/S	7.3%*	5. S/D/I	7.3%*	5. C/D/I	3.5%*
6. D/I/C	3.5%	6. I/D/C	3.5%*	6. S/D/C	6.4%*	6. C/D/S	6.4%*
7. D/S/C	6.4%	7. I/S/C	28.5%	7. S/I/C	28.5%*	7. C/I/S	28.5%*

Source: Target Training International   *Previously shown in another category

These two charts depict the percentages of each blend within the general population. As a reminder, "blend" signifies that these traits vary from "above average" to "high" in predominance. (On a Style Analysis graph, these traits appear above the midline.) Note the small percentages that are purely one style and not a blend of styles. Most people are a blend of two or three styles. When the side bar notes "ANY D/I/S," it refers to any above-average mixture of "D," "I," and "S" traits, including high "D" with "I" and "S," and high "I" with "D" and "S," and high "S" with "D" and "I." This is also true for the "ANY D/S/C" and "ANY I/S/C" side bars.

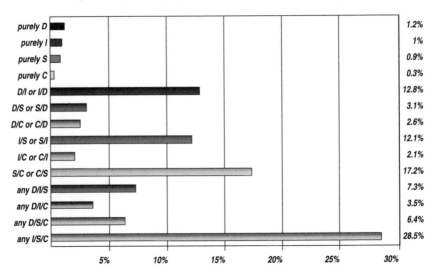

purely D	1.2%
purely I	1%
purely S	0.9%
purely C	0.3%
D/I or I/D	12.8%
D/S or S/D	3.1%
D/C or C/D	2.6%
I/S or S/I	12.1%
I/C or C/I	2.1%
S/C or C/S	17.2%
any D/I/S	7.3%
any D/I/C	3.5%
any D/S/C	6.4%
any I/S/C	28.5%

5%   10%   15%   20%   25%   30%

Chapter 3

"Combinations" of Styles

The most valuable aspect of the Model of Human Behavior is *not* in finding out what "type" you are. After seminars, participants come up to me and say, "I'm not sure but I think I'm a 'D' with a little 'I.'" Or after completing their own *Personality Insights Style Assessment,* they may say, "I thought I was all 'C,' but I found out I have a lot of 'S,' too!"

This is good information to possess — even a hermit might enjoy knowing more about himself — but the greatest value in using this material is *learning to understand others* and *becoming skilled at adjusting and adapting yourself* when you are in their presence.

A noted psychologist, Dr. Charles Lowery, once stated, "Sometimes we make personalities a *topic* rather than a *project!*" I agree. That is definitely not the purpose of this book. Although it is interesting and entertaining to discover who we really are (and learn about other personality types as well), we should not be satisfied with that discovery alone. It is after we "learn" about our own personality styles that the *real* learning begins. If we are wise, we begin the process of working on our personalities, in order to adjust our behavior to be the best person we can be. This is our goal.

For years, I have asked this question in my seminars: "If I understand you and you understand me, doesn't it make sense that we can be in a position to have a better relationship?" Learning to understand myself and then beginning to understand you increases our chances for success.

You have a distinctive behavioral style, composed of "D," "I," "S" and "C" traits. So do I, but my style is not *exactly* like your style. Our life experiences have not been *exactly* alike, either. So when we consider all of the various factors that come together to create your own special personality, we find that you are a complex individual. Me, too!

When your *blend* of traits (*your* "personality style") and my *blend* of traits (*my* "personality style") come together, they create a **combination**. For you and me to work together and become a "winning combination" will require adjusting and adapting from both sides.

Have you ever wondered why you "get along" well with some people and have such a hard time with others? Well, this is why: As we shall see, some combinations simply work together more harmoniously, while others require more effort, time, and understanding. It all boils down to this one truth: *We don't see things as **they** are… we see things as **we** are!"*

Most people do not know a great deal about personality styles. Any of their adapting and adjusting occurs haphazardly, maybe accidentally — and perhaps, begrudgingly — because they do not understand why they think, act and feel the way they do. They have even less understanding of why other people "choose" to act they way they do. We see this in marriages, work groups, classrooms, sport teams, business partnerships, volunteer committees, church boards, social organizations, and everywhere else that people must interact with each other.

We Act… React… and Interact

Do you remember hearing the expression, "Two's company but three's a crowd"? Its truth springs from the dynamics of personality *combinations*. Chances are, this expression has taken on a deeper meaning for you as you have learned about the differences and similarities of styles.

I am struggling to understand MYSELF…
I am trying to understand YOU, too…

Now I am going to try to understand US...
Just as it seems WE are making progress, here comes SOMEBODY ELSE to change OUR balance...
Now I have to think about ME... think about YOU... think about US... think about the NEW GUY... think about the NEW GUY and ME... think about the NEW GUY and YOU... think about ME and YOU and the NEW GUY... and think about ALL OF US...
And now, WHO do I see walking up to the THREE OF US...?
I think I need a nap!

Any time two or more people come together, we experience and observe *combinations* at work. "Combinations" refers to how people relate to each other. Each of us has a distinctive, individual blend, but when we begin to interact together, we become a combination — in other words, how does your behavioral style *combine with* my behavioral style? As we work together, we produce a combination that is *unique* to us. How we act *around* each other, how we react *to* each other, and how we interact *with* each other are influenced heavily by our own *blend* of traits *combining* with other individuals' *blends* of traits. We each bring benefits and pitfalls into every relationship.

It is with our unique differences that we can help, support and strengthen others. Our *differences* seem to attract us to others, more than our similarities. We tend to seek out what is missing in ourselves, to replace it with the assistance of other people.

We can see this relationship principle demonstrated in marriage — in fact, a term for "spouse" that has fallen into disuse today is "helpmate." Originally, this word was "help-meet." It did not mean a servant but "an appropriate helper," one who *completes* rather than *competes*. Almost every marriage relationship begins on a great note — few people marry someone they do not like! Most people marry someone they love deeply, with whom they plan to spend the rest of their lives. But the symphony turns sour when their mate's differences become irritations — and this well-known concept kicks in: "opposites *attract...* and then opposites *attack!*" Differences create disharmony and mates can become frustrated. This thought is familiar to every married person: "You're not the person I married! Why can't you be *normal... like me?!"*

I like this reply by Ruth Bell Graham, wife of evangelist Billy Graham, when a reporter asked her if she and Billy had similar personality characteristics. She answered, "Of course not — I'm nothing like him. But after all, if two people are just alike... all the time... about everything... one of them is unnecessary!"

The same is true in the business world (customer relations, employer and employee interactions, labor negotiations), the school (between teachers and students, administrators and faculty), the home (parents and children, brothers and sisters) ... and the list goes on! Whenever people interact with each other, you will find combinations, and you will find differences.

To be effective in life, we can *learn* to adjust our own behavior style, adapting smoothly to our environment. When we focus only on our own perspective, we become one-dimensional. But as we understand and work with our differences, we can create new dimensions. We can strengthen relationships and improve our chances for success. This concept is what *combinations* is all about.

Observe and Understand Others

Regardless of which personality types we deal with, we need to provide an environment that encourages their growth and makes it easy for them to deal with us. Understanding where others are coming from makes us twice as effective.

As you become more familiar with this information, you will be able to apply "D-I-S-C" principles in your personal and business relationships. When you observe others, ask yourself these questions:

Is this person's approach to life more outgoing, or is it more reserved?
Is this person task-oriented or people-oriented?
How does this person approach a task?
How does this person determine a goal?
How does this person learn?

What are this person's attitudes and preferences?
What are this person's motivational "hot buttons"?
What communication style does this person employ?
Where is this person's ideal environment?

Your answers to these questions may enable you to identify and predict many responses and behaviors as you work with and relate to other people. (Later in this book, we will give you tips to help you in all of the above areas!)

The purpose of this information is not to "label" others, nor to put limitations on their performance or capacity to achieve in any given endeavor — as we have said before, "labeling is disabling." Rather, your objective should be to become "people smart" as you learn to *observe* and *understand* others in practical ways.

Tools, Not Weapons

Before we jump further into all this great information, we need to emphasize this in plain language: *These "personality insights" are tools… not weapons!* The great value in understanding yourself and others is creating "win–win" opportunities, not using other people's strengths and weaknesses against them in order to get them to do your bidding or bring you success.

For example, picture a high "D," hormonal, controlling, teenage boy who, knowing this information, sets out deliberately to find a high "S," vulnerable teenage girl. Her great strengths are her desires to cooperate and to please people, and her greatest weaknesses involve her reluctance to speak up for herself and to say 'no.'" The potential for physical, emotional, mental and spiritual abuse in their "relationship" is very high.

Can you see how this controlling boy's intentions and actions are not significantly different from any others who would use personality styles information to get what they want from family members, friends or business associates? We must guard against using people to feed and support our own weaknesses. We must control ourselves, rather than controlling others.

So, in this section, we will establish the principles relating to predictable patterns of behavior — how we can expect "D's" to work with and relate to other "D's," "I's," "S's" and "C's." (And of course, how "I's," "S's," and "C's" may work with and relate to other "D's," "I's," "S's" and "C's" as well.)

To accomplish this, we will utilize a "**Trilogy Perspective**" — meaning *three different approaches,* revealing similar material in *three different ways* — none of them exactly alike — to provide a basis for understanding and to reinforce the teaching. The purpose of using **three viewpoints** is not simply repetition. Although repetition is a great tool in the learning process, you will see that the first view involves "sociability" issues, applying more readily to family and friends. The second view will include simple graphs that deal with the dynamics of interaction in work and personal life. Finally, the third view is business related, targeted toward building professional rapport and posture in a sales or negotiation setting.

At the same time, you will discover information in each of these contexts that can work well in the other areas of your life. The best preparation for living is knowing as many answers as you can ahead of time... and knowing what questions to ask when you don't exactly know what is going on! As you return to this section again and again in your lifetime, you will grow to appreciate its contexts and contents. Using these insights can help you to "engineer success" for everyone involved. After all... "If I understand you and you understand me, doesn't it make sense that we will be in a position to have a better relationship?"

The following pages present a general overview of the personality styles, answering in chart form the "people questions" we highlighted on pages 50 and 51.

Adjusting to Others' Styles

As we stated earlier, these charts will show you how "D's," "I's," "S's," and "C's" tend to relate to each other in social and work situations, but as noted, these are "unadjusted" situations — in other words, how, where, and why I can expect to get along with you if both of us are untrained in understanding different personality styles and building successful relationships.

Please note: This "Trilogy Perspective" information (three different approaches) will suggest guidelines for adjusting your own style to deal effectively and cooperatively with the four predominate styles. These guidelines are not presented as (nor should they be interpreted as) criteria or indicators for potential relationship success. While compatibility is important, so is commitment — both of which can be experienced if we work at it and understand what is going on in the relationship. Whether socially, in our personal life, or in business, success can be achieved as we work toward understanding ourselves and others and seek to grow together.

The "D" in Combination

"D" Relationships with a "D"

Just think about the situation you have when two "D's" get together... that's right — a battle! There is an old saying, "Anything with more than one head is a monster!" This is true in real life, as well as in science fiction. Have you noticed that few companies or organizations have two equal co-presidents? They understand what that old saying means!

Both "D" types want control. Both are unafraid of conflict, and both like a challenge. "D's" are committed to "making things happen." They can enjoy being with each other because they are so active and outgoing, but when there is a situation that calls for control, both will want to take over and be in charge. Both of them usually have the confidence and ability to achieve their goals. If they fail to make the right decision, they can find a way to make their decision right. To succeed in this relationship, they must agree together on who will lead and who will support as different situations arise. If they can eliminate a constant jockeying for position, they will have a dynamic relationship!

"D" Relationships with an "I"

Both types are active and outgoing. Both enjoy variety and upbeat lifestyles. However, each is motivated in different ways. The "D" is task-oriented and has a need to control. The "I" type is more impulsive and feels a need to be free of control. The "D" type is often short on words and big on results. The "I" personality sometimes thinks talking and doing are the same thing!

The "I" can help by demonstrating good relational skills. If the "I" can focus on producing rather than simply talking, they will help build an effective, energetic team. Be sure to publicly recognize "I" contributions and validate the "I" with encouraging feedback as a valued member of the team.

"D" Relationships with an "S"

"D" types like to lead and be in charge. "S" types tend to be followers and enjoy their supportive roles. "D's" make things happen — they are self-starters. "S" types are a little more reluctant to jump into "unknown territory." However, they are more than willing to help "D's" reach a goal and complete a task. Interpersonal relationships can unravel because "D's" enjoy constant change and variety, while the "S" prefers things to remain the same. Also, without making a careful effort to avoid doing so, "D's" can become abrasive and overbearing in dealing with "S's," who do not fight back but tend to "stuff" everything in.

Slower-paced, people-oriented "S's" can be a terrific balance to a "D's" fast-paced, task-oriented style if the "D" does not run them off or wear them out. Because "D's" and "S's" are opposite types, "D's" must be especially sensitive to their needs. "D's" can learn about loyalty and long-term people skills by observing the "S" style.

"D" Relationships with a "C"

This combination can sometimes be difficult. "D's" tend to like change and operate on the basis that "the end justifies the means." But "C" types do not like change unless they know exactly where it will take them. They would rather maintain structure while sticking with the tried, proven and known. Also, while "D's" tend to be direct and to the point, "C's" are extremely sensitive and do not take well to criticism.

Because both styles are so task-oriented, they can make a dynamic team. But because task issues are usually more intense and demanding than casual relationships, this "D–C" combination can get out of hand easily. "D's" create things; "C's" improve and perfect them. However, expect them to struggle in their relationship because both of them have vastly different expectation levels. "D's" should "shoot from the hip" a little less and take better aim at their target.

The "I" in Combination

"I" Relationships with a "D"

"I's" think in terms of people; "D's" think in terms of projects. "I's" make decisions based on how they feel other people will be affected by the outcome. "D" types think in terms of what is best for the whole company or operation. They want the entire process to succeed. Because both are outgoing, they usually develop good friendships. "D" types are bottom-line oriented — if they can "warm up" and be a little more friendly, they can have a good relationship with an "I." "I's" will win "D's" over if they focus more on "doing" than on "talking."

"I's" tend to look to others for validation and acceptance. In relationships with a "D," they need to focus more on *producing* results and less on *receiving* emotional gratification. Rather than looking for praise or recognition, understand that the "D" type expresses itself in terms of *respect* for your achievements and ability to go the distance.

"I" Relationships with an "I"

If anything with more than one head is a monster, anything with more than one "I" is a party! When two "I" types get together, you can bet there will be a lunch involved! "I's" love to celebrate, and sometimes they do better in planning the victory party than leading the team to victory.

Two "I's" will enjoy socializing and having fun. This means they can turn drudgery into play, and can inspire and induce others to join them in reaching the goal together. Unfortunately, their ability to accomplish a task is not a top priority. When two "I's" work together, they desperately need to develop personal responsibility and accountability. This combination is very capable of achieving great goals if they can manage to stay focused on the objective. Just be aware that their frenetic style needs to find balance.

"I" Relationships with an "S"

This combination works very well together. "I's" are great starters but tend to be poor finishers; "S's" tend to be great finishers but are slow starters. "I's" see their ideas in "technicolor" and can present them with enthusiasm. "S" types will help "I's" make sure all their talk is backed up and their work is completed satisfactorily.

Sometimes, conflicts occur when "I's" change plans impulsively, while "S's" are trying to stabilize the situation. In working with "S" types, "I's" should remember that change is not always progress, and that the tortoise often beats the hare in a long-distance race. "S" types will follow and support the "I's" imaginative plans, but they will shy away if "I's" bounce impetuously from one scheme to another.

"I" Relationships with a "C"

This combination is like the "little girl who had a little curl." When it is good it is very, very good, but when it is bad it is horrid! "I" types have great people skills but lack the "C's" natural capacity for giving attention to accuracy and details. "C" types are detail-oriented but lack the "I's" natural capacity for giving warmth and attention to people. "C" types love structure and hate surprises, while "I's" hate structure and love surprises.

In order to be organized, "I's" needs "C" type qualities in their life. In order to lighten up and enjoy the journey, the "C" needs the "I's" qualities. If the two can connect, they will make a good team. To facilitate this, "I's" can control their tendency to think out loud; presenting ideas less emotionally and more rationally. They can make lists and prioritize actions, so they are less distracted. They can listen more and talk less. Doing so will create confidence that the "C" is involved with someone who is sensible and self-controlled. Together, they can be a well-rounded team.

The "S" in Combination

"S" Relationships with a "D"

An "S" is initially drawn to "D" types because of their confidence. "D" types know how to start projects; "S's" know how to follow things up. However, after a while, "S's" may find themselves worn out by the "D's" kinetic power and energy — they are always on the go!

Their expectations are very different: "D's" like action and independence; "S's" enjoy calmness and close relationships. They do not share a common "vocabulary" in the language of living — they will have to learn how to communicate effectively. It is fair to say they will always speak each other's "language" with an "accent," but both will benefit by learning to understand each other. The "S's" ability to exercise patience and flexibility is important to the success of this relationship. "S's" can learn to be more outspoken and clear about their expectations — if they stand up for themselves, they will earn the "D's" respect. While they seldom admit self-doubt, "D's" will learn to value "S's" contributions in keeping them on course.

"S" Relationships with an "I"

"S's" and "I's" are warm and friendly. Both enjoy people and close friendships. "I's" are impulsive and like spontaneous activity; they sometimes have difficulty keeping their focus. On the other hand, "S" types prefer stability and calmness; they keep their focus well. "I" types are great starters and poor finishers; "S's" tend to finish well once they get past the starting point.

The challenge for "S's" and "I's" in a relationship center around the "S's" need for sameness and the "I's" need for variety. Even in friendships, "S's" look for quality and commitment, while the "I" looks for quantity and diversity. "S's" should learn to be more demonstrative and outgoing with "I's," and be more assertive in helping them to be accountable.

"S" Relationships with an "S"

"S" types get along great with other "S" types. This is perhaps the most compatible combination of all. Both enjoy people — their stable, caring, giving nature makes them easy to be around. But if two "D's" are a monster, and two "I's" are a party, two "S" types can be a stalled car! All right — that's *too* dramatic, but the point is that leadership and direction can be lacking in this combination. Because both of them prefer to follow, they have a tendency to put off plans while waiting for a leader to tell them what to do.

When they have an agreed objective, the two "S" types will work together very pleasantly and will make life go better for everyone else. The challenge for them in this relationship will not be in learning to get along — it will be in setting goals, starting plans, and venturing outside of their comfort zone. They should encourage each other to stretch, to be more bold, concentrating on accomplishing tasks, knowing that they will attend to the needs of others almost automatically.

"S" Relationships with a "C"

An "S" focuses on individuals and makes sure that people are getting along. "S's" will find that "C" types focus on the task at hand and all the details that must come together for completion. Generally, these two types will work well together. Since both are reserved, they will not risk being overly pushy. The "C's" will remain committed to excellence, and "S's" will pursue their commitment to keeping everyone happy. This produces a dynamic team!

"S's" will communicate better with "C's" as they think in terms of how the "S" contributes to the *process*. Efficiency is important to "C's," so "S's" should not become too emotional in dealing with them. "S's" tend to be sentimental, and "C's" do not understand this. On the other hand, "C's" are sensitive and easily offended, so "S's" must use their skills in helping to correct them, rather than simply pointing out their error.

The "C" in Combination

"C" Relationships with a "D"

"C's" and "D's" are task-oriented, but it is here that similarities end! Their potential for conflict is in *completing* tasks. "C's" plan their work and then work their plan. "C's" follow directions. If they start something, they finish it. "D" types change directions in midstream. They anticipate the bottom line rather than planning how to get there. They'll do whatever it takes — "the end justifies the means."

"C's" anchor this relationship and keep the ship from going aground in a storm, but they must be careful not to drag their anchor when it is time to set sail! Accountability is important for both — "C's" can help the "D" accept the responsibility that accompanies leadership and provide an objective measure of results. "C's" have difficulty recognizing their own mistakes and tend to judge others by their own exacting criteria. Both of them will benefit by becoming a little more people-oriented.

"C" Relationships with an "I"

"C's" and "I's" have a strange and wonderful relationship — "C's" think "I's" are strange and "I's" think they, *themselves,* are wonderful! Perhaps more than any other combination, they need each other desperately! "C" types are weak in the "I's" inborn interpersonal skills, and "I's" lacks the "C's" cautious nature and concern for quality.

"C's" can follow through on projects that "I's" only talk about. When working together, "C's" must understand that "I's" think with their mouths open — that's the way they process. But "C's" hear those words as commitments. So, "C's" must guard their expectations and be clear on exactly what both are agreeing to do, decide which issues are worth dying over and which they can live with. When the two "meet in the middle," they can be dynamic... if only they will meet!

"C" Relationships with an "S"

"C" types go well with "S" types because both are reserved. They do not want to overpower each other. Both prefer the tried and proven to the new and unknown. "C" types appreciate exacting quality while the "S" strives to please everyone and will be more deadline conscious. The danger is in bogging down in the details, but the friendly "S" will help "C's" complete a task in order to keep peace.

"C's" must make room for emotions. "S's" are far more sentimental than "C's," looking for reassurance that they are appreciated. "C's" should try to become more expressive and not expect "S's" to take the lead in a business or social setting — when a "C" is willing to do so in an appropriate manner, an "S" will march to the drumbeat. Encourage "S's" to speak their mind, since they will not do so willingly. Use a softer approach in dealing with them to achieve desired results.

"C" Relationships with a "C"

"C's" relate well with each other because both can understand the importance of quality work and good value. They may have difficulty completing projects on time because they are perfectionists. Both feel they could improve if they could only go over it "one more time!" In social settings, it is hard to be a host because they feel everything must be perfect. And it is hard to be a guest because they feel obligated to do that perfectly, too!

Both will benefit from learning that there are varying degrees of excellence. They can learn to trust each other and not spend all their time proofreading each other's Xerox copies! Their ability to negotiate through disagreements is a real asset. They respect each other's opinions and "space." As a team, they should work at getting outside themselves, practicing spontaneity. They must have fun, even if they must plan it in advance. As they improve their "friendliness factor," they will become tremendous assets to themselves and others.

Combination Dynamics

A Visual Chart of Interaction

When dealing with **Combinations**, keep in focus that it is with our unique differences that we strengthen and support one another. To be effective in life, we must learn to adjust our own behavior style. If we always focus on seeing things only from our own perspective, we will be one-dimensional.

Regardless of which personality type we deal with, we need to provide an environment that encourages their growth and in turn makes it easy for them to deal with us. Understanding where others are coming from makes us twice as effective. Remember the key: *"If I understand you and you understand me, doesn't it make sense that we can have a better relationship?"* Understanding this concept is what **Combinations** is all about.

These charts show how one style commonly interacts with the other four styles. Please keep in mind that we are referring to your *most predominate trait* as it interacts with another person's *most predominate trait.* Also, two areas are being measured:

1) How they interact on a business level to accomplish the task at hand, which most often involves their **Environment** style; and 2) how they combine on a personal level, which most often involves their **Basic** style.

Please Note: The following information suggests guidelines for adjusting your own style to deal effectively and cooperatively with the four predominate styles. They are presented with the thought "…unless you learn to adjust your behavioral style, this is the relationship these people will probably experience." They are not presented as (nor should they be interpreted as) criteria by which to predict or determine potential success in any particular relationship.

The "D" graph: *How these strong-willed and adventurous types live and work with others*

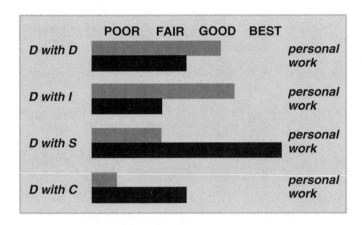

"D" with "D" — *"Good"* on the personal level because they have similar likes and dislikes, but only *"Fair"* in working together because they both want to be in charge.

"D" with "I" — Better than *"Good"* on the personal level because they have fun and are outgoing, but barely *"Fair"* in working together because they clash on work habits.

"D" with "S" — Barely *"Fair"* on the personal level because they are opposites and "wear" on each other, but *"Best"* in working together because they complete each other.

"D" with "C" — Very *"Poor"* on the personal level because both are strong-willed and divided in the area of risk-taking and compliance, and *"Fair"* in working together because they can usually find a middle ground.

The "I" graph: *How these fun-loving and imaginative types live and work with others*

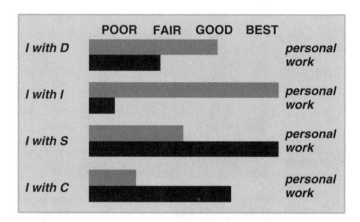

 "I" with "D" — *"Good"* on the personal level although the "I" wishes the "D" were more fun and less intense, but barely *"Fair"* in working together because they clash on work habits.

 "I" with "I" — *"Best"* on the personal level because they have the same excitement about life, but *"Poor"* in working together because they are easily distracted from accomplishing the task at hand.

 "I" with "S" — *"Fair"* on the personal level because one is outgoing while the other is reserved, but *"Best"* in working together because they combine creativity and responsibility.

 "I" with "C" — *"Poor"* on the personal level because their "gears" run in different directions, but *"Good"* in working together because one creates and the other improves; one "envisions" and the other delivers.

The "S" graph: *How these calm and steady types live and work with others*

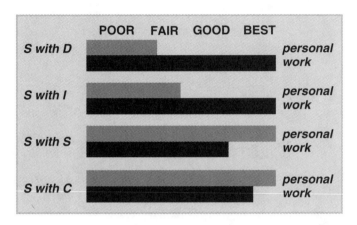

"S" with "D" — Barely *"Fair"* on the personal level because they are opposites and sometimes get "weary" of the other's energy level, but *"Best"* in working together, as long as there is mutual respect, because they complete each other.

"S" with "I" — *"Fair"* on the personal level because one is outgoing while the other is reserved, but *"Best"* in working together because "I's" enjoy starting and "S's" enjoy finishing.

"S" with "S" — *"Best"* on the personal level because they are both supportive and loyal, and *"Good"* in working together because they accomplish their tasks even though they will not set ambitious goals.

"S" with "C" — *"Best"* on the personal level because they respect each other's rights and privacy, and very *"Good"* in working together because they can dedicate themselves to meeting the task with a pleasing balance of people-centeredness.

The "C" graph: *How these quiet and detail-oriented types live and work with others*

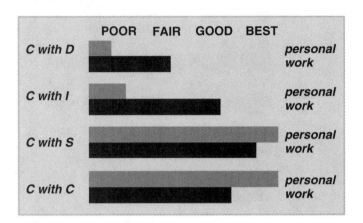

"C" with "D" — Very *"Poor"* on the personal level because both are strong-willed and have opposite approaches in the area of rational and objective decision-making, and only *"Fair"* in working together because they tend to clash in areas of accountability and respect for each other's values. One wants to be right, and the other wants to be "more right."

"C" with "I" — Only slightly better than *"Poor"* on the personal level because of their reasoning style (one "thinks" and the other "feels"), but *"Good"* in working together because their opposite skills of tactical planning and free-thought brainstorming enable them to deliver what they dream up!

"C" with "S" — *"Best"* on the personal level because they respect each other and avoid giving offense, and slightly less *"Best"* in working together because they give great attention to detail with a concern for its impact on people.

"C" with "C" — *"Best"* on the personal level because they are "cut from the same cloth," and very *"Good"* in working together because they often find agreement on methods and procedures, double-checking each other for accuracy.

The "D" Business Environment

Working with Others

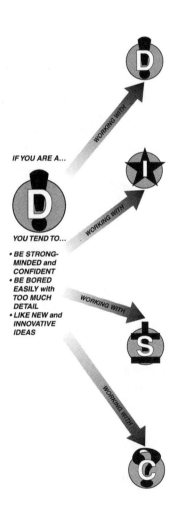

IF YOU ARE A...

YOU TEND TO...

• BE STRONG-
MINDED and
CONFIDENT
• BE BORED
EASILY with
TOO MUCH
DETAIL
• LIKE NEW and
INNOVATIVE
IDEAS

WORKING WITH

WORKING WITH

WORKING WITH

WORKING WITH

D — Do not be too strong or overbearing... just be yourself. "D" types see eye-to-eye pretty quickly. Let them have some control.

I — Go out of your way to be extra friendly. Let them talk and tell their latest story, joke, adventure, etc. Be a little less "businesslike." You should hit it off well.

S — Slow down a little bit and do not scare them. Your strong style may intimidate them. Be friendly. Give them a chance to digest the facts. Do not stress the "new." They like the stability of the tried and proven.

C — Answer all of their questions. Give facts, figures, comparisons, charts, graphs, etc. They love proof. Take things a little slower. Do not be pushy. Give them time to think. Answer their objections. Do not be phoney.

The "I" Business Environment

Working with Others

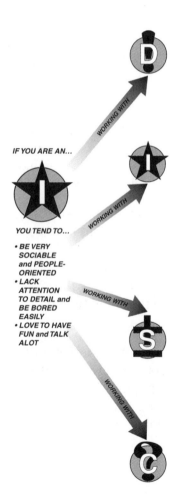

IF YOU ARE AN...

YOU TEND TO...

• *BE VERY SOCIABLE and PEOPLE-ORIENTED*
• *LACK ATTENTION TO DETAIL and BE BORED EASILY*
• *LOVE TO HAVE FUN and TALK ALOT*

D — Cut the jokes and the small talk. Get to the bottom line quickly. Be businesslike. Stress results. Do not waste time.

I — Remember, you're not there just to visit! Be careful not to talk each other to death! Remember to "ask for the order" or schedule a follow-up meeting.

S — Talk in terms of people and stories. Use facts along the way. Provide basic training and product knowledge. Earn their trust. Be careful not to "come on too strong" or be overly friendly too soon.

C — Cut the socializing. Cut the stories. Do not waste their time. Give facts and figures. Do your homework. Do not be silly. Provide proof. Raise your "C." This can be a real challenge for you... concentrate!

The "S" Business Environment

Working with Others

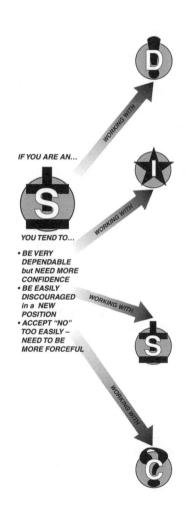

IF YOU ARE AN...

S

YOU TEND TO...

- BE VERY DEPENDABLE but NEED MORE CONFIDENCE
- BE EASILY DISCOURAGED in a NEW POSITION
- ACCEPT "NO" TOO EASILY – NEED TO BE MORE FORCEFUL

WORKING WITH

D — Try to have more confidence. Be a little more assertive. Recognize that they may challenge you. Do not be intimidated by the strong-willed "D."

I — Do not lose control by letting them "ramble." Keep the direction of the meeting focused. You both like people and should be able to relate well. Watch out for their "over-friendly" attitude.

S — They, like you, need reassurance. Be a little more confident than usual. You will get along well. Do not forget to be brave and "close the deal."

C — Answer their questions. Be confident in your product and plan. Remember that "C" types will challenge you with skepticism. That is normal. Firmly present facts and figures. Your slower approach will work well in your favor.

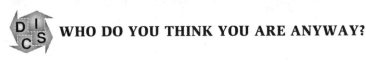
The "C" Business Environment

Working with Others

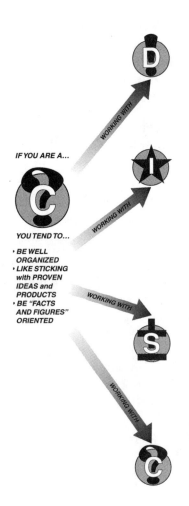

IF YOU ARE A...

C

YOU TEND TO...

- *BE WELL ORGANIZED*
- *LIKE STICKING with PROVEN IDEAS and PRODUCTS*
- *BE "FACTS AND FIGURES" ORIENTED*

WORKING WITH

D — Head to the bottom line. Do not overwhelm them with facts and figures. Give the big idea. Have more courage in what you are doing. Show results, goals, and achievements.

I — Let them talk a little more. Laugh at their stories. Show enthusiasm. Do not overwhelm them with facts and figures. Give them the experience and fun of "trying out" one of your products for themselves.

S — Be friendly, not too businesslike. Give them the "space" they need to accept your presentation. Talk about family. Do not be pushy. Slow down a little.

C — You will be right at home. Your thorough and precise presentation will be appreciated. You will see the same issues. This should be your best proposal/ sale/meeting.

Accurate Expectations

Contrasting the Differences of Styles

A Latin proverb says, "Everyone excels in something in which another fails." But we have difficulty when *others* fail in something in which *we* excel. Much of our anger and disappointment in dealing with others is caused by *their* failure to live up to *our* expectations. So, it is important that we enter into relationships (personal or business) with *reasonable expectations* concerning our roles, our accountability, our performance duties, our stability — in short, for our "team" to win, we must know our players!

George Bernard Shaw was not really contradicting the Bible when he said, "Do not do unto others as you would that they do unto you. Their tastes may not be the same." While we recognize that we must treat individuals with the sensitivity that we expect for ourselves, we also understand that we must treat them *individually.*

As we promised earlier, we will provide specific tips to help you in applying this information in your personal and business relationships. The following seven pages highlight major differences in the four basic "D," "I," "S," and "C" types. But as you look at them — and flip back to page 28 to see how each type can make a unique contribution to every event — begin asking yourself: *"Who do I know who has this style? Where can this person's special contributions be most effective? How can I position myself to help them win... and win in the process myself, as well?"*

Al LeBlanc, a friend in Massachusetts, has built a very successful and profitable business by developing his "people skills." Knowing how easily relationships can be harmed through misunderstandings, he cautions, "Don't do permanent damage to a temporary situation." Our personality differences can create either "problems" or "opportunities," depending on our skill in handling them. Robert Redford's observation is true: "Problems can *become* opportunities when the right people come together." This information helps us *become* the right people.

WHO DO YOU THINK YOU ARE ANYWAY?

TASK METHOD

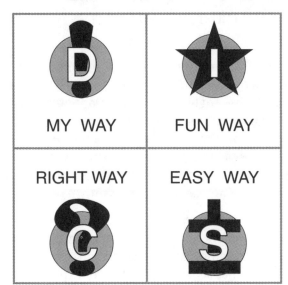

| MY WAY | FUN WAY |
| RIGHT WAY | EASY WAY |

Each personality style has a preferred approach to doing a job. "D's" have confidence in "conquering" a task. "I's" look at it as a game to win and make a task enjoyable rather than boring. "S's" want the least stressful way to do a project, and they may sacrifice in order to avoid conflict. "C's" plan their work and then work their plan.

GOAL SETTING

Each personality style has a different approach to setting goals. For a "D," it is the meeting of a challenge that is important. For an "I," the goal should be reached in smaller steps, accompanied by immediate rewards. The "S" believes that "slow and steady wins the race." The "C" can appreciate future distance rewards.

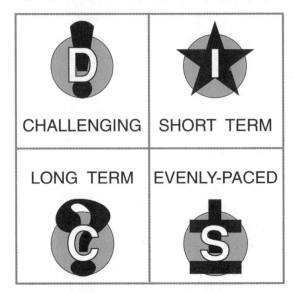

| CHALLENGING | SHORT TERM |
| LONG TERM | EVENLY-PACED |

LEARNING STYLES

Each personality style approaches instruction differently:

"I want to do things my own way!"

"What is this material about, bottom line?"
"Let me help teach the class."
"Be quick and to the point."
"Let me be in charge."

"I want to do things the fun way!"

"I learn best in a relaxed atmosphere."
"Let's learn by playing games."
"I enjoy being creative."
"I'll understand if I can see it."

"I want to do things the right way!"

"Answer my questions with quality information."
"Give me facts and figures."
"Let me do extra credit work."
"Explain your expectations."

"I want to do things the easy way!"

"Slow down a little, so I can process these changes."
"Go over it one more time."
"Help me understand this."
"I want to please you."

ATTITUDES & PREFERENCES

The likes and dislikes of each personality type are very different:

 "I like to win!" | **"I like to be liked!"**

I like to think about the future. *I like new ideas.* *I like a challenge.* *I like activities that change a lot.* *I like projects that produce results.* *I like to be my own boss.* *I like to move fast.* *I don't like to be under anyone else's control.* *I don't like to get bogged down in details.* *I like to be evaluated on results.*	*I like practical ways to do things.* *I don't like conflicts with people.* *I like to express my ideas and feelings.* *I like being part of a group.* *I don't like details.* *I dislike a lot of control or pushy people.* *I like people to agree and get along.* *I enjoy peace and harmony.* *I like a lot of social activity and fun.* *I like surprises.*
I like practical ideas and suggestions. *I like to know exactly what is expected of me.* *I don't like a lot of clutter.* *I like to finish whatever I start.* *I like an established routine.* *I don't like conflicts.* *I like technical things that require thought and planning.* *I think I worry a lot.* *I like specialized tasks.* *I like clear instructions.*	*I like teamwork and cooperation.* *I like predictability.* *I like to work on one task at a time.* *I like sticking with what I know will work.* *I don't like arguments.* *I like things to stay the same.* *I love practicality — the more practical, the better.* *I don't like conflict.* *I don't like sudden changes.* *I like knowing what is going to happen in advance.*

 "I like to be right!" | **"I like to be accepted!"**

MOTIVATIONAL TIPS

Each personality style has different "hot buttons." They might say:

I like to be in charge. *I like situations that change a lot.* *When I work hard, I work hard.* *When I play, I play hard.* *I like to have power.* *I am not afraid to take risks.* *I like to make decisions.* *I don't like the same routine.* *I don't like doing slow or repetitive tasks.* *I like new challenges.* *I like to solve problems.* *I like to be in authority.*	*I like a lot of friends.* *I like acceptance.* *I like other people to handle the details.* *I like a friendly environment.* *I like encouragement.* *I prefer short projects to long ones.* *It is important to me to be popular.* *I don't like a lot of rules.* *I like to "go" and "do."* *I dislike too many regulations.* *I like public recognition.* *I am easily distracted.*
I like quality. *I don't like a lot of silliness.* *I like detailed tasks.* *I like logical information.* *I like charts and graphs.* *I like to find creative solutions.* *I like to be reassured.* *I like to be organized.* *I have high standards for myself and others.* *I tend to be a perfectionist.* *I like to be commended for doing good work.* *I like to know things step-by-step.*	*I like a stable lifestyle.* *I like to please others.* *I enjoy people enjoying life.* *I don't like starting new projects.* *It makes me happy to see others happy.* *I don't work well with aggressive people.* *I like to feel appreciated.* *I like routine procedures.* *I don't like "daring" events.* *I like to feel secure.* *I enjoy finishing a task.* *I don't mind being told what to do.*

COMMUNICATION TIPS

When talking to each of the personality types, it is best to:

Get to the main point.
Be brief and specific.
Think in terms of answering the "WHAT?" question.
Focus on action-based results.
Solve problems.
Be logical.
Agree with objective facts — not subjective people.
Look for obstacles to overcome.
Support your statements credibly.

Keep a friendly environment.
Let them express their ideas.
Think in terms of answering the "WHO?" question.
Help them turn their talk into action.
Tell them what others have done.
Allow time for socializing.
Have short term projects with incentives.
Indicate mutual friendship.
Focus on their accomplishments.

Supply clear, accurate data.
Eliminate surprises.
Think in terms of answering the "WHY?" question.
Create a "Pro/Con" balance sheet for suggested actions.
Be specific on points of agreement.
Show how they fit in.
Anticipate their questions and have credible answers.
Be patient and speak slowly while providing details.
Review your thoughts clearly.

Be agreeable and nonthreatening.
Show sincere interest.
Think in terms of answering the "HOW?" question.
Demonstrate patience.
Be clear and explain details calmly.
Allow time to adjust to changes.
Explain their contribution and valued service in the plan.
Provide follow-up and transitional support.
Show them the benefits of their actions.

IDEAL ENVIRONMENT

Each style has a "comfort zone": "I like an environment where…"

I can be in charge of myself and others.
There are a lot of different activities and challenges.
I have freedom to set my own priorities and pace.
I can see that I am growing.
The bottom line is important.
I have good opportunities for advancement.
I can look good.

There are people to talk to.
Good work is recognized and praised.
There is opportunity to influence others.
Everyone has a good attitude.
People are accepted.
There are positive working conditions.
I am free from a lot of details and repetitive tasks.

There is a specific plan.
I don't have someone looking over my shoulder.
There is no "hurried" activity.
There are exact roles and job descriptions.
Expectations are clear.
Changes are made slowly and carefully.
I can be rewarded for new ideas and improvements.

I can identify with a group.
Sincere appreciation is shown.
There is a regular routine of events.
I don't feel rushed and under pressure.
There is not much change.
We specialize in a doing a few things well.
I know what and where my boundaries are.

SECRET TIP

Each style has a "blind spot" that requires special attention...

SECRET TIP:
Before you can be IN authority, you must first learn to be UNDER authority.

Learn to *follow* in the process of learning leadership

SECRET TIP:
It's NICE to be important, but it's more IMPORTANT to be nice.

Learn to keep egos in check when involving others

SECRET TIP:
Don't be afraid to say, "What part of NO don't you understand?"

Learn to be more assertive and in control of their lives

SECRET TIP:
People don't CARE how much you know until they KNOW how much you care.

Learn that "people skills" are as important as technical skills

Chapter 4

Traits of
Different Styles

In *Positive Personality Profiles,* we looked at some of the "natural tendencies" that accompany the "D," "I," "S," and "C" personality styles. And in the last chapter, we have just demonstrated how each style tends to have its own "comfort zones" — in facing daily situations, our natural tendencies search out areas of comfort and safety.

Remember, no one is purely a "D," "I," "S," or "C" type. Each of us has our own unique mixture of these qualities and traits. Our "Environment" may call for one type of behavior, while our "Basic Style" might or might not fit well into that setting. You have heard that someone is "the *wrong person* for this job." We prefer to say, "This is the *wrong job* for this person!" People have strengths and weaknesses that may or may not be helpful in their personal lives or vocations. I read once that the average American makes several *career* changes (not just job changes) in his or her life. Could it be that everyone is looking for a better fit, a better match for his style? This material can help all of us to improve by understanding ourselves and making necessary, appropriate adjustments in life.

You may have come to see why you may be less comfortable in certain environments. If you have completed a *Personality Insights Style Analysis,* you may have seen that your "Environment Style" graph looks strikingly different from your Basic Style graph. Perhaps a "light bulb has clicked on" in your brain, and you can see now why you may be feeling "stressed out." You can use up a lot of energy when you have to make yourself as flexible as Gumby!

Chapter 6 of *Positive Personality Profiles* provides some descriptive images to help you remember the orientation and characteristics of the "D," "I," "S," and "C" personality styles. It features a chart showing each style in quick reference form. In this chapter, we will follow a similar course with information that will help you identify "comfort zones" for yourself and others.

Again, the purpose of this information is not to label or limit anyone. Rather, you can use these insights to understand and relate better to people — picking up clues to their way of seeing things and expressing ideas and processing information. You will learn to recognize patterns and predict characteristic responses, so you can "create a climate" for success rather than failure, for cooperation rather than conflict.

Given the same "facts," let's see how different personality types respond to situations, based on their own perspectives. (An overview chart for the following information appears on page 84.)

Outlook or Orientation:

D – **Money, profit, the "what's in it for me?" bottom line.** They tend to see things in terms of personal competition, and every situation is an opportunity to conquer and win. They tend to be "me-oriented," but not necessarily selfish.

I – **Fun, travel, position.** They tend to be self-promoters and enjoy people-centered activity. Meeting powerful people and having stories to tell about their experiences promote feelings of prestige that boost their self-image.

S – **Helping people and building friendships.** Their peace and enjoyment is derived often from others, so they are more concerned with comfort and environment. They gain satisfaction in helping others to win.

C – **Product value and excellence.** How well policies are followed and procedures are handled is a "big deal" to these exacting people. They do not want to move until they are sure they have found the best option.

Blind Spot:

D – **Appreciating others' feelings.** They tend to "take charge" and assume that everyone else will follow along happily. Because *they* speak up or challenge whatever is not to their liking, they assume others will, too.

I – **Disorganization.** They tend to be sporadic and impulsive in their work habits. They have "piling systems" instead of filing systems — and while it may work for them, it is not duplicatible and may create extra work.

S – **Possessive.** They tend to be generous until they feel taken for granted, and then they guard their territory. Their desire for peace and predictability is very strong and they can become passive-aggressive to ensure it.

C – **Critical, demanding of self and others.** They tend not to wonder why the *glass* is half-empty but why *you* chose what was obviously the wrong-size glass. Even when given excellence, they still expect perfection.

Excesses:

D – **Directs too much.** Without meaning to, they tend to be bossy. "Nature abhors a vacuum," and if they see one in leadership, they fill the gap whether invited or not.

I – **Talks too much.** They tend to chatter when things get too quiet and that makes other people nervous. Under pressure, they become glib and their credibility suffers.

S – **Agrees too much.** They tend to feel guilty when they say no, and they frustrate themselves and others in trying to please everyone. They want to be appreciated.

C – **Questions too much.** They tend to probe and examine beyond others' comfort levels. When they ask probing questions others haven't thought about, they can make some people feel stupid.

Clues to Look For:

D – **Big desk, nice office, "whirlwind" action.** When you observe "trappings of power" and the kinetic activity surrounding it, recognize this person as task-oriented and fast-paced.

I – **Picture of family and disorganized desk.** This individual will have some great anecdotes and enjoys leaping from project-to-project with frenetic energy. Know that this is a people-oriented, fast-paced person.

S – **Charts nearby and manuals neatly organized.** A comfortable and reassuring "feathered nest" for its occupant. Items needed for reassurance may be within reach, along with a welcoming candy dish for visitors. This person is people-oriented and slower-paced.

C – **Neat and tidy, everything filed.** Visual clutter causes this cautious individual emotional and even physical discomfort, and they like to feel well-prepared and in control. This is a task-oriented, slower-paced person.

When Cornered:

D – **Fights their way out.** They enjoy challenge and conflict, and may not "take it personally" — they may seem surprised if you do. They like to win.

I – **Talks their way out.** They want to give and receive reassurances that you are still friends, and they may be devastated inside while seeming less concerned outside.

S – **Don't put them in a corner!** Sometimes they may crumble, and other times they may claw like a cat getting a bath. They take disagreements very personally. They usually end up with hurt feelings.

C – **Defensive — acts like a "D."** Allow them a way to "save face" or they may even defend being wrong. They don't have to "win," but they are not going to "lose."

Likes to Do Things:

D – **The fastest way.** They may not look before they leap. If they did not make the right decision, they will make their decision right. Knowing they can "pull it off," they follow their instincts and then move on to the next project.

I – **The fun way.** They do not like boring, repetitive tasks, so they will find a way to make a "game" out of it — but they will try to be practical since it's no fun to do it over again if it's wrong.

S – **The traditional way.** Their first response will be to do it the way they have always done it. If it is new, they tend to resist it or try to make a familiar method work. Experimentation is uncomfortable.

C – **The proper way.** They admire those who follow established procedures, and even if the result is right, they are not happy if protocol was not followed. They do not believe "the end justifies the means."

Approach to Tasks:

D – **Get it done now** ...and preferably by someone else. They tend to see the big picture but not the details, so they delegate readily.

I – **Put it off until later.** They are distracted easily and bored quickly. If they remember to start, they may switch to another task while they let this one simmer until deadline.

S – **Get help from others.** There is security in being part of a team — they can share the responsibility and the credit. They appreciate validation and reassurance.

C – **I'll do it myself.** They tend to think even a copy machine can skip a detail, so they view cooperative efforts skeptically. They may revise up to their deadline to make it perfect.

Primary Style:	D	I	S	C
Outlook or Orientation:	Money, Profit Bottom Line	Fun, Travel Position	Helping People Building Friendships	Product, Value Excellence
Blind Spot:	Appreciating Others' Feelings	Disorganization (Piling Rather than Filing)	Possessive (Lives by Order, Tranquility)	Critical (Demanding of Self & Others)
Excesses:	Directs too much	Talks too much	Agrees too much	Questions too much
Clues to Look For:	Big Desk, Nice Office "Whirlwind" Action	Picture of Family Disorganized Desk	Charts Nearby Manuals Organized	Neat and Tidy Everything Filed
When Cornered:	Fights their way out	Talks their way out	Don't put them in a corner!	Defensive — acts like a "D"
Likes to Do Things:	The Fastest Way	The Fun Way	The Traditional Way	The Proper Way
Approach to Tasks:	Get it done now	Put it off until later	Get help from others	I'll do it myself

Predictable Patterns

The following pages deal with "predictable patterns" — how you can expect "D's," "I's," "S's," and "C's" to behave according to their personality styles. Again, it is important to note two things about this information:

1) This information is not intended as a "predictor of success" in any area of performance. It is simply a "heads up" that will help you know when someone is in danger of veering off-course — even yourself!

2) What may appear to be a negative comment is not meant to be taken as "wrong." It is simply the way an individual is predisposed to behave. Knowing this information, we can change or adapt our behaviors in order to succeed. Even when we speak of "weaknesses," we say in our Personality Insights Seminars that "weaknesses are strengths pushed to an extreme, and therefore become out of control."

So, our goal will be learning to move confidently into relationships with both eyes open — understanding that "labeling is disabling." If we know what we can expect and what to guard against, we will be able to adjust our style for better results.

The Way They Process Information:

D – **"Let's just do it — get finished!"** This style tends to hear what it wants to hear and may "suppose" more than it learns. If this is your style, practice listening more closely and thinking more critically. In teaching people with this style, ask them to repeat what they have heard you say and what they believe you mean, to make sure you are communicating accurately.

I – **"Let's have some fun!"** This style tends to become restless when handling statistics and data, and is not skilled at auditory learning. If you have this style, be more methodical in taking notes so you can refer to them later on. Try to see the underlying principles that explain "why" and can be applied in other situations as well. In teaching, encourage this style to take notes, and relate what you are teaching to real-life experiences. Plan "hands-on" opportunities for learning.

S – **"Slow down — help me!"** This is a style that thinks and considers at a slower pace. They are not less intelligent; they process information differently and want to be sure they understand. If you have this style, do not be afraid to ask for further explanation. In teaching this style, exercise patience and pace yourself. Ask clarifying questions in a nonconfrontational manner.

C – **"Answer my question!"** This style may grasp the basic information quickly and begin probing for background details before others are up-to-speed. They want quality answers to their in-depth questions. If you have this style, get your additional facts at appropriate times and be sensitive to others. In teaching this style, you cannot be only "one page ahead of the student." Be over-prepared.

How They Handle a Budget:

D – **Go over it briefly.** Not you... them! Budgets are targets at best to this style. Their real goal is doing the deed, and financial details tend to be of lesser concern. They may glance at a budget, but they will not refer to it often. Someone else will be needed for this area.

I – **What is it?** A budget is a mystery to this style. They are not necessarily spendthrifts, but they must learn to "make do" with whatever they have. Financial projections and statements are abstracts to them and they prefer flexibility to limitations.

S – **Stay under it.** Because they are team players, they do not want to shortchange anyone. So, they may hesitate to spend money and put off making purchase decisions. Ultimately, they will try to come in under budget so there is a little left for unplanned expenses and so they will feel they have been wise. They do not want to make decisions about budget cuts, especially those that impact other people.

C – Stay within it. These are analytical people, so they will have reasonable projections of income and outgo. They will find value for their dollar and they will not be afraid to spend what they've got. If they find a bargain, they will apply the savings to upgrade another budgeted item on their list.

Driven By Their:

D – Will. By sheer force of will, they can find ways to accomplish what others find impossible.

I – Feelings. Under impulse, they are influenced to do many things that just seem to be right at the time.

S – Emotions. Easily swayed by sentiment, their mood often determines their performance.

C – Mind/Intellect. Distrusting emotion, they let logic and data dictate their views and decisions.

Key Strength:

D – Firm. Not subject much to peer influence, they set their own course and are able to stick to it.

I – Fun. Their perspective is optimistic, and they encourage others to have hope for the future.

S – Friendly. Basically agreeable, they "cool down" hot people and situations, and "warm up" cold ones.

C – Factual. Well-grounded in who they are, they are not easily excited or distracted by the temporary.

Key Weakness:

D – Not very friendly. Because they are fast-paced and task-oriented, it is more difficult for them to slow down and think of others. They seem less sensitive to their own feelings and they may not consider others' feelings.

I – **Not very factual.** Because they are fast-paced and people-oriented, they are easily distracted by others. They are stimulated easily by their senses and tend to be impressed more easily by the new and different.

S – **Not very firm.** Because they are slower-paced and people-oriented, they are heavily influenced by peer pressure. Others' expectations guide actions and opinions.

C – **Not much fun.** Because they are slower-paced and task-oriented, they seem to have an eternally present sense of self-control and duty. They are not amused by nonproductive entertainments.

Key to Success:

D – **To be under authority.** This type really enjoys autonomy and exhibits little in the way of self-doubt. To protect themselves and others from potential abuse of their power, they need to learn how to submit to others.

I – **To be more credible.** It is easy for this gifted and spontaneous type of person to be seen as a "flake." Learning to "hold their tongues" and control impulsive actions will create the respect they crave.

S – **To be more decisive.** To be seen as a team player and included in decisions, they must show more *ability* to make decisions and *adaptability* to change. Learning to do this will also ease their inner turmoil.

C – **To be more supportive.** This type is good at pointing out what is wrong or could be improved and enjoys working alone. Learning the give-and-take of teamwork will create a more well-rounded and free individual.

Motivating Statement:

D – **"I want you to be in charge!"** They love to give orders and meet a challenge. What de-motivates them is laboring in obscurity for someone who is not a leader.

I – **"You can do it!"** They love opportunities to shine and encouragement. What de-motivates them is lack of recognition or someone who doesn't believe in them.

S – **"I need your help!"** Their sense of self-worth is tied to service. What de-motivates them is being unappreciated or taken for granted when they reach out to help.

C – **"I need your best thinking!"** They engage in critical thinking with motivated enthusiasm when they are invited, but with de-motivated pessimism if they are not consulted.

Killer Statement:

D – **"You can't do that!"** Whether you meant they are not allowed or don't have what it takes, you waved a red flag at a bull. You kill the relationship because they will do it (just because you said no!) and then show you no respect for saying they couldn't do it.

I – **"You think that's funny?"** They want you to think of them as sincere, honest and winsome; under pressure they become inappropriately glib. This phrase will kill the relationship because it says you see them as a fool or clown and no longer respect them.

S – **"You are not very nice!"** They care so much, and if you imply (or if they infer) that they are being selfish or unkind, they will shut down emotionally as they add up how nice they have been to you — or occasionally, they may even show you how "not nice" they really can be, so you will appreciate the difference!

C – **"You made a mistake!"** They have a need to be right, and you can provide opportunities for them to discover their mistake and correct it. But this phrase will kill the relationship because you are striking at their identity, their considerable pride, and their sense of self-worth.

WHO DO YOU THINK YOU ARE ANYWAY?

For Increased Productivity, They Should Learn to:

D – **Communicate often.** They tend to change their plans in midstream, without getting input or letting others know. This can destroy team spirit and cause wasted effort.

Reward achievement. They tend to believe falsely that giving praise and recognition will make someone think he has "arrived." So they may withhold honor, thinking their actions will motivate higher performance standards.

Practice patience. Indecisive people bother them, as do those who are slower-paced or do not serve their agenda. Practicing patience will remove stress, make them more relatable, and inspire others to trust them.

Improve listening skills. Again, they tend to hear what they want to hear. Because they are bottom-line people, they tend to cut others off when they think they have heard enough. They need to gather information carefully and make efforts not to offend others by their inattention.

Display more empathy. This suggests being more sensitive to others, whether their needs, their emotions, their circumstances, their complaints... This will require lifelong effort — unlike the others, this is not just a *skill*. It is an *attitude* that goes beyond a task.

I – **Use short-term goals.** They succeed by breaking projects into tasks and assigning deadlines to each. When the first is completed, some small reward or recognition is appropriate. Then a short-term goal is set for the next phase, with ongoing accountability and appropriate recognition.

Behave responsibly. They most resemble Peter Pan — who makes even a duel to the death with Captain Hook a game. The alternative is to be held responsible for actions and decisions, with clearly stated rewards and penalties. They need encouragement, friendship and accountability while learning this new behavior.

Follow written plans. They tend to "shoot from the hip," and because they can be both flexible and spontaneous, it usually seems to work out. However, people around them may feel terrorized in the process. So, written plans will help them to think things through, will establish an objective minimum for expected results, and reassure others that things are on track.

Keep commitments. They talk so much, and in the heat of the moment they say things they really mean, and they make promises they intend to keep. But the difficulty in remembering what was said, meant and promised can be mind boggling. They should be slower to commit themselves to a course of action, be sure of what they are committing to, and make it a matter of personal integrity to do as they say.

Focus on listening. They "think out loud." When others are speaking, they are either formulating their next "out loud" thought, interrupting someone else's train of thought, or just getting ready to talk. As memory expert Jerry Lucas says, they need a mental picture of wrapping their own "elephant ears" around the person who is talking to them, to really concentrate on what is being said.

S – **Accept challenges readily.** They do not like either kind of challenge: new efforts they have not succeeded in before, or when someone questions what they have said or done. They can develop confidence to attempt *new* challenges and to withstand *questioning* challenges.

Demonstrate flexibility. When they feel pressure to accommodate someone's wishes, they tend to give in. But when they are asked voluntarily to adapt their comfort zone or adjust their disposition, they often feel put-upon. More flexibility would show that they can be positive about change, rather than resigned to accept it.

Voice opinions and ideas. They have a lot to contribute because they look for ways to help everyone win and they are not easily swayed by the shiny and new. But they tend to hold back because they feel verbally assaulted if asked to defend their ideas. They can learn to take a posture that does not feel or give offense.

Concentrate on deadlines. They tend to hesitate rather than act. They do not do well under deadline pressures, but face them often because they are not good starters. Establishing a timetable or enlisting someone to "jump start" their project could help in this area.

Exercise assertiveness. They are afraid others will think they are being "pushy." But at the same time that they think they're being too strong, others are just starting to notice them. They can learn to say what they mean and what they want, without being offensive.

C – **Show more optimism.** They think they are "realistic" when others think they are pessimistic. Often, it is not what they say but how they say it. They can use the same creative energy to suggest ways that ensure success or improve the product, rather than explaining why it will certainly fail. Many great advances can be made by asking positive "what if…" questions.

Act more spontaneously. They tend to be more rigid in their planning — some actually *schedule* the day they will buy an ice cream cone "impulsively." Being spontaneous does not mean they will combust, and they can learn to be more comfortable trying it out in measured doses so they can examine the results. (One "C" type told us she even planned when to have fun in her day. I was shocked — I have never "planned" fun in my life — it just happens!)

Simplify their ideas. They see layers and layers beneath every concept because they understand the underlying principles. But explaining them to people who do not think critically can be frustrating to everyone. They can learn to break ideas down into simple components and to speak in "sound bytes" with simpler vocabulary.

Decide more quickly. When they are "in their element," they can be very decisive, but outside of their specialty or expertise, the "paralysis of analysis" holds them back. They can learn to analyze the information, collect informed opinion, weigh the pros and cons — and go with their decision. If they make a wrong one, they can enlist other styles to help them "make it right."

Control perfectionism. Their standard exceeds "mere" excellence, and they look for perfection in themselves and others. They can be more generous in the acceptance and evaluation of themselves and others, and they can learn to set more reasonable expectations without abandoning their standards or values.

On the following page, you will see a chart that capsulizes these adaptive skill concepts for quick review and ready reference.

WHO DO YOU THINK YOU ARE ANYWAY?

Primary Style:	D	I	S	C
The Way They Process Information:	"Let's do it — get finished!"	"Let's have some fun!"	"Slow down — help me!"	"Answer my question!"
How They Handle a Budget:	Go over it briefly	What is it?	Stay under it	Stay within it
Driven By Their:	Will	Feelings	Emotions	Mind / Intellect
Key Strength:	Firm	Fun	Friendly	Factual
Key Weakness:	Not very friendly	Not very factual	Not very firm	Not much fun
Key to Success:	To be under authority	To be more credible	To be more decisive	To be more supportive
Motivating Statement:	"I want you to be in charge!"	"You can do it!"	"I need your help!"	"I need your best thinking!"
"Killer" Statement:	"You can't do that!"	"You think that's funny?"	"You are not very nice!"	"You made a mistake!"
For Increased Productivity, They Should Learn to:	Communicate often Reward achievement Practice patience Improve listening skills Display more empathy	Use short-term goals Behave responsibly Follow written plans Keep commitments Focus on listening	Accept challenges readily Demonstrate flexibility Voice opinions and ideas Concentrate on deadlines Exercise assertiveness	Show more optimism Act more spontaneously Simplify their ideas Decide more quickly Control perfectionism

Chapter 5

Recognizing Tell-Tale Traits

Utah business leader Randy Haugen once told a group of business owners, "We relate most to our peer group. The problem is, you can't build success only with people you relate to. You run out of people who think that way. Figure out a way to open up *your* personality enough to relate to other people."

How *can* you recognize another person's style, so you can open up to them and relate according to their "language"? The answer is important because, as Randy said, it will determine your success in every relationship with people.

If you have been asking yourself this question, you are going to enjoy this "fun" chapter. It is filled with ideas to get you thinking about some ways different personality styles may express themselves. And along the way, you will be challenged with how you can adapt yourself to relate in more positive and productive ways.

In *Positive Personality Profiles*, we introduced our own "personality symbols": the "D" type exclamation point, the "I" type star, the "S" type plus-and-minus, and the "C" type question mark. And we also talked about how different people see the "half-glass of water" — some say it is *half-full;* others say it is *half-empty.* Some think it actually is the *wrong-size* glass. Others think it's a stupid question! (One weary mother just wanted to know who had left it on the counter and said, "I don't care what *size* it is or if it's got *anything* in it — *I'm* not washing it!")

Other Images

Since that book was printed, we have had fun with the new images on these next pages. In asking people to tell us what personality styles they saw in these pictures, we have collected some entertaining answers.

 The stopwatch suggests great accuracy and split-second timing to many viewers. If this is the case, does this image describe someone who is very task-oriented or someone who is very people-oriented? Think about who you know who could be represented by this image. What personality style does this individual have? This image reminds of us of two quotes. The first is for a task-oriented, fast-paced individual — the highly competitive "D," who sees the stopwatch in terms of a contest or race. Humorist Will Rogers said, "Even if you're on the right track, you'll get run over if you just sit there." The second quote is attributed to Secretary of State Henry Kissinger, for a task-oriented, slower-paced individual — the highly organized "C," who views the stopwatch as a master: "There cannot be a crisis next week. My schedule is already full."

 Now look at the "wedge of Swiss." What does it suggest to you? Some have answered, "The big cheese!" If so, you are probably thinking of someone who takes charge in a bossy manner. (Noting the Swiss holes, one person commented that the "big cheese" was also "full of air!") Does a "big cheese" person tend to be fast-paced or slower-paced? Task- or people-oriented?

 What about the boxing gloves — is this someone who likes to "mix it up?" If so, you are probably *not* thinking of an "S" type individual who avoids conflict and seeks to please everyone. Typically, someone who enjoys conflict and challenge is a "D" type. However, even an "S" can lash out when security or stability is threatened. As

Frederick Hayes observed, "There is no way to *make* people *like* change. You can only make them feel less threatened by it." With this thought in mind, what could you do when you encounter behaviors represented by this picture?

This pacifier inspired some people to think about "big babies" — those who tend to pout if they don't get their own way. Again, certain styles fit this image well, while others do not. (Often, "I" types are so quick to respond that they sometimes "whine" unnecessarily.) Others see this image as someone who calms and reassures others when they need to be pacified. What styles might fit these descriptions?

This parking meter suggests "I have time for you, but my meter is running!" It may remind you of friends who are very task-oriented and organized in the use of their time. Also, there is no "gray area" for a parking meter — you either are in compliance with time left on the meter, or a red flag is letting everyone know you are in violation. What style would this describe? Both scenes fit a "C," but a "D" type person on a deadline can fit this description, too. Under what circumstances might you feel similar responses from an "I" or an "S"? Think about it.

How about an open heart candy box? Physicist-mathematician Blaise Pascal wrote, "The heart has its reasons which reason does not understand." Most of the people to whom we showed this picture thought immediately of an "S" type person — generous in the extreme, open for acceptance, sweet. However, *you* may have thought of Forrest Gump's mother who said, "Life is like a box of chocolates... you never know what you're gonna get." So, this box of chocolates could represent someone who looks good on the outside, but is unpredictable on the inside. What other behaviors would you look for in order to know if the "open heart candy box" was a person's real style or a behavior that masked another purpose?

 The safety pin reminds many of someone they can count on in an emergency, or someone who can hold it all together. But others might see someone who is sharp and pointed unless they keep themselves under guard. Another view is an individual who will not give up safety and security. With this in mind, The First Century historian Tacitus wrote, "The desire for safety stands against every great and noble enterprise." What behaviors and styles can you think of for this "safety pin" image? How might you adjust your own style when confronted by these cautious behaviors?

 To some, these "beagle-puss glasses" — the funny nose, moustache and spectacles — represent a comedian, like Groucho Marx. Others see a disguise to hide behind, or an impostor who is not what he seems. (For example, an "I" type jokester may hide behind humor when he feels "attacked" or under stress. We may interpret this individual's response as showing they have no concern for our criticism, even though they may be "dying inside.") Remember this observation by Cyril Connolly: "All charming people have something to conceal, usually their total dependence on the appreciation of others."

 A magnifying glass suggests a detective, or someone who is preoccupied with details. Of what personality type does this remind you? How can you expect such a person to approach data relating to a new or changing project? How can you adjust your own style so that someone who is careless about details may become more thorough in this area? (In *The Magic of Thinking Big,* Dr. David Schwartz wrote that the two failure diseases are "excusitis" and "detailitis.")

The "propeller beanie" probably reminds you of an "airhead" who is not much for critical thinking and analysis, going through life on the surface of things, rather than thinking about long term consequences. Or maybe you thought of a childish adult who is

fun-loving and has never grown up emotionally. F. Scott Fitzgerald wrote, "Grow up... that is a terribly hard thing to do. It is much easier to skip it and go from one childhood to another." In either case, the picture does not suggest someone who is task-oriented or slower-paced. By process of elimination, what style remains? ("Not task-oriented" means more people-oriented. "Not reserved" and "not slower-paced" means more outgoing and fast-paced. Hint: these traits are found in the upper right quadrant of the pie!)

A "spark plug" is an "igniter" that gets things started. "Spark plugs" can be people who are "shocking" or "fun" — perhaps a "D" or an "I." But spark plugs are also "consistent" and "long-term reliable." They *keep* a car going — more like "S" or "C" type behavior. However, spark plugs must be controlled when in a volatile situation. And they don't do much good when their "timing" or their "gap" is off. All of these traits remind us that looking below the surface can help us to understand each other more completely. Remember, there always is more to a person than what we see.

When we showed it to most people, the skeleton suggested a person who is interested in only the "bare bones" of a situation. Others thought of someone who wants to get all the way down to the "nitty-gritty." But our personal favorite observation is, "no guts, no glory!" How can you adjust your style to motivate or work with people whom you view as fearful or reticent to take a risk?

Lastly, we see a life-jacket. Many said they could count on such an individual to rescue them when they "got in over their heads." But others saw that this image could also represent someone who "stays afloat" in rough seas, who is tough-skinned and prepared for calamity.

Judging Versus Observing

Whatever words we use to describe the "personalities" of these thirteen items, our interpretation is not really based on their "behaviors," is it? They are, after all, inanimate pictures of inanimate objects. Rather, we assign them a style and value based on how *we* view *them* — *our own* personalities interpret *their* personalities. And therein lies the problem!

This is an important distinction. While it is just a game when we look at pictures, it is serious business when we look at people and assign motivations to them based on what we see. We must be careful not to "label" people based on our own viewpoint or our tendency to stereotype behaviors — even some "I's" wear vinyl pocket protectors filled with pens and pencils (though not many)! In 1869, the English preacher Charles Spurgeon wrote, "Don't rely too much on labels, for often they are fables."

Well, if prejudging is bad, how can we use this information to build good relationships? Remember, our goal is not to "pigeonhole" or manipulate people for our own benefit or comfort. Rather, we want to **understand** their basis in relating to us — and us to them. Then we will be able to have better teamwork and cooperation in whatever we do.

So when you first meet any individual, ask yourself two questions to identify their style of behavior:

1. **Does this person appear to be *fast-paced and outgoing* or is this person *slower-paced and reserved?***
2. **Does this person appear to be more *task-oriented* or more *people-oriented?***

You will recognize the following illustrations from pages 6 through 8 — they are the "mental picture" we should have in mind when we are meeting a person for the first time.

Question 1 determines which part of our "first pie" this individual fits into: either the top (outgoing) or the bottom (reserved).

Fast-paced, outgoing people tend to speak and move with more energy. Even their gestures and facial expressions have more "passion" than a slower-paced individual. Their natural inclination is to be more fast-paced. Outgoing people are "D's" and "I's."

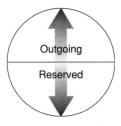

Slower-paced, reserved people tend to speak more quietly, less forcefully. Their gestures and facial expressions seem more "guarded" than the fast-paced individual. Their natural response is to be slower-paced. Reserved people are "S's" and "C's."

Our answer to Question 2 will tell us to which part of the "second pie" this individual belongs: either the left (task-oriented) or the right (people-oriented).

Task-oriented people tend to focus more on the job to be done or the goal to be accomplished. They seem to be less influenced by the opinions of others and more logic-based in their approach. They tend to be loners rather than joiners. Task-oriented people are "D's" and "C's."

People-oriented individuals tend to enjoy the company of others and seem to see them as a priority, rather than their project at hand. They seem to be more influenced by the opinions of others, less "fact-based," more sensitive or emotional. They tend to be joiners rather than loners. People-oriented individuals are "I's" and "S's."

According to the pie, you know that someone who is outgoing and task-oriented is a "D." If an individual you have just met appears to behave in this manner, it is safe to assume that his behavioral style is "D." If he behaves like an outgoing but people-oriented individual, it is safe to begin understanding him and responding to him as an "I." If his behaviors tell you that he is people-oriented but seems more reserved and slower-paced,

you can't go too far astray treating him like an "S." And if he seems reserved but more task-oriented, relate to him as a "C."

How can you find the answer these two questions? The easiest way is by observing the behaviors we have just discussed, while reviewing the assembled pie mentally when you meet someone for the first time (more about this on page 104–105).

Switching Gears

Of course, appearances can be deceiving, so it makes good sense to continue looking at an individual's responses, adjusting your view according to the most complete, up-to-date behavioral information you can observe, until you have a reliable understanding of their style.

During the 1996 Olympics, Chris entered a local contest to win an antique Corvette. It was a "come-on" to collect names for a timeshare development in Orlando. Both he and his wife Cindy enjoyed the salesperson's "I" type behavior. Then they saw it switch to "D" type behavior as pressure was applied to close the sale — when the salesperson's orientation moved from "people" to "task." Then, when it became apparent that money was not changing hands on that particular day, the salesperson's emphasis changed to moving them out in order to make room for more potential buyers.

Our point here is not that sales people are "bad" or "pushy." Rather, we are saying that first impressions can help you know how to respond to people, but appearances *can* be deceiving. Be ready to "change gears" as you observe changes in the other individual's behavior style. After all, you are seeking to adjust *your style* to *their style* for maximum, *mutual* success in your relationship together. If you cannot recognize their shift, you may wonder what you did "wrong," or why it happened.

Taking this example one step further... If you knew you were an "S," you probably would have enjoyed the warm reception given you by an "I-mimicking" salesperson. And you might have let down your guard since many "I's" seem to care more about remaining your friend than signing the contract. Both of you would have been in a "people-oriented" mode. And if you did not reevaluate the salesperson's behavior as he put it into "D" for drive, you might have been run over!

Remember that "S" types have a great deal of difficulty saying no. So, at such a time, it would be appropriate for an "S" to shift into more "C" type behavior — cautious, careful, critical thinking. A "C" would ask: *Exactly how much will this one-week lifetime vacation cost me with the $5,000 down payment, the $350 escalating annual upkeep fee, the $10,000 balance financed with a loan at 18%, compounded over 7 years?* As an "S," you would need to "raise" your own task-oriented skills to survive against such salesmanship! You would want to balance your strong desire to please this stranger with an objective view of the facts.

As an aside, this is one reason why equal partners so often have difficulty after the honeymoon phase of their business is over. Frequently, opposites attract in business as well as in romance. And a supportive "S" has a hard time saying no to a determined "D" who generally gets his way or makes the "S" feel like a traitor. The great philosopher Anonymous put it this way: "When two friends have a common purse, one sings and the other weeps." The "D" will sing because he is happy he has won, and the "S" will cry because he is afraid they will lose down the road — and he will probably be left holding the bag!

We saw this recently in a married couple who are close friends. She has a D/I type blend, and he has an S/I blend. When there is a power struggle or decision to be made, their secondary "I" traits do not get together and induce an imaginative, inspiring solution. Like an algebra problem, their "I's" cancel each other out, leaving a "D" and "S" to work things out. Until they learned about their styles, this couple did not understand what was happening in their decision-making process.

Learn to Ask People Questions

Another way of discovering a person's style is to ask the "FORM" questions used by many salespeople. As you talk with someone, ask questions that relate to these four topics:

F: Family — ask about their spouse, children or grandchildren because family issues reveal a lot about how people-oriented they are. Or they may describe a task-oriented lifestyle and provide clues for an effective approach.

O: Occupation — what they do for a living can tell you about their task and people skills, and whether they work at a faster or slower pace.

R: Recreation — what they do for relaxation and why they do it may indicate whether they are fast- or slower-paced, whether they enjoy tasks or people more. You are also looking for "common ground" upon which to begin building your relationship.

M: Motivator — is their "hot button" reward, recognition, achievement, appreciation, correctness, challenge? What motivates them to excel? Again, you are simply collecting information that will help you determine where this person fits best in the Model of Human Behavior, and what common bridges you can use to establish rapport.

Another way is to *ask...* That's right, simply *ask* someone these two simple questions:

1. **Do you feel that you are more *fast-paced and outgoing* or would you say you tend to be *slower-paced and reserved?***

2. **Do you think you are more *task-oriented* or are you more *people-oriented?***

Are you surprised that you can simply *ask* people what they think about themselves and get the answers you are looking for? In asking these two questions out loud, we have never heard anyone say, "That question is too personal!" Most people really enjoy talking about their favorite topic: themselves. In fact, they seem genuinely pleased when you show interest in them.

The only people who might not warm to your questions

would be very private, very reserved, very task-oriented "C" types — and their response would provide the information anyway!

Ask with sincerity at the proper time; you may even hear some interesting stories along with their reply. If they ask why, explain that *you* are interested in what interests *them,* and that friendships are built by understanding each other. They might even ask you the same two questions. If you ask a few "icebreaker" questions in the "F–O–R–M" series, people should be very willing to answer these two questions as well.

Be aware that even reserved, task-oriented people may *tell* you they are outgoing and people-oriented. This is because they may not have thought about the issue until you ask — and most people think it is a good thing to be outgoing and like people, as opposed to being a recluse who hates people! Back up what they say about themselves with your own observations and you should have a fairly accurate picture.

Finally, you can learn about your behavioral style through assessments that reveal your characteristics in very accurate terms. Personality Insights provides such assessments for companies, teams, families and individuals. One such assessment can be completed and scored yourself, resulting in Environment and Basic Style graphs along with an overview of your style. Another assessment yields a computer-scored report with graphs, action plans and very specific information.

When our friend Jim completed one of these computerized assessments, he asked, "How is it that I selected answers from just 24 little questions and I got a report that says if you want to talk to me, don't get within three feet of my face? That's always bothered me, but how did the report know that? Is that on everyone's report?"

No, it was the specific level of "D" and "C" in Jim's report that triggered this computer comment. As a "D," he was likely to feel crowded and challenged, although not consciously, if someone got too close physically. In "cave man" days, an acceptable response might have been to push that person away to a "safer" distance. But having read Dale Carnegie's *How to Win Friends and Influence People,* Jim knew instinctively that this was not a modern-day option! So, his natural response was to pull himself back emotionally and create distance for himself.

In addition to his "D," Jim also possesses a strong "C." (Remember, *no one is purely a "D," an "I," an "S," or a "C."* We are all a *blend* of these characteristics to a greater or lesser degree.) Jim's critical thinking and analytical skills want objectivity — he feels a need for space so he can see the big picture and know that he has not missed any details. So, when he is physically crowded, Jim's ears and eyes tend to shut down the flood of incoming information. He tends to eliminate whatever is not basic, bottom-line information (a "D" trait), and he reacts with greater skepticism to what he has heard and seen already, or what gets past his protective filters during this time (a "C" trait). Therefore, as the computer says... if you want to communicate effectively with Jim, don't get within three feet of his face!

It's amazingly simple when you understand the idea. Jim's business associate, Peter, had wondered why he was sometimes unable to overcome these obstacles during some of their meetings. Since Peter has such a high "S," he naturally assumed he was doing something wrong. ("S" types expect things to be their fault.) Now Peter understood that it really wasn't bad breath or some other error on his part. Neither Jim nor Peter were at fault. They simply had different communication styles, and their occasional "wall" was just a matter of bad location. If Jim had exercised his strong "D" with Peter, a similar invisible wall could have been erected on Peter's side. In their conversations, Peter now tries to give Jim more of the physical "space" he requires. And he has been able to understand and reject the easily occurring "S" feelings of self-doubt that he had previously experienced. Both men have been close friends for years, but a *Style Assessment* released this valuable information.

One of the best things about understanding personality

styles is that everyone wins when we apply the information with a right heart. Jim wins because he understands himself better and is aware of his tendency to shut down — and he knows how it may come across to other people. Peter wins because he stopped looking for shortcomings in himself and found a simple, workable solution. And *we* are winners because we have another excellent story for this book, and an example that helps you become more sensitive to the unseen issues that are all around you all the time.

Chapter 6

The Truth About You

Benjamin Franklin wrote, "Years have taught me at least one thing and that is not to try to avoid an unpleasant fact, but rather to grasp it firmly and let the other person observe I am at least treating him fairly. Then he, it has been my observation, will treat me in the same spirit."

Great insights into living come as a part of your particular personality style. But blind spots come with it, too. Over the next few pages, we are going to explore how you get to know yourself — how you see yourself and how others see you. Franklin was right: if there are any unpleasant facts about us, it is best to face them and deal with them — they don't go away when we ignore them. And others see us as having true character when they know that we are working to be fair and honest about ourselves and with them.

Knowing Yourself

You have heard people who *should* know better try to explain their feelings or actions with the phrase, "If I know my own heart, and I believe I do…" And then they followed with their own "take" on why they "felt led" to do something they wanted to do anyway. As Dwight Morrow observed, "We judge *ourselves* by our motives and *others* by their actions." This is a false and double standard.

At the risk of being misunderstood, I am going to suggest that you cannot truly understand another individual's heart motivations for what they do. But I will go a step further to suggest that we probably do not know our own hearts very well, either.

We'll "prove" this point in just a second, but just so you'll know where we are going with this, I believe we *can* know and understand and monitor our *behaviors* — and this helps us to be aware of our blind spots and deal effectively with our limitations. Bob Waterson said, "You can succeed so far on your strengths, then you must overcome your weaknesses." What I am saying is that we can fool ourselves about what areas we need to work on when we try to judge our *motives,* but we can get a truer, more objective view of our situation when we look candidly at our *behaviors.* Now let's see if I can back this up in a way that will make sense to you.

Misjudging Character

When we observe someone's actions, we feel we know him. 17th Century philosopher John Locke wrote, "The actions of men are the best interpreters of their thoughts." As we watch someone "behave" according to their style we are able to say, "This individual is acting like an outgoing, task-oriented person, so he is probably a 'D.'"

On the other hand, we might see this same "D" person behaving in a way that is out of control and think "this guy really is a pushy jerk!" But we cannot say being a "D" is what makes him a jerk. We cannot say, "All 'D's' are jerks — so this guy is a jerk!" Whether or not he really *is* a "jerk" is hard for us to judge. An individual's personality style does not determine if he is of good or bad character. His *character* determines how he handles his *personality* style. (In fact, we have all *behaved* like jerks at one time or another without thinking we *are* jerks!)

So, we may look at an individual's *actions* as a way to interpret his *thoughts,* but we do not have a way of looking at the "why" of his heart *motivations.*

When we have a false view of others because we do not understand their behavioral styles, or when we view them through the cracked lenses of our own style, or when we falsely believe we can discern their hearts based on this flawed information, we sabotage our ability to create healthy, long-lasting relationships.

British Prime Minister Benjamin Disraeli knew the ease with which we misjudge the character of others, based on whether we feel we are "getting along" with them. He said, "My idea of an agreeable person is a person who agrees with me." It really is easier to find "good character" in those who are most like ourselves.

Again, we need objective sources of information and interpretation. One objective source is a *Style Analysis,* and much of this book explains how and why it is effective. But another source for understanding much about human behavior is the Bible. William Lyon Phelps said, "You can learn more about human nature by reading the Bible than by living in New York." So, here are some excellent Bible references regarding our "heart condition" and motivations:

In Jeremiah 17:9, the prophet wrote, "The heart is deceitful above all things, and desperately wicked; who can know it?" We infer from this that no one can *really* know us, except God, whose "lamp searches our inmost parts" (Proverbs 20:27 NIV).

The Psalmist wrote, "Search me, O God, and know my heart; test me and know my anxious thoughts. See if there is any offensive way in me, and lead me in the way everlasting" (Psalm 139:23–24 NIV). This was not said in an attempt to justify himself — it was a plea that God would help him to see himself as he truly was. This requires time, patience, and cooperation on our part. Both of these writers were saying, "God knows the *real us* in a way that no human being can, including ourselves."

Saint Paul wrote that in his attempts to be upright and good, he found obstacles: "For what I do is not the good I want to do; no, the evil I do not want to do — this I keep on doing" (Romans 7:19 NIV).

The Bible teaches that we do even good things for our own gain, that our outlook is self-focused and our goals are self-oriented. Isaiah wrote that even at our best, "all our righteous acts are like filthy rags…" (Isaiah 64:6 NIV). Before you take offense or feel your character has been besmirched, remember that admitting these truths puts us in some pretty good company.

Think about the last time *you* got upset with someone. Chances are it was because what *they* did caused *you* a loss of some kind — at the very least, your distress was because *they* did not fulfill *your* expectations. You took it personally. But Jan Christian Smuts explains it this way: "Men are not *against* you; they are merely *for* themselves." My friend, Charlie Boyd, author of *Different Children, Different Needs,* says, "People don't do things *to* you or *against* you but *for* themselves.

Outside Scripture, we find many sources on this theme of acknowledging personal challenges. Hopefully, these won't depress you or make you feel like you have fatal character flaws, but they are worth thinking about because they challenge us to grow:

The greatest of all faults is to be conscious of none. (Thomas Carlyle)

Great abilities produce great vices as well as virtues. (A Greek proverb)

All men are evil and will declare themselves to be so when occasion is offered. (Sir Walter Raleigh)

If you wish to be good, first believe that you are bad. (Greek proverb)

Everybody has a little bit of Watergate in him. (Billy Graham)

We are not sinners because we sin; rather we sin because we are sinners. (Charles Spurgeon)

Whatever you may be sure of, be sure of this: that you are dreadfully like other people. (James Russell Lowell)

Now that we have "proven" that you are a dirty, rotten scoundrel, where are we going? As I said earlier, this is not the point. You may be a scoundrel or you may not, but your behavioral style does not determine that. You would still have issues to deal with in your life *regardless* of which personality style you might possess.

It is not fair for me to judge your *heart* simply by observing your actions. I cannot say your *motive* is good just because I am comfortable with your behavior style, and I cannot say your motive is bad just because your behavior style makes me uncomfortable. And I am not a good judge of my own motives, since I am skilled at rationalizing my own thoughts and actions... as are you!

The Mirror of Truth

If you will allow one more scriptural reference, James the Apostle wrote that even when we are exposed to the truth, we tend to misunderstand it, forget it, or ignore it: "Anyone who listens to the word but does not do what it says is like a man who looks at his face in a mirror and, after looking at himself, goes away and immediately forgets what he looks like" (James 1:23–24 NIV).

I love what my friend Dexter Yager once said: "Every morning when I wake up and stand in front of the mirror, I see a 10 year old kid... blocked behind some old guy!" A mirror is supposed to show us what others see, but most people tend to replace *reality* with their own *image* of themselves. The mirror is objective, but we are subjective.

What I am saying is that we need something more objective than our own prejudices and misconceptions when it comes to understanding ourselves and others. "D-I-S-C" is a tool we can learn to use with confidence.

Reflecting the Truth

As an example, Chris and his wife Cindy were having a disagreement a few years ago. (Back then, Chris did not know what a "high I" was, but now we know that his "I" goes off the top of both his Environmental and Basic Style graphs.) No matter what Cindy said in this disagreement, it seemed that Chris had a self-justifying response and a reason why Cindy should see and do things his way. Cindy finally told Chris, "You are the most manipulative person I have ever met." What was Chris' response? Of course, he denied it, said she had misunderstood him, and he felt hurt.

When Chris completed a *Personality Insights Style Analysis,* one of the things it pointed out is that under pressure people see him as manipulative, and in another place it revealed that he was capable of being highly manipulative in using his people skills to get what he wanted.

Now it is one thing to disagree with your wife, but it is quite another thing to try arguing against a computer! After all, computers do not speak in anger or say things under the influence of emotion. They do not try to justify or excuse themselves. And there it was in black-and-white: *Chris has all the makings of a master manipulator!*

He swallowed hard when he read the words. Maybe what Cindy had said was right. But then, he thought, "Even if this is true, I'm sure I only manipulate people for their own good..." In other words, "my motives are good, anyway... and I'm still right."

This is an example of how we can believe we know and understand ourselves when, in reality, we do not have a clue. Chris had to face a truth about himself: he had a tremendous "I" virtue in being able to inspire and induce, but with it came the "I" vice of being manipulative when he got out of control. For Chris to continue denying this truth would continue to harm himself and others. For him to admit this truth gives him the insight to be sensitive to it, to avoid it, and to quickly correct it when he is aware of it. And it makes him more open to Cindy, who may be able to see him manipulating a situation when he does not see it himself.

Circumstances and Excuses

Jerry Meadows, a Nashville-based business leader, has said this about people who make excuses for their behaviors: "Some people say, 'Well, that's just the way I am...' Well, 'the way you are' got you where you are — aren't you embarrassed? I don't really need to understand your circumstances [that made you the way you are]; it wouldn't do any good. It's irrelevant. The only thing that matters is if you have a purpose big enough to overcome those circumstances and change the way you are..."

You have heard people say, "I'm doing all right under the

circumstances." Utah-based businessman Don Wilson says, "Well, what are you doing under there? Get out from under them! It's better on top of them!" In other words, we all have circumstances that influence us — and our behavioral style is one of the main influences. Our goal should be to get all those circumstances — including our personalities — under control. Whether you are a "D," "I," "S," or "C," the view is better from the top! Jerry Meadows completed his talk by saying, "Circumstances *break* people, or they *make* winners."

We won't belabor this point except to say that ignoring how truly "human" we are in our behaviors is not the way to understand ourselves. Let's just agree that with all the wonderful attributes of your style found on pages 32 and 33, you were also able to check off a few traits that can be improved upon — or at least made more readily adaptable for serving others.

In my seminars, I show how the four styles acknowledge their mistakes. First, I act like a "D," offering an almost belligerent "Sorrrrry...!", as if it is *your* fault that *I* have to apologize to *you.* As an "I," I make a little joke of it to show that I did not do it on purpose: "I'm sorry — do you like me now?" As an "S," I seem even more troubled by the error than you: "I'm sorry. Please forgive me. It was all my fault and I will never do it again. I am *really* sorry." And then, as a "C," I just stand there, with a blank expression on my face, because this type of person is "never" wrong and certainly does not want to admit making a mistake to anyone else!

We all make mistakes. If you have ever played basketball, you know that when the referee blows his whistle, all play stops because someone has committed a foul. There is going to be a penalty of some kind because the rules were broken, but the referee does not want the player who committed the foul to quit the league — just raise his hand, acknowledge the foul, take the penalty and get on with the game. Some of your "blind spots" can be treated the same way. When your personality is out-of-control, acknowledge the foul and get back in the game! Facing the truth about you gives you freedom to improve your "game," while denying the truth keeps you "stuck on the bench," where you are.

Changing Our Ways

Our patterns and behaviors are ingrained. Once Chris hired a bookkeeper for a business he owned. "Kim" held a masters degree in accounting. He was from the People's Republic of China and educated in the United States. As a very high "C," he had difficulty finding work because he had not adjusted well to his adopted American culture. Kim had enrolled in further postgraduate work to improve his people skills and worked for Chris's business several days each week while in school. His English was quite good, so it was surprising that he performed all his mathematical calculations in the Cantonese language. Kim explained to Chris's wife Cindy that he could express *words* in English, but his *concepts* were Chinese. To do math in English, he would have to translate too much!

"Translation" is often a challenge when dealing with others — when we are learning to speak their language. If we have "D" concepts, it is hard to think or speak in "I," "S" or "C."

Chris was involved for three tumultuous months in a business partnership with a very high "D." We'll call him "Stan." Chris already had owned this business for seven years, but three weeks into their partnership, Stan whispered to a prospective employee, "Take whatever Chris says with a grain of salt — I let him be president..." Frequently, Chris felt Stan was pulling "power plays" in his desire to succeed. Finally, he brought in a board member to arbitrate their impasse. Chris told Stan, "You bully your way through everything we do." Stan was offended and said he was being misunderstood and misjudged. When the soft-spoken arbitrator agreed that Stan actually was a bully in all his relationships, Stan thought about it for a moment, slammed his hand down hard on the table and said, "All right — I repent! Now let's move on..."

None of the people involved had an understanding of personality styles at that time, but two of them recognized this fact: Stan was weak in caring for others and being fair in his dealings with them. His "D" was out of control and he abused people in order to "win." Often, his defense was that he was doing it for their mutual benefit, and he was offended that they would take offense.

When Stan said, "I repent… let's move on," he revealed that he did not really see the problem. He only knew "God talk," a method of using spiritual sounding words to get his own way. He needed to change his *actions* on a daily basis. When we hear the referee blow his whistle, we must do more than just acknowledge the foul — we must continue in the game, playing by the rules.

What was required was a *change of behavior*. In order to do this, Stan needed to understand that "gracious" was not his native language. Like Kim, he had a "translation problem," too. He *could* learn to "speak" that language to people, but he would always speak with a bit of a personal accent. He would have to concentrate on speaking it carefully and clearly, because his mental concepts were in a "different language."

Our point is that it usually takes more than "changing your mind" to change your behavior. It takes an understanding of how you are actually behaving, the behavior you want to demonstrate instead, and conscious effort in that direction, with course corrections to help you stay on target. All of this requires time and accountability to others — something none of us wants but all of us need.

"Spiritual" Behaviors

Recognizing our behaviors for what they are is a big step. It is necessary in making changes in our lives. Here are two more quick examples that relate to our "language."

A Christian financial counselor presented a seminar about money management. At the beginning, he spoke a little about the "D-I-S-C" Model of Human Behavior and how it applies to teaching your child to handle money. Later on in the presentation, he explained how God loves orderliness and fiscal responsibility, and there seemed to be an implication that balancing your bank statement pleases God. Afterwards, he and Chris discussed motivations — does a "C" really justify his bank statement because he is "spiritual" and wants to glorify God? Is it any kind of "sacrifice" for a "C" to do this? Probably not. He would do so anyway, because he cannot tolerate disorder in the details of his life. Now, for an "I" to do so voluntarily ranks with Abraham's willingness to sacrifice his son Isaac!

Thinking of our natural strengths as signs of spirituality is another example of equating actions or behaviors with motives. They are not the same. It reminds me of Ambrose Bierce's definition of a Christian: "One who believes that the New Testament is a divinely inspired book admirably suited to the spiritual needs of his neighbor." We must apply truth impartially to ourselves before we judge others.

"S" type people have a style that gets along with people and goes along with the plan. Does this mean that they are more "spiritual" than others? With strength in this area, they also have some weakness in other areas. A "D" type person with "missionary zeal" has no difficulty telling others exactly what he believes, but does this mean he is more spiritually attuned than people who are quiet examples of what they believe? Or is there room for *both*?

Favorite Bible verses of many "S" type Christian people are Galatians 5:22 and 23 (NIV): "But the fruit of the Spirit is love, joy, peace, patience, kindness, goodness, faithfulness, gentleness and self-control..." These are strengths they can identify with. But it was the Apostle Paul who wrote those words, and he was a "D" — off-the-charts! (Read more about this in *Positive Personality Profiles*, page 32.) When Paul wrote this, he was saying, "Look, this is not how I am naturally. But I see this 'fruit' of how God is working in me to help me become more like this."

Now I wouldn't want to start a whole new denomination over this, but I believe if he really had been an "S," Paul would have had a different list of fruit — he might have talked about having confidence, commitment, boldness, far-reaching faith, and courage. Why? Because these are things "S" types do not possess in their natural "Basic Style." What do you think he might have seen God working on if Paul were an "I" like Peter, or a "C" like Thomas?

To take spiritual credit for what is more or less "native" to us is like taking credit for having green eyes! You are not a better person just because you have green eyes, although many people may find your eyes attractive. And you are not a better person just because you have certain traits or characteristics, although many of those characteristics may be attractive.

All this is just to say that the "language" we speak is understood easily by those who also speak that language. Just as I can bless God or curse people with the English language I was taught by my mother, so I can help or harm others by the behavioral "language" with which I communicate to them. We can learn to speak and listen and understand the "languages" of other personality styles, too. That's part of the goal — so, repeat with me: *"If I understand you and you understand me, doesn't it make sense that we will be in a position to have a better relationship?"*

The Truth About *Us*

John Godfrey Saxe's poem became a favorite when I first heard it years ago. I found it again recently in *The Best Loved Poems of the American People*. It demonstrates how the limited experience and vision of even the wise can be hindered by an inability to see the "bigger picture." I think it is fitting to conclude this chapter with a humorous commentary about all of us.

The Blind Men and the Elephant

It was six men of Indostan
　To learning much inclined
Who went to see the elephant
　(Though all of them were blind),
That each by observation
　Might satisfy his mind.

The First approached the elephant,
　And, happening to fall
Against his broad and sturdy side,
　At once began to bawl:
"God bless me! but the elephant
　Is nothing but a wall!"

The Second, feeling of the tusk,
  Cried: "Ho! What have we here
So very round and smooth and sharp?
  To me 'tis mighty clear
This wonder of an elephant
  Is very like a spear!"

The Third approached the animal,
  And, happening to take
The squirmy trunk within his hands,
  Thus, boldly up and spake:
"I see," quoth he, "the elephant
  Is very like a snake!"

The Fourth reached out his eager hand,
  And felt about the knee:
"What most this wondrous beast is like
  Is mighty plain," quoth he;
"'Tis clear enough the elephant
  Is very like a tree."

The Fifth, who chanced to touch an ear,
  Said, "E'en the blindest man
Can tell what this resembles most;
  Deny the fact who can,
This marvel of an elephant
  Is very like a fan!"

The Sixth no sooner had begun
  About the beast to grope,
Than, seizing on the swinging tail
  That fell within his scope,
"I see," quoth he, "the elephant
  Is very like a rope!"

And so these men of Indostan
  Disputed loud and long,
Each in his own opinion
  Exceeding stiff and strong,
Though each was partly in the right,
  And all were in the wrong!

Chapter 7

25 Great Insights About Personalities

I have had the pleasure of teaching college level summer courses for educators as part of their ongoing certification requirements. Recently, I asked one class to list the insights they discovered while learning about the personality styles in our in-depth 40-hour course. They are worth sharing with you in these pages, and I think they will encourage you to keep going and growing! Here they are:

1. **It will always feel uncomfortable to adjust your personality style.**

    Speaking this new language, as we discussed in Chapter 6, will always require some purposeful thought, especially when we are under pressure — that's when we tend to revert to the behaviors that make us comfortable or have seemed to work for us in the past. Expect to be stretched. People and rubber bands have one thing in common: They must be stretched to be effective. And as you know, when something is stretched it never quite returns to its previous small size!

2. **It helps when you appreciate the differences in others, rather than resent them.**

    You can encourage others by appreciating and accepting them, rather than resenting and rejecting them. Often, they become more cooperative. You also save yourself anxiety. Comedian Buddy Hackett said, "Don't carry a grudge. While you're carrying the grudge, the other guy's out dancing!"

3. Our secondary traits often "kick in" when pressure occurs.

When there is a job to be done, we have a host of less predominate skills available to us through our secondary traits. We can use them to achieve our goals. Again, refer to pages 28 and 29 for more information on how our secondary traits can support us.

4. We need all different kinds of personality types.

The phrase "Together, Everyone Achieves More" is a wonderful acrostic — it spells out the word "TEAM." As you look over the contributions on page 28 and the list of traits on pages 32 and 33, you can see how we complement each other when we decide to "complete" and not "compete."

5. Children, like adults, have different personality styles as well.

Some children, Bill Cosby insists, come into the world complaining about the bright lights and the cold delivery room, wanting to know who is in charge and who let the father into the room! Following one of my seminars, a pediatric nurse told me that she had seen over two thousand births, and, by knowing what behaviors to observe, she believed she could identify most infants' basic styles while they were still in the delivery room.

We have developed a *"Style Analysis for Children"* following the "D-I-S-C" model that uses cartoon robots and short stories. Many parents have said it was very helpful in understanding their child's makeup. We also recommend your reading *Different Children, Different Needs* (dealing with the personality styles of children) and *Tales Out Of School* (200 teachers explain how they use "D-I-S-C" in the classroom). These materials are available from Personality Insights — see the information pages at the end of this book.

6. Any personality style or type can be a leader.

"D's" and "I's" may appear to be leaders because they are more outgoing by nature. However, "S's" and "C's" can be leaders, as well. Their hearts are full of desire to help others and follow a correct course of action to produce the desired outcome. Leadership skills can be learned and demonstrated by any personality style. My longtime friend, motivator Charles Tremendous Jones, includes all personality styles when summing up leadership qualities: "The size of a leader is determined by the depth of the conviction, the height of the ambition, the breadth of the vision, and the reach of the love."

7. **People with the same personality style still may vary in intensity.**

I played football in college with Billy Green, one of the best running backs in the country. Once, I asked him what he thought about before a game. He replied, "Well, no matter how good I am, I know there is someone on their team who is better than me. My job is to overcome that opposition so we can win." In other words, if you are a "D," sooner or later, you will meet someone whose "D" traits are stronger than your own. The same is true for "I's," "S's," and "C's," as well. Seeing our behaviors in others helps us get ourselves under control.

8. **Our culture and environment influence our personality style.**

Again, pages 2 and 3 list fifteen factors that influence who we are. We are more than our behaviors or our intelligence or our experiences or our heredity. We can adapt our behaviors to accomplish certain goals or tasks in our environment.

9. **You need to understand your own personality style as well as the personality style of others.**

Unfortunately, we are not taught how to do this in school, so we must dig out these insights on our own. In that regard, Henry L. Doherty said, "It is the studying you do after your school days that really counts. Otherwise you know only that which everyone else knows." This truth seems more evident to task-oriented people. Yet, simply collecting data without empowering people is not productive.

My friend Ron Ball cautions, "Don't get *fanatical* about

this personality information — get fanatically excited about your life, your family, your hopes and dreams for the future. That is where you *put this information in practice,* and having your 'why' will show you 'how.'"

10. Understanding personality styles allows you to give people the freedom to be all they were meant to be.

Admiral Richard E. Byrd, who conquered the North and South Poles, believed that "few men during their lifetime come anywhere near exhausting the resources dwelling within them. There are deep wells of strength that are never used." Learning to understand ourselves and others shows us how to release those resources and strengths.

Elbert Hubbard, a publisher and motivational writer who lived at the beginning of this century, wrote, "There is something that is much scarcer, something finer by far, something rarer than ability. It is the ability to recognize ability." Grasping this personality styles information allows us to accept people as they are and recognize the contributions they have been gifted to make.

11. When dealing with several different personality styles, remember that there will be several different views expressed.

Ron Ball, in talking with a group of business owners, showed four different views based on personality styles: A "D" is self-sufficient and thinks, "I'll make it okay." An "I" is optimistic and thinks, "It'll be okay." An "S" is patient and thinks, "I will make it okay... someday." A "C" tends to be critical and thinks, "He will *never* be okay!" In other words, each of us looks at life through our own personality lenses — so we should expect and understand that different perspectives will be presented. We should prepare for them so we can respond thoughtfully as they are presented. This actually helps us increase our productivity by seeing challenges in advance, before they "ambush" us later on.

12. It always helps when you know what your own strengths and weaknesses are. Your strengths will carry you — your weaknesses should concern you!

We are not talking about being a negative thinker when we discuss weaknesses. In our *Personality Insights Seminar* presentations, we define weaknesses as strengths that have been abused or taken to an extreme. They indicate areas in our life that need better balance. André Maurois said, "We are always glad when a great man reassures us of his humanity by possessing a few peculiarities." So, we should expect to discover areas for improvement in ourselves.

Executive Search recruiter John Warren said, "Only a few people are winners, and only a few people are losers — most people are 'at-leasters.'" This is the type of person who compares his shortcomings to others and says, "*At least* I'm not like him..." In response to our weakness, remember that long-range goals can help you overcome short-range failures. If you raise your problem too high, you lower your potential. Our long-goal in looking for personal improvement is overall mastery of the personality "wiring" God has given each of us — not creating obstacles and excuses for failing to live our lives well.

13. If you are working with "S" types, you may have to look closer for leadership qualities.

This is similar to statement number 6, but it is worthy of emphasis. Even an "S" can be a leader, although his methods may not be as "showy." Indira Gandhi said, "I suppose leadership at one time meant muscles; but today it means getting along with people." Of course, "S" types are great at getting along with others and bringing a sense of cooperation.

A kite has to be anchored by a string in order to fly high. And an "S" leader can learn how to do this for "D" and "I" followers. It requires knowing how and when to be assertive (one type of leadership) as well as how and when to be a servant (another type of leadership, at which many "S" types excel). Sometimes an "S" leads by appearing to follow.

14. In many situations, your personality style can feel threatened.

If you were to say to a room full of people, "After this meeting is over, we need to stay and clean up this room," the initial reactions of each personality style would be different.

A "D" type's instinctive response might be, "Hold on! I didn't mess it up — I'm not cleaning it up!" This request might be view as a challenge or "control" issue.

An "I" type's instinct probably would be, "Hey, we can order a pizza and have a party while we do it!" As long as they are having fun — even if it is work — they are happy.

An "S" type usually will go along with the plan, saying, "I'll do it. I don't mind..." They will want to do their part. They are sometimes stuck with the dirty work because they are willing to help get things done. Their greater difficulty would be in asking others to stay and help them.

A "C" type reaction probably would be to question the appropriateness of the request: "Isn't there a maintenance staff to take care of things like this? Didn't I pay a fee to attend this meeting? Why ask me? It's not my responsibility."

The aspect of responding to people may challenge the "task-oriented" individual. Similarly, aspects of a task may a challenge someone who is more "people-oriented." When we say a personality style can feel threatened in a situation (an "environment"), understand that it may require people to adjust their styles in different ways. Recognize that most "situations" are not intended as personal "threats" to you, and try to adjust your style to cooperate in the process.

15. Everyone naturally thinks that his or her own way is the best way and the right way.

When our staff works together on a project, there has to be give-and-take among us. So, we have developed a little "check" that helps us know how to offer suggestions in a way that is nonthreatening. We want to be open-minded and work together for the best outcome, rather than being close-minded or trying to protect our own view or interests.

So, we ask this question: "How are you holding this?" What we mean is, "Are you holding this issue clasped to your heart, shielding it from attack and criticism, or are you holding it loosely and at arm's length, so we can all be objective when we examine it?"

We ask this because we know that anyone who has invested time and effort in a project wants to believe he has thought it through and come up with the best solution, that his is the best way. Asking this question reminds us that we can let go, step back, and see things from another perspective. Then we can create a "win-win" opportunity. This is exactly what understanding personality styles is all about. We are persuaded to see other points of view and work with them.

16. It takes a lot of concentration to adjust your personality style. You can use self-talk to help it along.

I remember hearing about a little boy who found himself falling further and further behind in a foot race. Suddenly, as he began "mouthing" something under his breath, his legs picked up speed, and he won. Someone asked what he was mumbling about and he said, "I've been talkin' to God. I told Him, 'Lord, you pick 'em up and I'll put 'em down... you pick 'em up and I'll put 'em down...!'"

What you tell yourself is very important in overcoming frustration, exhaustion and discouragement. You need encouragement as you develop new personality strengths, too. After all, your personality style and behaviors have been "imbedded" over a period of years. So, it will take time to gain strength as you exercise new "personality muscles." Do not "beat yourself up" emotionally as you develop these skills. Emphasize your progress, rather than your shortcomings.

Remind yourself that "people are not *against* you but *for* themselves." Congratulate yourself *out loud* (really!) when you adjust and adapt your style appropriately. Rather than telling yourself negative messages (like "I've never been very good with people"), begin telling yourself positive messages: "I have what it takes to build good relationships..." and "I'm building stronger people skills every day!" If you have a particular blind spot, begin talking to yourself about how much better you are getting in this area. This may sound like a silly idea if you have never tried it, but you will raise your own confidence and expectations for success. While it requires concentrated effort to change at first, many of the details involved in adjusting your style will become second nature and you will be able to do them almost without thinking.

17. When you take on another personality style, you may feel very uncomfortable. You are not being a hypocrite — you are simply being responsible.

This information is especially helpful for a "C" type to understand. In our seminars, we ask people to cross their arms over their chests in a relaxed posture — set this book down right now and do it, too! How does it feel? When you look down at your arms, is your *right* forearm crossed over your left, or is your *left* forearm crossed over your right? Now, do it again, but this time in the opposite way... Uncomfortable, isn't it?

Clasp your hands together on your lap, in front of you. Is your *right* thumb on top of your left, or is your *left* thumb on top of your right? Try it the other way. Some people say it feels as if they have too many fingers! The point is this: neither way is right or wrong, but they are different — and you probably have a distinct preference between the two. Learning to do it the other way is not comfortable for you, but that does not make your way better.

Aristotle wrote, "We become just by performing just actions, temperate by performing temperate actions, brave by performing brave actions." Someone who acts bravely in spite of fear is not a hypocrite. Rather, he is doing what must be done, even if it makes him uncomfortable.

In adapting or adjusting your personality style, remember that your purpose is not manipulating or deceiving people — or compromising what is important — but rather, your goal is *serving* people and doing the task-at-hand in a responsible manner. Thomas Jefferson said, "In matters of style, swim with the current; in matters of principle, stand like a rock." We can all learn how and when to adjust our styles.

18. Sometimes we are not as much fun, or as mature, as we think we are.

Balance is important in our lives. People who are task-oriented or reserved should practice becoming more people-oriented or outgoing. Emotional spontaneity can make them more fun to be around. Chances are, they are not as much fun as they think they are — and their inability to "go with the flow" may be a sign of emotional immaturity they cannot recognize. Joseph Collins said, "By starving emotions, we become humorless, rigid and stereotyped; by repressing, we become literal, reformatory and holier-than-thou. Encouraged, [emotions] perfume life; discouraged, they poison it."

On the other hand, some people who are naturally people-oriented or outgoing are not nearly as much fun as they think because they don't know when to turn it off. They may "wear" on people and make others uncomfortable when their behavior is not appropriate for the time and place. They may consider themselves mature, but they should practice being more task-oriented and reserved. Playwright Arthur Miller said, "Everybody likes a kidder, but nobody lends him money." Biographer André Maurois commented, "It is not enough to possess wit. One must have enough of it to avoid having too much." Among outgoing or people-oriented types, demonstrating this side of the balance can reveal true maturity. No matter how you slice it, there are always two sides — we *all* have areas we can be working on!

19. Our environment mixed with our own personality style may create some real challenges for us.

Dennis Peacocke says: "When you set a goal, understand that power and success are guarded by problems. Problems are God's barbells." Every normal individual would like to be a well-rounded person. But we will always find a challenge in the events and people around us. Challenges make us strong, and integrity does not come without a struggle.

Just as we build our physical muscles through resistance, we build spiritual muscles by facing our fears and doubts, moving ahead anyway, by faith:

Doubt sees the obstacles,
 Faith sees the way;
Doubt sees the darksome night,
 Faith sees the day.
Doubt dreads to take the step,
 Faith soars on high;
Doubt whispers, "Who believes?"
 Faith says, "I."

— J. Oswald Sanders, *Robust Faith*

This is why historian James Anthony Froude wrote, "You cannot dream yourself into a character; you must hammer and forge one yourself." Novelist Joan Didion wrote, "Character — the willingness to accept responsibility for one's own life — is the source from which self-respect springs." Since we know that different personality styles experience discomfort in different environments, we can welcome the challenges of "fitting in" as seeds for growing character and self-respect.

If you truly want to succeed in this area, add this thought to your own self-talk: "A person who is successful in any area has simply formed the habit of doing things that unsuccessful people will not do."

20. When our personality style is out of control, we can hurt our life.

I wish I knew the source for the following quotation I found in a church bulletin. It is filled with wisdom. "One man gets nothing but discord out of a piano; another gets harmony. No one claims the piano is at fault. Life is about the same. The discord is there and the harmony is there. Study to play it correctly, and it will give forth beauty; play it falsely, and it will give forth ugliness. Life is not at fault."

In disappointment, it is easier for us to blame our circumstances or other people. But many of our problems lie in our inability to control our own personality and behavior. "Life is not at fault." When we look honestly at our lives, we can see how self-discipline — learning to *do appropriate things* even when they are uncomfortable, and learning to *avoid inappropriate things* even when they are desirable — is a key to avoiding harm and achieving success. My friend Zig Ziglar says, "Discipline weighs ounces; regret weighs tons."

21. The first step in maturity is recognizing the strengths and weaknesses of our own personality style.

Arkansas business developer Ed Courtney tells the story of an old fisherman who had survived 14 shipwrecks and was asked if he was a good swimmer. He said, "No, the swimmers think they can make it on their own. They rely on themselves, and they wear out and drown. I just look for something bigger than myself that floats, and I just hang on until somebody comes and rescues me." The old fisherman knew his limitations and did not exaggerate his strengths. And he recognized an immediate source of safety while looking for eventual rescue.

In relationship skills, we need to do the same. We should understand our strengths and weaknesses. We should know what to do when we "get in over our head" — what skills we can hang on to while we search for a way out. This book is filled with techniques and ideas for working well with others, even in unfamiliar waters.

22. Our goal is to be so balanced with "D-I-S-C" traits — not just skilled with one set of traits — that people cannot pick out our basic style because our behavior is always appropriate for the occasion.

It is easier for us to recognize in others when a trait has gotten out of control than it is to detect when one is operating appropriately and under control. So in becoming balanced, one goal is checking the weaknesses or blind spots in our own personality style. A second goal is developing the traits with which we are least comfortable, outside of our personality style. But if we accomplish one without the other, we run the risk of having no distinguishable traits, rather than becoming a "well-rounded" person with a variety of outstanding and appropriate behaviors.

A very successful man once said, "In reading the lives of

great individuals, I found that the first victory they won was over themselves; with all of them, self-discipline came first." Being able to discipline and control our personality style appropriately is a demonstration of real maturity.

23. Being in a position of leadership will force you to work with other personality styles.

Dale Carnegie taught about leadership and human relations, and his book *How to Win Friends and Influence People* is filled with many valuable insights. He wrote that leadership requires patience and understanding: "When dealing with people remember you are not dealing with creatures of logic, but with creatures of emotion, creatures bristling with prejudice, and motivated by pride and vanity."

Because true leaders are not "picked," but pick themselves to lead, it is important to know how to work with a variety of personality styles. You don't want to lose a "leader in the rough" because you cannot work with that individual. Rather than looking for "weaker" people you can lead, look for "stronger" people you can develop — and you will find leaders in every imaginable personality style. Prejudice has no place when you're looking for leaders.

24. We all tend to be "territorial" concerning our own personality style.

A special program on cable television's *Discovery Channel* told about mountain goats that walk in very steep, narrow places yet keep their balance and footing. Occasionally, two mountain goats come face-to-face on a narrow precipice, where neither goat can pass. At this point, they have three choices: First, they can fight it out, butt heads, and try to run each other over. One, if not both, will fall to its death or be severely injured. Second, one goat can back down from the cliff as the other pushes it aside. But stepping back is both hard on its pride and awkward — the goat may slip and fall. The third choice is for one goat to *lie down* and let the other goat walk over it. Then both can go on their way unharmed. This is what they do most of the time, and it is the *more mature* goat that makes this choice. We can choose to be territorial and risk great loss, or we can choose to make way for others and win together.

Dr. Martin Luther King, Jr., said, "If a man hasn't discovered something that he will die for, he isn't fit to live." The pity is what some goat-headed people are willing to die over! According to a United States Supreme Court ruling, if we are not willing to die for something, it is not a true conviction but a preference. When we feel defensive and territorial, we can ask, "Is this something I am willing to die for? Am I willing to 'kill' over it? If not, can I learn to live with it?"

25. Oftentimes, the way we act is determined by our moods, when in reality, we should learn to harness our personality to display self-control and maturity.

Ohio businesswoman M. J. Michael told a group that, according to Oswald Chambers, in *My Utmost for His Highest,* "Moods never go by praying, but by kicking. A mood has its seed in the *physical* condition, not the *moral*. Make a continual effort not to listen or submit to a mood's physical power for a second. Grab yourself by the scruff of the neck and shake yourself."

My friend Ron Ball told a similar group, "Your emotions are *responders,* not initiators. They ebb and flow, they come and go. They are undependable — you cannot build on them. They can be mistaken, so don't give them too much power. They have only as much power as you give them."

Peter J. Daniels graduated from high school functionally illiterate. He was doomed to failure according to all his teachers and everyone who knew him. Today, he is one of the wealthiest men in Australia and is a trusted advisor to many Fortune 500 companies in the United States. He has made millions of dollars, lost them and started again — several times! When asked how he battles discouragement and frustration, he says, "Emotion is not always subject to reason, but emotion is always subject to action."

Bestselling author Chuck Swindoll wrote, "This may shock you, but I believe the single most significant decision I can make on a day-to-day basis is my choice of attitude. It is more important than my past, my education, my bankroll, my successes or failures, fame or pain, what other people think of me or say about me, my circumstances, or my position. Attitude in that 'single string' that keeps me going or cripples my progress. It also fuels my fire or assaults my hope. When my attitudes are right, there's no barrier too high, no valley too steep, no dream too extreme, no challenge too great for me."

As you continue to work through this book's tremendous information on personality styles, we hope you will return again and again to this chapter for encouragement.

Chapter 8

DISCover Your Child's Design

"A family," wrote Ogden Nash, "is a unit composed not only of children but of men, women, an occasional animal, and the common cold." There are viruses at work in some families more damaging than the common cold — unhealthy relationships between parents and children that infect their homes and threaten their existence. We hope to provide a cure for some of that *"dis-ease"* in these next pages.

If you are a parent, you do not need any explanation for Sam Levenson's famous statement: "Insanity is hereditary; you can get it from your children." If you are not a parent, there is no "complete" explanation. Parents who understand their children's personality styles possess a magic key to these young hearts. So, while much of this chapter will be "fun," you will find it filled with serious ideas, concepts and consequences.

Teachers, too, are in need of this information. Mark Twain quoted a teacher describing her first day back in grade school after a long absence: "It was like trying to hold 35 corks under water at the same time." Again, if you have ever taught a class of wiggly kids, you need no explanation.

Reaching a child's heart and mind is the necessary goal of every effective parent and teacher. Our goal in this chapter is not to provide all the answers to every question you may have about your child's personality style, but to point you in the right direction and give you confidence that you *really can* discover many of these answers for yourself.

Train Up a Child

Proverbs 22:6 is familiar to most people, regardless of their religious training. The *New International Version* (NIV) translation of this Bible verse says, "Train a child in the way he should go, and when he is old he will not turn from it." The original Hebrew text literally means, *"start a child according to his own way..."* In my first book, *Positive Personality Profiles,* we explored the difference between encouraging a child to start on the road that is right for his particular personality style versus "scripting" him according to a way chosen, prescribed and imposed by the parents. This verse recognizes a child's special, God-given disposition, talents and gifts — it does not treat all developing personalities the same. It does not say that parents should choose their children's paths, but it instructs parents to encourage, nurture, guide and inform so their children will be prepared to choose and follow the right paths even when they are grown.

19th Century humorist Josh Billings reminded us, "To train up a child in the way he should go, travel that way yourself once in awhile." So another purpose of this chapter will be to help you see things through your child's eyes while discovering how to model a balanced personality style for your child.

This is easier said than done. As Mignon McLaughlin noted, "Most of us became parents long before we stopped being children." Novelist Peter de Vries wrote, "Who among us is mature enough for offspring before the offspring themselves arrive? The value of marriage is not that adults produce children but that children produce adults." In other words, while we are bringing up our children, we, too, are "in process." *(some people never grow up)*

We also want you to get excited about the possibilities of your relationship with your children. Of course, your kids may not want you to be their constant companion, but they do *need* — and *want* — you to be their guiding light. Finding your rightful place in that relationship is a fulfilling experience!

And, if that is not enough, we will give you help in harmonizing family relations. You will find aid in dealing with teen rebellion, as well as how to get your eight-year-old to take out the trash.

Put "D's" In Charge

Positive Personality Profiles and *Different Children Different Needs* (coauthored with Charles F. Boyd) provided several examples of "D" type behavior observed in my family as we raised our oldest daughter. (I recommend both books for a more thorough understanding of working with children according to their personality styles.) Out of a growing respect for my growing children, we will not add further to the Rohm Legend by recounting a lot of family stories in this volume, but I do have a favorite that shows how "D" type children not only like to be in charge, but want to get every task accomplished *now...*

One day, I told Rachael, my oldest daughter, that I wanted her to be in charge of cutting the grass. To me that meant, *"I* want *you* to cut the grass."* To her it meant, "Dad wants *me* to be *in charge* of cutting the grass." Such an open-ended request created a whole new opportunity! When I returned from my errands, it looked to me as if every other "row" in my lawn had been cut at a different height. I had never seen stripes like that before, and I asked her, "What's the story with the yard? I noticed the grass is uneven." Matter-of-factly she explained, "Dad, *you* put *me* in charge. I got our lawn mower and Esther (her high, high "I" sister) got the neighbor's lawn mower, and we cut the lawn together, at the same time. I thought it would go faster that way." I asked, "Didn't you notice that every other row is a different height?" And she said, "Isn't it radical?" To her, she *conquered* the project in record time with a *distinctive* outcome. What more could she want?

"D's" Need A Job

I heard about a business owner who hung a "Boy Wanted" sign in his window, looking for after-school help. A long line of applicants answered his appeal. One boy scribbled a note, pushed his way through the crowd and handed it to the owner. It said, "Don't do anything till you've seen me. I'm the last in line, but I've got the goods." You can be sure he was a "D"!

I was speaking at a conference where the emphasis was on helping children. I mentioned how "D" type children have a strong need to be in control. I suggested that the best way to help a "D" child function correctly within a group is to give him "a piece of the action" by letting him be in charge of something. Several months later I ran into a gentlemen who had attended that seminar. He told me when he first heard my comment, he thought I had lost my mind. But then...

He told me about a group of children he met with once each week. One little boy in the group misbehaved so badly that he often prayed the child would not even attend the meeting. The boy disrupted everything. Because the man had listened to my presentation, he realized he was working with a high "D" child. He thought he should at least give my idea a try — what could it hurt? He asked the child to come early the following week to help him, making sure all of the mats were distributed for sitting on the floor, and several other projects.

To his astonishment, a transformation came over the child almost overnight. Rather than being a problem-maker, he became a problem-solver! The man said, "I watched as he brought more of his friends to the meeting than everyone else in the room combined. No one was more astonished than me, watching the transformation in this young boy! I discovered that the real problem was not the child — it was me!" (Insight such as this takes a lot of humility!)

How sad and yet how true it is that often we create our problems by not handling personalities correctly. We try to force compliance by using our own methods and techniques, rather than understanding the needs, desires and motivations of others. Oftentimes, when we acknowledge a "D" child's need to be in control and her eagerness to take on a challenge, we create a basis for cooperation and relationship.

"D's" Enjoy Conflict

Musician and speaker Derric Johnson tells a story from childhood in his book *Easy Doesn't Do It!*, about when his four-year-old brother was in a fight, sitting on top of the other boy and swinging his fists wildly. Derric's mother came running to break up the fight, and held his arms back so he would not be able to reach the other boy as she tried to pull him off. She was shocked as he leaned forward and bit the other little boy's nose. Scolding him severely, she said, "Satan must have made you fight like that!" Derric's little brother replied, "Maybe Satan made me hit him, but biting his nose… that was my idea!" "D" type children so enjoy a good scrap, and they never seem to run out of ideas for getting in one. They love conflict and challenge. They can get "stirred up" about almost anything, and if you have one in your home, you know that they want to call the shots all the time.

One night I was in Charlotte, North Carolina, having dinner with my good friend, Steve Yager, who is Senior Vice President of InterNET Services Corporation. Steve has six brothers and sisters, and since I am an only child, I find the contrasts very interesting. We were talking about growing up in such a large family — where, I imagine, "survival of the fittest" is often the rule. I was very amused at one particular story he told me about his brother Jeff. I appreciate very much their giving me permission to share it with you.

Steve told me that he was the baby of the family and Jeff was a big brother. When they were kids, it seemed like Jeff beat him up almost every day. Steve told me that after getting "thumped on," he would sit on the floor, crying. Within two or three minutes Jeff would look over at him and say, "Hey, you wanna play checkers?" Steve would reply, "No, I don't want to play checkers with you. I never want to see you again!"

It has always fascinated Steve how quickly Jeff could get over what had happened in the past and move on to new territory. I shared with him that this is one of the great qualities of the "D" personality. They may be upset with you one moment, but after it is over, it really *is* over for them. They aren't the type to hold grudges or want to live in the past. Their desire is to move on to bigger and better things and let bygones be bygones — forget the past. The future is where it's at! Steve told me he wished he had known about the "D" type personality growing up, but it still would not have helped him feel any better after he had been beaten up!

Jeff, of course, is still an intense "D" — only now, he has a focus for his intensity as president of InterNET Services. He is my good friend as well and has certainly learned to bring his "D" under control to become a dynamic leader!

"D's" Need to Understand Themselves

One morning I was leading a seminar for 450 teenagers at a high school in West Palm Beach, Florida. We spent all morning working through personality styles and "How to Understand Yourself and Others." After our "assembly program" had finished, the school administrator made the comment that he had never seen 450 teenagers sit from 8:30 till noon in one place and behave so well. I knew it was because they were interested in the topic... themselves!

Later the next day one of the mothers told me that she had been asleep at home, late on the previous night, when her son came home from school. After participating in the seminar, attending the rest of school and going to athletic practice, he burst through her bedroom door, jumped onto the bed and shook her, exclaiming, "Mom, mom, wake up! I've got to tell you something!"

She told me, "I was scared and startled! He was so worked up I thought something awful had happened. So I asked him what was wrong. He said, 'Mom, guess what? I'm a high 'D'!'" She told me that her son began telling her how he finally understood his personality and why he felt, thought and acted the way he did. He also had the opportunity to look at his possible work preferences and was on a new course of action with goals and a real sense of purpose in life.

When she told me this story, the mom had just completed one of our training seminars for herself. She smiled and said that now she understood exactly what he was talking about. "He was right — he is a high 'D' and I'm grateful that he understands that and has direction and purpose in his life." If parents and teachers taught their sons, daughters or students this information, children could move in the right direction and find success by understanding their personal behavior style and working *with* themselves (instead of *against* themselves).

A study at Ohio State University found that one of the greatest problems in America is job dissatisfaction. Americans change *careers* four to seven times, trying to find a *job* they enjoy. If workers were taught this information early in life, they would have a better understanding of who they are and which avenues are best-suited for their behavior styles.

Sometimes schools try to provide students with this direction in the form of technical skills assessments or psychological profiles. But a "D" type person is very bottom line-oriented, and complex reports tend to confuse or bore them. One of the sharpest young men I know is Andy Thoms. Unable to hear as a young boy, he did not learn to speak until he was in the upper elementary grades. But he had a tenacity even then that was not going to be denied — you would never have any idea of the obstacles he has worked to overcome, unless someone shared the details with you. Andy's parents feel they have benefited greatly from this *Personality Insights* information in their family, as they have learned to understand each other. When Andy was a high school Senior, his school gave all the graduates an extensive profile assessment that was not related to the "D-I-S-C" system. His mother told me that when he got home with all the pages and pages of information and coined phrases to explain his makeup, she asked him how it turned out and what it meant. He replied, "Mom, you *know* I'm a 'D!'"

The great thing about the "D-I-S-C" system is that it offers a language that is easily learned and communicated, that does not carry any stigma on its own, and offers practical insights for improving self-image and personal performance.

A mother who works with the Archdiocese of New York called our office very excitedly because her daughter had completed

WHO DO YOU THINK YOU ARE ANYWAY?

Get Real!, our self-scoring *Style Assessment* for teens and young adults. Their communication had not been good, and in high school, her daughter seemed lost and lacking direction. In fact, the mother *paid* her daughter twenty-five dollars just to complete the fifteen-minute assessment questionnaire. When the teenager had worked through the information, she came to her mother and shared enthusiastically what she had learned. She called her best girlfriend and told her about it — and asked her come over and complete an assessment for herself. And then she gave her mother back the twenty-five dollars! Gaining understanding is a powerful experience!

"I's" Need a Focus

"D" type children seldom lack confidence. They tend to be independent and do not care too much about peer pressure. Whether or not your "D" child *joins* a gang probably will not be a major worry in your life... However, "D" types are the ones who *start* gangs!

Unfortunately, not all children have the drive, determination or diligence of "D" children. For instance, the other fast-paced, outgoing style is the "I," who is very influenced by others and tends to ride an emotional roller coaster. Because "I's" are impressionable, impulsive and illogical, they often feel like "the life of the party" ...looking for a party!

It is not that they are stupid — far from it. They are usually very quick-witted and imaginative, but often they have a short attention span. I have said jokingly that sometimes (as an "I" myself) "I's" have the attention span of a gnat! We have an incredibly high ability to be involved mentally in a project *if* it is something in which we are interested. That is the key... the higher our interest level, the more committed we are to the learning process. We are distracted easily; our minds wander, we get off track, and the smallest thing that catches our imagination diverts our attention. "I" type children have all their marbles. It is just that their "shooter" is missing! Because of this, they need help in the form of short-term goals and immediate feedback.

"I's" Feel, Rather Than Think

I remember once telling my youngest daughter Susanna to lay out her school clothes before going to bed, so she would not be in a panic the next morning, looking for her things. I figured if she knew what she was going to wear and had her books and lunch collected in one place, she would get off to school without our customary confusion. When I checked on her at bedtime, I found her clothes literally *laid out* on the floor, looking as if she had lain down on the floor and fallen through, leaving only her clothes behind! While this was not what I had intended, the following morning she discovered that getting organized ahead of time really was a big help, and she received immediate feedback and validation when it worked.

Of course, "I" types love to go and do. People think of them as "busy bees." But Kin Hubbard says, "Bees are not as busy as we think they are. They just can't buzz any slower." This well describes the "I" type child.

And they love to talk. Vice President Hubert Humphrey was this kind of "I." Once, as his speech went on and on and he became more and more emotional, his wife Muriel remarked, "Hubert, to be eternal, you don't have to be endless!" Even as children, "I's" tend to be talkative and sociable. Their constant chatter wears down their parents and teachers. Most of the time, they even "think out loud." Teachers pick this type of child as class spokesperson. They often get the lead in school plays. Their emotional zeal and energy is amazing — and if "D" is their secondary trait, being around them will make you feel like a mobile home in tornado country!

They tend to be experience-oriented. Critical thinking is not a natural skill for them. Existentialist Sören Kierkegaard claimed that "Life can only be understood backwards; but it must be lived forwards." And this describes the fast-paced, outgoing child. They cannot truly understand life until they have lived it. So, the parent of an "I" child must make special effort to explain underlying principles and results, to show this child how "cause" and "effect" are connected.

"I's" of any age are embarrassed easily, but "I" children feel it acutely because many of their friends have not learned "sophisticated" methods of teasing yet. They do not like to feel silly or stupid or awkward or immature in front of their peers. A good quotation that you can share with them comes from Ethel Barrett: "We would worry less about what others think of us if we realized how seldom they do."

"I's" Need a Pattern

Because they are not task-oriented, assignments that seem obvious and simple to a parent may frustrate an "I" child. Chris's oldest daughter Jessica is an "I" who is full of fun and laughter and music. Emptying the kitchen trash was not only one of her chores as a seven-year-old — it was also a major source of conflict between his wife Cindy and Jessie. As any mother understands, there is more to taking out the trash than taking the trash bag out to the garbage can — it also involves replacing the trash bag in the kitchen. Jessie was good at taking out the trash when she was asked, but she often forgot the second part of the task. Finally, Cindy and Chris sat down to look at the job from her perspective:

Jessie took the trash bag out of the kitchen trash can. Then she tied the bag closed. She carried it through the kitchen, into the family room, past the television and games and her younger sister. She opened the french doors to the patio and carried the trash bag out to the garbage cans near the wooded area in the back yard. Then she had to remember to put the lid back on the can, walk back to the double doors, wipe her feet, pass back through the family room — uh oh! television and games, or distractions upstairs if she went the other way because she thought she heard her little sister calling. Then into the kitchen, past the refrigerator, the telephone and another television to complete the task: go to the pantry, find and install a new trash bag in the can.

"I" type children are easily distracted anyway. By viewing the assignment from Jessie's perspective, they saw that the act of "closing the door" when she returned from the back yard spelled *finito* in her mind. Constantly reminding her that her work had not been finished was frustrating both Jessie and Cindy. Everyone understood that the goal was getting the job done, not causing friction. So, they simply moved "completion" closer to the beginning of Jessie's task: Take the full trash bag out of the trash can... Look — a hole! The trash can is empty! It needs to be filled up! Get a new bag and put it in! The part that she forgot was now placed where she could not forget it, because she was not allowed to tie the full trash bag and carry it to the can until she had replaced it. Then she could take it out to trash cans, so when she came back inside and closed the door, it really was... *finito!* Of course, they are still working on teaching her to observe for herself when the trash needs to be emptied and not stepping around a full can when she is trying to get to the dinner table. But that will come in time, with a little more maturity.

Set Up an "I" to Succeed

Cyrus Ching said, "I learned long ago never to wrestle with a pig. You get dirty, and besides, the pig likes it." The point is that even if you win, you may lose. There is another "country proverb" that says, "Never try to teach a pig to sing. It frustrates you and irritates the pig." This means you will get frustrated trying to do what cannot be done and you will make even the object of your labors unhappy in the process.

If you are highly task-oriented and reserved, parenting your "I" child may be the most demanding job you have ever attempted. You will not succeed in turning an "I" into a "C" — no matter how hard you try. Your child has been "wired" by God to be inspiring, interesting, imaginative, influencing, impressive and illogical. You can nurture and develop the skills you believe are important for your child's success, but in the process of wiping out the "I" characteristics you do not like you may also lose the spontaneity, resilience and open heart that make "I" children so refreshing.

The tendency of a frustrated parent is to instruct and correct to the point that children hear the "noise" instead of the "words." So, we are suggesting that you give Cindy and Chris's "trash can philosophy" a try the next time you run into a challenge with your

"I" children. Do everything you can to see it from their perspective — not to make an *excuse* for their failure, but to make a *way* for their success.

Helping Teachers See "I" to "I"

Ralph Waldo Emerson wrote, "I pay the schoolmaster, but 'tis the schoolboys that educate my son." "I" type children are outgoing and people-oriented, and they are far more influenced by their peers than most parents wish. I have never researched this, but I believe most of the children who are labeled as "Attention Deficit Disorder" (ADD) or "Attention Deficit Hyperactive Disorder" (ADHD) are found in the higher ranges of "D" and "I" behavioral styles. Think about it... are schools designed for their learning styles? Rules say: stay in your seat, raise your hand to speak, stand in a straight line, sit and listen quietly while the teacher is talking, keep track of your assignments, listen well and take lots of notes... Does this even *sound* like a "D" or an "I" child? Or does this sound like a more comfortable environment for "S" and "C" students?

What passes for "success" in a classroom does not always succeed outside its walls. Cyrus H. Curtis said, "There are two kinds of men who never amount to much: Those who cannot do what they are told, and those who can do nothing else." To be successful in life, some students need to "rein in" their personalities, while others need to "loosen their grip" a bit more. Curtis' comment probably explains why there are many people who did not do phenomenally well with formal education but have succeeded stunningly in the "real world."

R. Buckminster Fuller, father of the geodesic dome and famous freethinker, said, "If I ran a school, I'd give the average grades to the ones who gave me the right answers, for being good parrots. I'd give the top grades to those who made a lot of mistakes and told me about them, and then told me what they learned from them." Albert Einstein said, "Imagination is more important than knowledge." But, sadly, schools are not set up to reward this type of learning style.

My book *Tales Out of School* is filled with wonderful examples of what happens when personality styles don't mesh in the classroom — and the great things that can happen when educators teach students according to their styles. One teacher's brief example is entitled...

"20-20 Hindsight"

Kenny was in my Kindergarten Class last year and I could not understand him at all. He was very argumentative — he always had to have the last word. I was so tired and frustrated at the end of each day from constantly "butting heads" with him. I thought, "Why is he so obnoxious?" He never raised his hand and he always had some comment to make, usually about how I could do things better.

I used every kind of discipline possible, but I could not get a handle on his behavior. I didn't understand it at all. Now I see that Kenny was a high "D" and didn't like control. If I had him in my class now, I would handle him differently. I would let him help the others with their writing and coloring (he was very neat). Boy, he would have thrived on that! Next time, I will try to nurture, rather than conform, this personality style.

Jordan joined us in the middle of the year. This is usually hard on a child who doesn't know anyone and feels insecure, having a hard time catching up. *Not Jordan!* After his mother left and we had him settled in, he began talking and carrying on — he had everyone laughing and liking him instantly. What a character! He had so much personality and the children took him in immediately. He was sharp and caught on quickly. However, he had trouble finishing his work and staying in his seat. He was always at someone else's table, talking.

Every time he got in trouble and had to sit at recess, he would cry and it would break my heart. I thought, "If you hate this so much, why do you keep doing the things that get you in trouble?" I didn't understand that Jordan had an "I" type personality. If I had, I would have let him get up and do something else to give him a break from class work.

Erica was the ideal student: smart, sweet, quiet, and loving. She was always willing to help and ready to please. To this day, she and I enjoy a wonderful relationship. Being an "S" type myself, I really relate to her. There were no problems teaching Erica. She was easy!

Karen was the most inquisitive child I have ever known. She was so intelligent, but she checked and rechecked everything she did and everything she was supposed to do. She seemed so afraid of making a mistake. She had to know the "why" to everything. It was so exasperating at times. She cried if she missed one question or forgot one little detail.

I would often think, "Karen, you are being ridiculous — no one is perfect!" Now that I know that being wrong is rare and hardest on a "C," I will try to help children like Karen to relax and understand that it really is okay to not always be right. They need to enjoy things more.

This course has opened my eyes so much and I am looking forward to starting over with a new outlook on teaching. This information would save so many people from "going gray" and pulling out their hair if every individual were required to learn it early in life — especially school teachers!

Assuming that you understand a good deal about personality styles by now, what do you think would happen if a teacher who did not know this information put two "I's" together and gave them an assignment…? Party time! Their whole experience would be like one long trip to Six Flags or Disney World. They would have a great time together but what would they get done? Not much. Would you want to put an "I" in charge of a high school yearbook? The school year would end and they would be thinking, "Man, was I supposed to do stuff all year? …Pictures? You mean I'm supposed to have pictures?"

Two "I's" together often demonstrate a poor work ethic because they enjoy socializing so much. As a result, they have little time for their task. If I were their teacher, I would surround my "I's" with "C's." When the "I" would nudge his neighbor "C," the "C" would respond by saying, "I can't talk, I have to keep working." Both "D's" and "C's" are task-oriented. They go to school to get the work done. (A "D" will probably complete a very concise term paper on schedule, and a "C" will meet the deadline, maybe ahead of schedule, with a full-fledged *document* in hand.) Both "I's" and "S's" go to school to see friends, so they have a more difficult time with these kinds of projects. (The "I" underestimates the work and may try to bluff his way to completion, while the "S" is a hesitant starter and will worry over meeting the teacher's term paper expectations.) So, "D's" and "C's" get to know the material and "I's" and "S's" get to know the teacher!

This is how a teacher can help "I" students overcome their struggles with term papers: Because "I's" learn best in short increments, they do not function well on a six-week schedule. "C's" can understand and function on that kind of schedule, but "I's" think in bite-sized thoughts and chunks. An informed teacher tells these students that she needs to review their note cards in two weeks, followed by a rough draft in two more weeks, a bibliography the following week, and then the final paper the next week. In "setting them up for success," she follows through to see that they are on schedule. In this way, she teaches them *success patterns.*

Even as a doctoral candidate, whenever I went to the library to study, I would spread my papers out on the table and then see someone I knew. Of course, I always felt I had to go visit with them. Of course, the librarian always thought I made too much noise. To this day, I have to isolate myself to get things done.

As a final word of encouragement regarding "D" and "I" types, it is good for us, as parents or teachers, to recognize and appreciate the resilience and winning attitude of these high-energy children. Economist Paul Zane Pilzer tells about a father who arrived home after a tough day at work and saw his eight-year-old son playing ball in the driveway. "Dad! Dad! Watch this…" The boy tossed the ball into the air, took a swing and missed. "Strike One…!" Gamely, he tossed the ball up in the air again and swung even harder, missing wildly. "Strike Two…!" The father shook his head and wondered how his son could be such a bad hitter yet so enthusiastic about it. Again, the boy tossed the ball into the air and swung so hard he spun around and fell on the ground. "Strike

Three...!" The father was trying to think of something encouraging to say, when the boy exclaimed, "I've been strikin' out like that all day — pretty good pitchin', huh, dad?"

George Bernard Shaw wrote, "Some see things as they are and ask why. I dream things that never were and say, why not?" This is the gift adventurous, young dreamers offer the world. As parents and as teachers, we are fortunate that we are trusted to nurture their special gift.

"S's" Seem So Simple

The thing "S" type children seem to concentrate on is "getting along" and "going along." They want everyone to be friends and they want to cooperate with everyone. For the most part, this is not an effort for them; it is part of their Basic Style. Both "S" and "I" types are people-oriented, so they tend to be very trusting, even gullible at times. They feel the emotions of others and are quick to come to the rescue.

I never will forget the night the Gulf War began. We were driving in our van, my two younger daughters in the back seat. We turned on the radio to heard live reports about missiles being launched against Iraq — we could hear them exploding in the background. At that moment, many Americans felt a sense of patriotism welling up inside because America was trying to help Kuwait and Saudi Arabia in their hour of need. But there was also a *moment* of need taking place in my car.

As I glanced in the rear view mirror, I saw tears streaming down the cheeks of my "S" daughter Elizabeth. I asked her what was wrong. In a broken voice she told me how sorry she felt for all the people who were dying. In fatherly tones, I tried to explain what the war was all about, but it didn't do a lot of good. She said to me, "I understand all that, Dad, but it still makes me sad to know that innocent people get killed in wars and I feel sorry for their families." Well, of course, I sat there and felt like a dog, but at least I understood her high "S" nature and where her concern was coming from. Regardless of whether the war was right, the real issue in her mind was the pain that sorrow and death brought to all families. It all can seem simple to a parent with a different style, but to an "S" child, life seems more complex because they consider *people* in the equation.

Not to be outdone, Susanna (my youngest "I" daughter) was jumping up and down with excitement. She told me that at school her friends had changed Saddam Hussein's name to "So Dumb Insane" because of all the trouble he was causing. We laughed as she told me and thought it was so funny, and it did help make the moment a little lighter for us, including Elizabeth.

As we got close to home, I looked in the rear view mirror again and wondered how the same gene pool could have produced two totally different children! The answer of course is that each child is "wired" with her own, unique makeup — and naturally, each sees life through her own, unique perspective. It is very important to understand this concept in raising children, as well as in marriage and business relations, in order to see things from the perspective of the other person, to build better relationships, and to appreciate what each contributes to life.

"S's" Have Sensitive Relationships

One morning I received a telephone call from a man in Mineral Wells, Texas, who told me he had just been to see his 95 year old mother. She lives in Ft. Payne, Alabama, and is a retired psychologist and teacher. After he visited with her a few minutes, he gave her a copy of my book, *Positive Personality Profiles,* and told her that it was all about how to understand yourself and others. He said she began reading and would not put it down. She told him he could go watch television or do something else — she wanted to read the book. He laughed as he told me the story because, he said, "Basically, that was the end of the visit with my mother!" She ignored him the rest of the weekend, but he told me it was a joy to see her enjoying something so much.

After she finished reading, they finally sat down and talked. Tears ran down her cheeks as she told him she had agonized all of her life over her relationship with Betty, his aunt who had died several years earlier from cancer. His mother had tried all of her life to have a close relationship with her sister Betty, reaching out to her in a warm, friendly manner. His mother then said, "I have finally discovered that I am a high 'S' personality and Betty was a 'D.' No matter what I tried to do to change myself or change her to make her act more like me, I never was able to do it. I now understand her and realize that it wasn't my fault — that's just the way she was. She wasn't good or bad, she was just different. I wish I had understood all this years ago."

From childhood, his mother had carried a heavy burden, and in a few minutes of reading, it was released. She was not exaggerating when she used the word "agonize" concerning her desire to have a good relationship. Her story is a healthy reminder that there are many people (especially people-oriented "S" and "I" types) who really do agonize over the value and quality of their relationships. Yet without this simple but specific information, none of their agonies, hopes and desires is capable of changing anything, until they understand how to focus correctly and adjust their own personality styles accordingly.

Self-image and confidence are two key concerns for parents rearing an "S" child. They need to identify their worth and value within the family and learn to see themselves as significant and important.

"S's" Need Help in Saying No

I do not endorse a book that was written years ago, but I like the title: *What You Think of Me Is None of My Business.* Both "I" and "S" children are people-oriented, and as we have said, they are usually more influenced by peer pressure than "D" and "C" task-oriented children. Since this is true, you need to help them establish boundaries in their relationships.

Because "opposites attract," an "S" type child often joins in with a "D" type who is more than willing to give orders and lead the way. An "S" child can fall under the control or domination of a strong-willed, destructive little tyrant-friend. It can happen easily if he views the friend's behavior as "masculine" or mature. So, you need to help your son or daughter establish expectations for (and limits on) his own behavior before he is "boxed in" by the expectations of peers.

Similarly, a teenage girl who is an "S" may be putty in the hands of a "D" teenage boy. As a parent, it is *your* responsibility to help her define her limits *before* she gets into a "just say no" situation. This is because saying "no" is one of the hardest things she can do. She does not want to cause disappointment for others or rejection for herself.

Helping people-oriented children face sexual pressures is easier if you discuss it beforehand. Help your child work on some good "no lines" she can use when she is feeling pressured. I heard about one girl who was being pressured sexually and morally by her boyfriend. She asked him if he would first take her to a drug store. He said, "Sure!" While he waited in the car, she went inside the store — and called her dad! In a few minutes, her father pulled up in a parking space beside the boy. When the young man glanced over... Well, I would like to have seen that, wouldn't you?

"S" type kids also tend to take on the problems of others. They may be expected to "fix" things that have gone wrong — probably because they are so quick to accept blame or responsibility for the situation. At times, their relationships take on aspects of codependency, since they tend to get their identity from how they help others and how they are valued by others. Unless this potential area of concern is addressed, some children with this tendency will enter into unhealthy relationships as adults, or they may become "enablers" of alcohol, drug or domestic abusers.

A man who said "yes" to everyone, from his early childhood on, spoke to me several years ago. He said, "Never stop sharing this information with people. Keep telling 'S' types it's okay to say no." Briefly, he said "yes" to everyone else's burdens, said "no" only to himself, suffered quietly in an abusive home, and drifted without plan or purpose in life. Then one day, as an adult, he "woke up" in his automobile, three states and many miles away from his home. He had no idea how he had driven there over a period of several days. A psychiatrist explained that he had experienced a *"psychogenic fugue"* — an episode wherein his conscious, critical thinking processes closed down because of his emotional overload.

I am not suggesting that doom lies in the path of every high "S" individual. But I am suggesting that you, as a parent or teacher, may be able to observe some of these behaviors. Here is one way you can "stand in the gap" for them, and while we *all* should learn to use this is a phrase effectively, you can teach "S" children to say, "Let me check — I would rather let you know than let you down." And then, you can be the "heavy" who helps them say no when they should. For the sake of healthy relationships in youth and on into adulthood, an "S" child's parent can plant and nurture many seeds for successful, helpful and independent relationships.

C's Seek Quality Information

When I spoke before several thousand teachers at a regional conference of the Association of Christian Schools International (ACSI), I described how each of the four styles responds to this "D-I-S-C" information.

I said "D" types were already tapping their feet with nervous energy, thinking, "Okay, we've got the idea — move on! What else? Let's go!" "I" types were laughing at every little joke, thinking, "I know people like he is describing! This is great! I've got to tell him my favorite story — I know he'll use it! Maybe we can go to dinner with him sometime!" The "S" types were just a little nervous about the noise and excitement level in the room, thinking, "Boy, I sure hope he doesn't call on me. Maybe if I sit really still, he won't notice me. Is there going to be a test on this?" And "C" types were skeptically evaluating all of it, thinking, "Who is this guy? How do we know this isn't *bogus* information? Where does he get his facts? Are we sure any of this is correct?"

After my talk, a lady introduced herself and told me what had happened during my speech. Their school's very high "C" science teacher had been sitting in front of her, squirming a bit because he had registered for the conference to learn more effective facts for communicating chemistry information to his students. He was not interested in watching some high "I" motivational speaker bounce all over the stage while telling silly stories about life. He had written four words in the margin of our seminar outline: *"This is bogus information!"* and put away his pen. When I began describing those responses, the lady said he reacted *physically* to the word "bogus." He started squirming in his seat again. Then he quietly reached back into his pocket, withdrew his pen and *scratched through* his marginal note.

"C" type children seem to have considerably more skepticism than others. They have an endless stream of questions for parents and teachers, many of which are impossible to answer. Comedian Bill Cosby said when he was in college, philosophy majors used to wander around in deep thought, asking "Why is there air?" But physical education majors, like himself, never wasted their time. They *knew* there was air to blow up basketballs, footballs, and volleyballs...!

"C" type children love simple questions requiring complex answers, if answers are known at all. Some of the following "C" questions have appeared in Marilyn Vos Savant's "Ask Marilyn" column in *Parade* magazine, and I have been asked the others by students over the years:

When a fly lands on the ceiling, how close does it get before it "turns over" and lands. And when it lands, does it flip front to back, or side to back?

How do they fit all that hot air into blow dryers, and why don't they ever run out?

Why does a wool sweater shrink when you wash it, but the same wool doesn't shrink on sheep when they stand in the rain?

Why do dogs hate it when you blow in their face but then they stick their head out the window when they ride in a car?

How come Mickey <u>Mouse</u> is taller than his <u>dog</u>, Pluto?

Why hasn't anyone ever thought of milking their pet cats and dogs?

Do oysters get bored? How can you tell?

When God made Adam, did He give him a bellybutton? And did the first trees have rings? Since we get half of our chromosomes from our mother and half from our father, and since Jesus was born of a virgin, did He have 23 or 46?

Why do all the fingers have special names (thumb, index, middle, ring and pinky) but only the big toe and little toe have names? (And "piggies" doesn't count.)

If M&Ms melt in your mouth and not in your hand, what about your underarm? I want to test it but my Mom won't let me.

As a parent or teacher on the receiving end of impossible questions, encourage these "inquiring minds" to write down their queries and seek out answers for themselves in reference books. Two things will happen as they realize you are going to refer them to other sources: they will learn to keep quiet about the trivial because they know you are going to say "look it up," and they will learn how to look for their own satisfying, quality answers. This is a true "win" for you both!

"C's" Seek Perfection

As we have said, "D's" and "I's" cannot seem to understand life until they live it. "S's" and particularly "C's" cannot seem to live it until they understand it. They are made very uncomfortable by unknowns.

A woman came to me after a conference to ask clarifying questions about personalities. According to my descriptions and the *Style Analysis* questionnaire she completed, she was a "C." But it seemed to her that some of the questions could have been answered in several ways. If she had made other choices, couldn't she have been a "D" or an "I"? I told her she could have chosen any answers she wanted to choose, but she still would have been a "C" — regardless of what false responses she might have selected on the questionnaire, or what she did to make her graph appear different, she still *really* would have been who she *really* was: a reserved, slower-paced, detail-concerned, task-oriented individual.

She was not convinced yet, so I explained to her that even the manner in which she was questioning her *Style Analysis* report was a typical, high "C" type behavior. "You are 'C-ing' right now," I said. She wrinkled her nose, cocked her head and squinted at me in suspicion. I played my trump card: "When you were a little girl and you were coloring pictures in your coloring book, what did you do if you accidentally colored outside the lines?" The woman responded, "I tore the page out of the book, of course." And then, she finally saw it. She understood what I was talking about.

A woman in San Jose, California, once told me how different her high "D" and high "C" sons were. She said, "Isn't it interesting how God can create two children who are so totally different, even though they come from the same parents?" Then she related this example of helping her children plant a garden:

After they had prepared the soil and made the rows, she told her two sons to put their seeds in the ground, two inches deep and spaced about two inches apart. Then she left them to complete the task. Within 10 minutes, her "D" son had finished and walked back inside their house — he had already planted all his seeds, covered them with soil and was ready for some action! After waiting for a much longer time, she went to check on her "C" son. She found him on his hands and knees, using a *ruler to* measure each hole two inches wide and two inches deep! He had taken her at her word *literally* and was being precise in all his calculations. "C" type children do enjoy doing things precisely, even to a fault.

When "D's" and "C's" grow up, they usually follow those same patterns. The "D" will continue to be quick, to-the-point, and ready to move on. The "C" type will be meticulous, careful and sometimes frustrated.

Actor-playwright Alan Bennertt said a perfectionist is someone who takes infinite pains and gives them to others. While this may describe "C" behavior at times, they usually do not make too many mistakes and are extremely proficient and conscientious in whatever they do. Understanding this characteristic, you can build a better, healthier relationship between yourself and your "C" type child.

Discipline and Nurture

Edward, Duke of Windsor once said, "The thing that impresses me most about America is the way parents obey their children." If the times in which he lived were seen as permissive, I wonder what he would say about parents and children today? Many people seem to suggest by their comments that parent–child relationships are at an all-time low. Take this little essay that I came across recently:

"Our youths love luxury. They have bad manners, contempt for authority; they show disrespect for their elders, and have to chatter in place of exercise. Children are now tyrants, not the servants of their households. They no longer rise when their elders enter the room. They contradict their parents, chatter before company, gobble up their food, and tyrannize their teachers." Actually, that was written about another generation — no, not our grandparents, but as Socrates viewed young people in 400 BC.! So, each generation has shared our concerns. As Solomon noted, "Nothing is new under the sun."

There is a story about a man who was riding his motorcycle one cold, cold night. He put his jacket on *backwards* in order to keep the wind from whipping through the opening. Suddenly, he hit a patch of ice, slid into a tree, and was dead when the ambulance arrived. A bystander told the rescue squad, "I thought he was in pretty good shape after the crash, but by the time we got his head straightened around, he was dead!" Is that how you feel about the kids in your charge — by the time you get them straightened out, will it be too late?

You know instinctively that there is a difference between *punishment* and *discipline*. If all we do is punish a child, we may be doing little more than "getting even." When we discipline, we should seek to correct behavior and build character.

More than twenty years ago, psychologist James Dobson authored a wonderful book entitled *Dare to Discipline*. Its thrust was that the greatest gift a parent can give a child is the ability to discipline himself. One day your child is going to be too big to swat on the rear end, and if he has not learned how to discipline and control himself, our society will do it for him. He will either end up working for someone else who has already learned the principles, or he will be locked away in a place where those decisions are made for him. If you do not learn to discipline yourself, sooner or later, someone else will do it for you!

Several years ago, Dr. Dobson published a revised *New Dare to Discipline*. Just after its release, he and Chris were riding in an elevator together at an Association of Christian Counselors conference. They discussed the book briefly, and as Dr. Dobson stepped from the elevator, Chris told him he felt the new edition was particularly effective... especially in hard cover! As the elevator doors closed behind him, the quizzical look on Dr. Dobson's face turned to a grin — he could picture the "effectiveness" of the hardcover volume sailing across the room toward a defiant child, as opposed to the "impact" of the paperback version! No, we are not suggesting physical abuse of your child or student. In fact, Dr. Dobson maintains that children respond better to our *action* than to our *anger*.

He spoke once in California to a convention of teachers, and afterwards a very large woman told him she loved teaching but felt is was too bad that she had to be angry all the time. Now, Chris has a very high "I," and it is possible that his version has "improved" with telling over the years, but this is how he remembers hearing Dr. Dobson relate the story:

As he explored the meaning of her comment, Dr. Dobson learned that this teacher allowed her students regularly to push her

WHO DO YOU THINK YOU ARE ANYWAY?

to her "boiling point." When she reached this limit, she would shove the items on her desk off to one side, pull out her chair and use it as a step up to her desk top. From that perch, she would reach down into her blouse to pull out her whistle on a lanyard. Then she would blow the whistle loudly and scream, *"I have had it!"* At this point, she said, the students quieted down and got back to work.

Well, why shouldn't they? After all, they had become bored, they had run her through her paces, she had performed her "trick" for them, and as a reward, they threw her a "treat" — they became attentive again. Of course, they also knew they were dealing with a psychopath by this time, and in the interests of self-preservation, they turned down the heat!

Dr. Dobsons's point in telling the story was that the students were not truly responding to the teacher's *anger* but to her *action*. He tried to show her how she could simply move up her "action line" so she could reach that point before reaching her "anger line." Most of us do not take action until we become angry, so we do not know that we are crossing two distinct lines at the same time. When we understand, we can take action designed to benefit and discipline, rather than respond in anger to punish or exact revenge.

For "D" parents and teachers, this is wonderful news, because it means they do not have to be confrontational or bullying, but firm. "I's" do not have to become a bad guy or a killjoy, but a guide. "S's" do not have to muster false bravado or create conflict, but draw attention back to teamwork and cooperation. "C's" do not have to lower their standards or settle for less than a reasonable response, but explain expectations and consequences, then follow through.

In each instance, for each style of parent or teacher, this is a major principle: *Take action.* You will not accomplish your objective if you *threaten* some vague action — you must actually *take action before* you get angry. And in that way, children will learn that you are a person of your word, and in turn, they will regard you more as a person of worth.

Appropriate Discipline

The following example also appears in *Positive Personality Profiles,* but it serves well to demonstrate appropriate discipline for an outgoing, people-oriented "I" type child. One day one of my daughters spoke disrespectfully to her mother. Her sassy reply was not a hideous outburst, but I felt it was important to alter her behavior before it became a habit. So I said to my daughter, "You can't talk that way to your mother. You are on phone restriction for the next three days." She was in shock — *three days with no telephone calls, for one little remark?* Of course, her protests were kept in check; what high "I" teenage girl would want to extend *this* discipline to a full week?

The following day, my daughter came to me more quiet and thoughtful. She made a very revealing suggestion: "Dad, I've been wondering... Do you think you could just *spank* me instead...?" I asked, "Why would you want me to spank you?" She replied, "Well, if you spanked me, then I could be off phone restriction. I've *got* to talk to people — I'm dying!" Well, spanking her would have been punishment, but I don't think it would have been as effective discipline. Her comment let me know that what she was experiencing had *power* to alter her thinking and her attitude. It was *appropriate discipline* for her personality, *properly aimed* at her behavior and *sharply focused* on her "out of control" speech.

If you are wondering what types of discipline may be appropriate for a particular child, you might want to ask him or her. I have heard numerous stories about parents who allowed their children a voice in identifying ground rules and choosing the consequences that would result from their disobedience. In most cases, the disciplinary measures suggested by the children were not only appropriate, they were more "severe" than the parents would have devised. This explains in part the meaning of these words by Eric Hoffer: "You can discover what your enemy fears most by observing the means he uses to frighten *you.*" While your goal is not to make your child fear you, children often have ideas about discipline that will surprise you.

Relatively Speaking

Chris has a young nephew who has a lot of "I" as his primary trait and a very strong "D" as his secondary trait. You can image his energy level. It reminds me of something once said by comedian Joe E. Lewis: "You only live once — but if you work it right, once is enough!" Being a verbal child with strong opinions, this seven-year-old can sometimes drive his "S" mom to distraction. One day he just couldn't seem to control himself, and his mother finally said, "That's it — now I'm going to have to spank you." He was not being "mouthy" or sassy when he made the following comment; it had been a hard day for him, too, and this was like the *coup de grâs*. He sighed and said, "Oh great! Now I have to *cry…!*"

Well, you could have spanked him until your hand hurt without affecting either his backside or his attitude. It did not communicate to him. But to make him sit quietly in a chair in "time out" is effective because he dislikes being still, he hates to miss the action, and he has time to consider his behavior and "come down from orbit."

Like many children, he is a picky eater. But at Aunt Cindy's house, kids eat what is on their plate. (Chris's wife has a "C" style that expects compliance with her rules and a "D" that is not shy about enforcing them.) So, he knows he is expected to make a valiant effort and at least sample something new, even when he thinks he will not like it. Again, we believe he responds this way to Cindy because she understands his personality style and takes action ahead of anger. Once he balked at the table and Cindy gave him three rules that could help him eat the foods he did not like. They were:

1. Concentrate on the foods you like on your plate, not just the foods you don't like.

2. Eat the foods you don't like in little bites, chewing them well and having a sip of water to "wash them down" if necessary.

3. When you say a blessing over your food, you are telling God

that you are grateful for what He has given you to eat. Ask him to give you a grateful heart for His blessings.

Imagine Cindy's surprise when her nephew called her on the telephone one evening around dinner time. He said, "Aunt Cindy, we're having tuna casserole for supper... What were those three rules again?" He had remembered two but wanted to check out all three, and his parents were impressed that he really did want to win this challenge in his life. Because she knew a "D" likes control, when Cindy removed his control over the menu, she gave him control over his attitude and the manner in which he ate what he did not like.

What's Eating You?

Here is an interesting example of "indirect" action: I was in a grocery store and observed a lady shopping with her high "D" child who was naturally trying to overpower his mother and put her under his control. He wanted one of everything in the store. I perceived this sweet lady to be an "under control, high 'S'" individual. She was very gentle and kind to her son, telling him that each item he wanted was either something they already had or something they didn't need.

Occasionally she would keep one of the items he brought to her — I suppose out of desperation. When she said "no" to him once too often, he fell on the floor, kicking his heels up and down. I had not seen someone "throw a tantrum" in a long time, and I wondered how the mother would handle it.

To *my* surprise, she calmly walked on to the end of the aisle, turned the grocery cart and walked up the next aisle. The boy continued all the while to have the "fit" (as we say Down South). In a minute, he opened his eyes and looked to see if his performance was having the desired effect. To *his* surprise he saw his mother was gone and apparently had not even noticed him. He looked up and saw me watching him, as he was lying there in humiliation and disgust. I smiled and said, "It isn't working, is it?" He never answered me. He just stood up, dusted himself off, and walked away. Under his breath, he muttered, "Good grief!" I couldn't help but think, "Way to go, Mom! Good for you!" That's a way to handle a child. Don't let them control you. You stay under control and deal with the situation according to what is right, even if it doesn't feel right at the time.

Have you ever wondered why the parents of "Dennis the Menace" sat him in his chair facing a corner so often in those comic strips? You know Dennis quite well yourself after all these years. Can you imagine *anything* that is more repulsive to him that sitting still, calming down and thinking about his disobedience — other than having to kiss nasty old Margaret? It is probably the most effective discipline his parents have ever found or used. They probably figure if he lives long enough to have a deep voice, he'll come out okay. Dennis is not malicious, just wired for high-voltage current.

Some children can be disciplined with a raised eyebrow and a look of disapproval. To them, this is "taking action." Many "S" types will crumble — but a "D" will think, "If you've got something to say, just say it!" It is not "taking action" to him. If you give that look to an "I," you may get a silly face in return. After all, disapproval may be translated by an "I" as "I don't like you or even want to know you!", and they will do something to break the ice or win you back. A "C" type response will more than likely be one of self-defense. Often, you do better *reasoning* things through with "C" children and helping them discover their error, rather than pointing out to them how far they have fallen short of perfection.

So, take action before anger, and do so consistently. Remember that animals on a farm periodically brush up against an electrified fence just to make sure it is still on. Even though it is a barrier to them, the presence of this "safety net" makes them feel more secure. Kids feel that way, too.

Convictions and Preferences

While this is not intended primarily as a book on discipline, one more thought is appropriate at this point: We do not succeed as parents when we punish our children for behaving only as children. Consequences should come as a direct result of disobedience rather than because a child has made childish mistakes. This is an especially important concept for parents and teachers who are more task-oriented and expect perfect performance. If you *discipline wrongdoing* and *forgive mistakes,* you maintain communication while helping a child understand that we are all trying to grow and get ourselves under control.

When children do childish things, you must decide about your own standards for their behavior. For instance, you might not be the type of parent who would walk away if your child fell down on the floor of a supermarket and kicked his legs in a tantrum. You might confront his misbehavior more directly. Either way, he will probably give up such public behavior by the time he is forty, but you may feel strongly about sanctioning his actions. Or you might feel even more concerned about public reaction to either your child's tantrum or your method of correcting his way of showing displeasure. Are there some things about which you have such strong convictions that you would identify them as *core beliefs* — the things you would be willing to "draw the line" and die for? Make sure you enforce those with love and child-appropriate disciplinary techniques.

There are other things you feel strongly about but they fall more into the category of preferences. If you would not die for them, are you willing to kill over them? In other words, are you damaging a relationship with your child (or spouse, or co-worker, or friend) with no clear end in mind, simply because this preference fits your comfort level?

Finally, if something is not worth dying for or killing over, is it something you can live with? According to each parent's or teacher's style, this line may have to be drawn at a different spot, but the important concept here is to draw your line consistently, and then put your "action line" in front of it, so you never get all the way to your "anger line" before you do anything about it.

We noted earlier that Dr. Charles Lowery said, "Sometimes

we make our personalities a *topic* rather than a *project!*" As you grow in using the personalities information, you will also see your "anger line" moving further and further away because you will understand yourself and others in deeper ways.

Tantrums and Teentrums

We have mentioned allowing a "C" type child to discover his own shortcomings when possible. I'm going to suggest that this can be a good strategy for working with almost any teenager. *Self-discovery and personal awareness* are effective teaching tools.

Here is an example: Rather than telling teens you think they have become intolerant and judgmental about parents, let them read the "funny article" on "How to Raise Your Parents," shown on at the end of this chapter, on page 176. Ask them how they liked it. In this way, you make them aware of their own behavior gently, without them "tuning you out" before you even get started! You can employ an indirect "asking" approach, rather than a direct "telling" approach.

Please understand, I am not saying you have to feel threatened by the task of parenting teenagers. However, because it is a difficult time for them socially, emotionally, and physically (remember hormonal changes?), it is a good idea to use an indirect approach to help them "listen" before they "close their ears" to what you are trying to tell them.

Child psychiatrist Dr. Ross Campbell goes even further, suggesting that the best way to get children to obey is to *ask*, rather than *tell*. For example, it is one thing to *tell* a child to take out the trash. It is another to *ask* in a manner that enlists help and encourages cooperation. *"Will* you take out the trash?" asks for a response from the child, while "Take out the trash!" is simply a statement of command.

When you say "will," Campbell believes, you are now hitting the real issue — namely, *the child's will.* If the child says "yes," then their *will* is clearly in harmony with your own. If "no," then the *focus* and *attitude* of their *will* is revealed. Either way, the underlying issues quickly come into sharp focus, and if there is an issue, you can deal with it accordingly — and appropriately.

There are intelligent limits, of course. Fran Lebowitz says, "Ask a child what he wants for dinner only if he is buying." However, in my personal experience as a parent and educator, I believe that 95 % of the time saying, *"Will* you get your homework finished? *Will* you be home on time? *Will* you take out the trash?" will produce a better response in children, teens and adults than being dictatorial or disrespectful of another person's freedom and dignity.

I am not talking about becoming a "permissive parent," because I believe that, to a certain point, God holds parents accountable for the training of their children. Of course you do have the authority as the parent to *tell* your children things without always *asking* them. But you know that some parents and children experience a hardening of the heart that becomes a wall of indifference. Asking for help or for an opinion can demonstrate to teens that you are coming to regard them as people of worth — a very sensitive area at this point in their development. It seems to reduce the "power struggle" and helps to focus much better on the issue of personal responsibility.

If you find a particular challenge in this concept of *teaming together* and *asking* your teen for help rather than demanding it, ask yourself if it is really a reaction based on a principle you would be willing to die for... If not, it simply may be your own "D" responding over a control issue.

Again, if our focus in discipline is giving our child the gift of *self-discipline,* we will want to train our children according to the way *they* should go, and do what works most effectively. To keep issues clear, lines of communication open, and the relationship growing, asking "will" questions is a handy technique to understand and use. In short, it works!

Frequently Asked Questions

Wherever we go, there are a few questions, repeatedly asked by parents, that fit neatly into the broad topics discussed in this chapter. These answers to these exciting questions reveal helpful tips that make issues easier to understand. So, we'll look at them together in these pages.

Q: How are different personalities related to Attention Deficit Disorder (ADD) or Attention Deficit Hyperactive Disorder (ADHD)?

A. We touched on this briefly in this chapter, but we will expand on the question here. We all know that school is designed primarily to be a learning environment. Although there are different ways in which people learn, the main method used in traditional schools is "rote memorization." Both "D" and "I" types have difficulty concentrating for long periods of time. They have short attention spans and become frustrated when things do not happen quickly.

Recently, I was talking with my daughter Rachael, and my mind wandered. I quit listening. When she "nudged" me back into reality, I apologized. I said, "Rachael, please forgive me — but you've got to remember, I have the attention span of a gnat!" She smiled and said, "Dad, I understand. I have the attention of a *newborn* gnat!" We both got a good laugh out of it.

I have a friend who specializes in learning disorders, and after a great deal of research, she has concluded that if a person has a genuine Attention Deficit Disorder, the problem usually can be treated with a specific prescription drug such as Retilin. This calms the nervous system and allows the individual to have greater periods of concentration. It is strictly a physiological phenomenon, rather than a social one. If the problem cannot be resolved with medication, then evidently it is not physiological in nature. I believe too many "D" and "I" type children get labeled with ADD and ADHD simply because they have a short attention span and difficulty sitting still.

It seems the school environment is better suited to "S's" and "C's" than to "D's" and "I's." How would the following sentence "feel" to an "S" or a "C"? *"Boys and girls, let's stay in our seats, sit quietly, don't talk, and learn this material together. If you have any questions, hold them until the end; then we will go over everything again together."* Now, reread the sentence with the mindset of a "D" or an "I." Do you notice any difference in the way you feel? Hmmmm?

This is a sensitive situation because some people take immediate offense with the issue if they know they have this challenge and have found help through prescription medication. I reiterate that a true ADD situation can be remedied with correct diagnosis and proper treatment. It is unwise to lump every problem into one simple solution. We are all too complex for that single, easy way out. Just because people (whether "D," "I," or any other personality style) have difficulty memorizing material or concentrating for long periods of time, they are not excused from self-discipline and hard work in order to achieve academically. If your child has difficulty concentrating, I suggests six ten-minute study periods, rather than a one hour of study time. Learn to work *with* your limitations, not *against* them. In extreme cases it is best to consult your own physician for further tests and/or referral.

I want to remind parents and teachers that "labeling" often can become "disabling." Currently, federal "special education" funds and other supplements are available to schools and families with ADD or ADHD children, so some observers see *incentives* for agencies to label children in this manner. I believe it is better to try alternative avenues that help the problem before labeling someone as ADD or ADHD too quickly.

Q. Do "twins" have similar personality styles?

A. After speaking with many, many parents who have twins, I conclude that there is no correlation between personality styles and twins, whether identical or fraternal. Research seems to indicate an unusual bond between twins. Studies have shown that twins who were separated at birth have later gone into the same profession or married people who had some of the same characteristics, etc. However, the aspect of similar personality traits is hardly ever mentioned. It almost goes without stating that each person is his or her own, unique individual self. Children of the same parents demonstrate different personality traits whether identical twins or simply siblings.

Q. Is birth order a factor in personality style?

A. This is another question that has been raised on many occasions. It seems that a lot of people want to believe that firstborn children have "D" type personalities because they receive so much perfectionist nurturing from parents. I once heard that firstborns are leaders and second-borns are competitors who fight with the firstborn leader. Third-borns go in an entirely different direction, seeking to be neither a leader or a challenger. That *sounds* really good and perhaps a child's environment would dictate such a scenario. However, while all of us have known firstborn "D's," we also know many firstborn "I's," "S's" and "C's."

A school teacher once told me that her firstborn daughter was an "S" and her second-born daughter was a "D". She said she spent her whole life trying to make her second daughter act like her first daughter. Of course, these two styles are so opposite that it would be impossible. You can't change a person's Basic personality style, regardless of birth order. Give your children life direction based on *who* they are rather than what number or position they occupy in the birth order.

Q. Is personality related to gender (male or female)?

A. Again, there is no correlation between gender and the traits of "D," "I," "S," or "C". I have know some incredibly strong male "D's," but I have also known some incredibly strong female "D's." The same is true among "I," "S" and "C" trait as well. In many cultures, females are subservient to males and assume an "S" type posture in their presence. However, when they are among only other females, their "D-I-S-C" personality traits are very marked. Studies have shown this to be true among African, South American, American Indian, Asian Indian, Oriental and Pacific cultures. Observe the way little girls and boys play with their toys and you will see that Basic Styles are not gender-based.

Q. **Is there any particular key that works well with children of all different personality types?**

A. Yes, definitely! One key helps in dealing with all personality styles, and it is this principle: *Ask questions, rather than making dogmatic statements.* When you make a dogmatic statement you set yourself up for ambush.

I remember saying, "You are always late!" to one of my daughters who was late coming home one night. She replied, *"Always?!?* I'm *always* late? I have *never* come home on time? Dad, you are *always* accusing me of something that is just not true!" And with that, she turned and ran up the steps crying. While I think that was a pretty good decoy for coming in late, I have learned that it is much better to pose questions rather than statements, as in the following manner: *"What time were you supposed to be home…? What time is it now…? Was the time you got home before or after the time you were supposed to be home? Did you come in when you were supposed to…? Do you think I should not worry when you have a certain time to come in and I have not heard from you…? Do you think this displays responsibility on your part…? What do you think should happen for your coming in at the time you did…?"* You get the picture. In each case, simply ask a few questions, not a lot, that leave the burden and responsibility for the infraction on the offending party.

It does not matter whether people have a "D," "I," "S," or "C" personality style — by asking open-ended questions, you create a situation where they have to think, accept responsibility, and focus on their own particular actions. You may have to discipline "D's" and "I's" more actively than

"S's" and "C's," because they are usually more outgoing and better able to "stir up stuff."

In any event, the best way to deal with people is to ask questions, rather than make dogmatic statements. Watch them squirm when you do this! As stated earlier in this chapter, when you ask what *they* think their discipline should be, people are often harder on themselves than you would have been. This can be a helpful tool as you learn about your child. It also helps to eliminate hollow threats or unfair punishment — and it certainly alleviates a lot of the arguments that occur when you slip words like "always" and "never" into your indictments and discussions.

Q: Why do some parents abuse their children?

A. These answers appeared in a church newsletter. As I read, I noticed how many problem areas originate in issues of understanding the differences in personalities. I have added emphasis to illustrate what I mean.

Often abuse is in reaction to past or present problems or stresses with which the parent cannot cope, such as:

Immaturity — Very young, insecure parents often *can't understand* the child's behavior and needs.

Lack of Parenting Knowledge — Parents *do not know* the various stages of child development and how to raise a child.

Unrealistic Expectations — Parents *expect children to behave like adults* at all stages of their development.

Social Isolation — There have no friends or family to help with the *heavy demands* of small children.

Unmet Emotional Needs — Some parents who *cannot relate* well with other adults may expect their children to take care of them, satisfying their need for love, protection, self-esteem.

Frequent Crises — Financial stress, employment difficulties, marital problems, legal situations, major illness, etc., can pressure some parents to "take it out" on a child.

Poor Childhood Experiences — Many abusive adults were *mistreated themselves* as children.

Drug or Alcohol Abuse — Such problems limit parental ability to *care properly* for children.

Notice in almost every instance the root problems can be traced back to some relational issue, i.e., someone has failed to *understand* himself or another person.

Q: Can a teenager's personality style change over time?

A: This is an important question, and it is asked often — especially by parents who see their teenagers doing strange things, and forget their *own* teen years. In *Get Real!,* our *Style Analysis* for teens and young adults, I explained it this way:

Does your personality change over the years? The answer is both *yes* and *no.* Over the years we should mature and grow wiser in decision making abilities. However, simply because your behavior is different from youth to maturity, it does not necessarily mean your personality has changed.

For example, if an 18 year old, strong-willed, high "D" teenager joins the Marine Corps, will his personality change? He will get himself under control during this time, maturing, adapting and adjusting to his environment, obeying orders and cooperating without questioning authority. However, his strong nature will still be present when he leaves the Marine Corps and gets back into the "real world." His behavior will return to its natural style — with the *addition* of maturity and discipline through experience.

So... yes, personality "changes" when it matures, adjusts and adapts. And... *no,* we do not become another person with a different outlook or understanding about life and how we respond.

Teenagers "try on" different types of behavior as they grow up. Have you heard of the "Terrible Twos," when toddlers push the limits on parents and others, trying to learn where the boundaries are? In adolescence, many mental, physical, emotional and spiritual changes occur. During this time, teens "try on" different behaviors to see how they feel, imitating people they admire. Usually, when an experimental behavior does not work well, or is frustrating and futile, they give up with little damage done. Any adult can look back on their teenage years and remember how they settled down to the "natural" style they had when they were younger. That's why the Bible says "Train up a child in the way he should go, and when he is older, he will not depart from it."

The basic personality we are born with is probably seen best between the ages of 4-14, then goes into a tailspin from 14-18, and then smooths out and produces a great life from 18 and older. Although they are not "required," the turbulent teen years seem to be a "fact of life" that most people experience.

Parent, can you remember your own energy at this age? How about your dreams for achievement or greatness in ways your family did not understand? As you matured, you put a lot of that "silliness" away. But in doing so, I hope you have not become like the people one teenager described when he said, "Most grown-ups are really given-ups!"

As your teenagers go through adjustments, keep your finger on their pulse — if their heart is still warm and tender, and their will is pliable, thank God. As my girls have grown up, I have checked on them by asking periodically, "How's your heart?" In other words, are things good between you and God? Between you and me?"

I like this thought from Logan Pearsall Smith: "Don't laugh at a youth for his affectations; he's only trying on one face after another till he finds his own." For added perspective as a parent, find *your own* face in an old high school yearbook! It may help you remember some of the experiences and phases you came through in order to become the reasonably sane and responsible adult you are today. In this way, while your children are "finding their face," you won't lose your mind!

Recommended Reading and Resources

The purpose of this information has been to demonstrate a few practical ways this "D-I-S-C" material can be applied in working with your children. I recommend *Different Children Different Needs,* a book on which I worked with my friend Charles F. Boyd. It provides more than 200 pages of practical insights, ideas and methods for parenting and educating children. I also recommend our self-scoring *Style Analysis* for elementary age children, *All About BOTS, All About You,* and our self-scoring teen *Style Analysis* called *Get Real!* These two products are designed to help children understand themselves and see areas in which they can grow and improve. And if you are a school teacher or work with groups of children, I am confident that you will gain additional, helpful information from *Tales Out of School.* Of course, all of these materials may be ordered from Personality Insights, using the order form in the back of this book.

How to Raise Your Parents

1. Don't be afraid to speak their language. Try to use strange sounding words or phrases, like "Yes…" and "I'll help with the dishes…"

2. Try to understand their music. Most of it isn't on CD, but you might find cassette tapes of what they used to call "records" that you can play until you get accustomed to the sound.

3. Be patient with the underachiever. When your mom is dieting and you watch her sneaking salted peanuts, do not show disapproval. Tell her you like fat moms.

4. Encourage your parents to talk about their problems. Keep in mind that things like earning a living, keeping a job, or paying the mortgage seem important to them.

5. Be tolerant of their appearance. When your dad gets a haircut, don't feel personally humiliated. Remember, in this phase, it is important for him to look like his peers.

6. Most important: Parents need to feel loved. If they do something you do not approve of, let them know it is their behavior you dislike and not that you dislike them.

7. *Try it!* Try these six rules in your home. You will like the results. You can never go wrong by raising your parents to be the best parents ever!

Chapter 9

DISCover Your Spouse's Design

Probably one of the Great Truths most married people have discovered is this: "opposites attract!" I was speaking to an audience of over 2,000 couples when I asked the question, "How many of you married someone who is totally different from you?" Almost everyone in the audience raised a hand. And most expressed that they were genuinely surprised at the great disparity in those differences that didn't just "work themselves out" during the honeymoon phase.

Why does it seem that almost everyone is totally blind when selecting a partner with whom to establish life's most important human relationship? I think much of it is because of the "deceiving process" we all go through in the dating game. We go out of our way to hide our weaknesses while exhibiting positive behavior. It's true that "Love is blind," and that "Marriage is an institution." Someone put these two thoughts together and quipped, "Marriage is an institution for the blind!"

There *is* an important reason why we *need* our differences, and it is the focus of this chapter. We are not going to explore all the complexities of communication and adjustment that successful marriages require — *oooh, another sequel!* But we hope to help you recognize and appreciate the assets our spouses contributed when they agreed to "pair" with us.

While physical attraction often is the catalyst in a beginning relationship, many unhappy couples can attest to the fact that "beauty is only skin-deep, but *ugly* goes clear to the bone!" The

"Hollywood ideal" of relationships is presented in film and soap operas often enough that many believe its lie. (A friend of mine says you would be better off taking cocaine than watching soap operas — at least cocaine is dependable!) In the years that actress Joanne Woodward has been married to actor Paul Newman, she has learned a great truth: "Sexiness wears thin after a while and beauty fades, but to be married to a man who makes you laugh every day — ah, now that's a real treat!" It's not the *laughter* but the give-and-take, the working together as a team, the shared experiences and the subtleties of commitment that can make marriage a *joy.* Truly, it is inner beauty that must last.

The goal of successful marriages is learning to *complete,* rather than *compete.* And as we demonstrate ways in which a couple can learn to *complete* each other, you will discover ways to improve your marriage relationship — regardless of its present condition — provided both of you are willing to adopt a fresh perspective and work together from that perspective, serving and helping each other.

Filling in the Gaps

In the first *Rocky* movie, the awkward Philadelphia boxer started dating a quiet, shy, plain-looking girl named Adrien, who worked away from people in a small pet store. Rocky's best friend was Adrien's brother, Pauly, who asked Rocky what he saw in her. Why in the world would he want to date *her?!!* In his simplistic manner, Rocky explained, "Because she has gaps!" Pauly looked dumbfounded and asked, *"What?"* Rocky replied, "You know, 'g-a-p-s...' She's got gaps and I got gaps. And between the two of us, our gaps meet and we sort of fill each other in."

Whether he realized it or not, Rocky had discovered a profound truth — everyone has gaps! I believe that is another reason why opposites attract. Whether we realize it or not, we are looking for someone to fill our own gaps, our own weaknesses.

When two things are different, it does not mean one *has* to be right, and the other *has* to be wrong. Although this seems simple enough, the root cause of many divorces is this basic problem: first, opposites *attract;* then opposites *attack!* At least one of two people who were enough "in love" to marry each other — one of life's biggest decisions — later changed his or her mind when the other person turned out to be too "opposite." Many divorcees have thought their own "gaps" were okay, but their partners' gaps were not okay!

How much better off we would be to accept the simple, evident truth that we have gaps and our mate has gaps — as well as our children, associates, teachers, parents and everyone else! Then we can help "fill" one another in, accepting the *possibility* that *their* contribution might fill our gap! Rocky saw "gap-filling" as a good thing — an advantage that would help both him and Adrien. Pauly could not or would not see it, and he stayed wrapped up in his own little existence all of his life. (You've probably heard that "a person who gets all wrapped up in himself has a very small package!) There may be more to that brief scene in *Rocky I* than most of us have realized!

I believe so many of us marry our opposite style because we are looking for someone who is strong in an area in which we feel weak. Whether we realize it or not, our "antennae" search for those who see another side of life, in order to open our eyes, to compensate for our blind spots, to help us see *both directions.*

If you and I stood back-to-back and I asked, "What do you see?", *you* would probably describe something entirely different from what *I* could see. Of course — we would be looking in *opposite* directions! And this is exactly my point about marrying our opposites: when two people are "back-to-back," they can see in two different directions, and they may *double their effectiveness* by sharing what they see, especially if they are willing to listen to one another.

The Art of Listening

If your marriage is going through difficulty right now, you may not want to hear about participating verbally with each other. You don't enjoy talking with your spouse if you feel your words are bouncing off a silent wall of resistance. You don't enjoy listening if you hear the same accusing words or empty phrases repeated endlessly. Your desire to understand your mate may have become a casualty in your war of words. If you feel your intent and meaning has been twisted or discounted with each attempt, you may not wish to exert any more of the energy that true communication requires. So, you may have fallen into silence and solitude.

The trouble is, as Stendahl wrote 150 years ago, "One may acquire everything in solitude — except character." We need give-and-take in order to grow together with others. Because I believe God has ordained a "two shall become one" kind of relationship — not one in which either partner loses identity, but in which husbands and wives maintain their own identities yet also join to create a new, *whole* unit — I also believe He has put the *hope* for such a relationship in the hearts of wives and the *need* for such a relationship in the hearts of husbands. If you have given up on your hope or need, understand that it *is* possible to achieve. Each of us has the *potential* to change and adjust. What we must develop is the *will* and the *courage* to do so. "Hope deferred makes the heart sick," says Proverbs 13:12, "but a longing fulfilled is a tree of life." You *can* find your answer!

Samuel Johnson was regarded in the 18th Century as an outstanding conversationalist and lexicographer. He observed that "Silence propagates itself, and the longer talk has been suspended, the more difficult it is to find anything to say." While it does entail some risk, perhaps this book will become your way to begin a conversation together. Chris and Cindy found it to be the case as he edited my first book, *Positive Personality Profiles*. The distance that had developed between them began to close as he worked on the book and as she helped him with proofreading and suggestions.

Dean Rusk said, "One of the best ways to persuade others is with your ears — by listening to them." If having four daughters has taught me anything, it is the necessity of listening. Listening to what is *said* and what is *meant*. Few of us say exactly what we mean in the first couple of sentences — we are not "bottom liners."

Often, it takes time for any of us to get to the point we are trying to make. Sometimes, it is the act of talking through an issue that brings us to an understanding of how we feel ourselves — besides helping us to understand how someone else feels. Being an "I" myself, the listening process has been slow, hard and painful — I prefer using my mouth to using my ears. No wonder the Old Testament writer stated, "The heart of the discerning acquires knowledge; the ears of the wise seek it out" (Proverbs 18:15).

We Are Different

A very popular book is Dr. John Gray's *Men Are From Mars, Women Are From Venus.* It has gained notoriety from its attempts to explain the ways in which the outlook, motivations, attitudes and actions of the two sexes differ. However, if some women had been allowed to determine the books title, they might have suggested *Men Are FROM Mars... Men Are LIKE Pluto — or Goofy or Donald or Mickey!* (In other words, men seem nonsensical, a cartoonish puzzle, and no one can figure out what they may do next.) As a man, I resent such an inference... until I recall that previous generations have suggested this of women!

Women who have an outgoing, fun-loving husband sometimes grow tired of the "fun and games" attitude with which he approaches almost every situation. They may wish they had married a man who has both feet on the ground. Other women have chosen men who are very organized, predictable and restrained — and some may respond, "Show me a man with both feet on the ground and I'll show you a man who can't put his pants on!"

Men and women communicate differently. A research study, several years ago, was designed to examine the communication styles of young males and females. A university's psychology department set up an observation room in which they could monitor the conversation and behavior of boys (as young as four) and teen males. They gave chairs to two boys in the same age group and told them to sit in the observation room until they were called. The boys believed they were waiting for the study to begin, not knowing that it was already progressing nicely!

Invariably, they found that even when the boys arranged their chairs in proximity to each other, their conversation "bounced off" walls and ceilings — they did not make frequent or intense eye contact with each other. The content of their conversations seemed less vulnerable, more competitive. This behavior also can be observed in adulthood. Think about the ways most men communicate with their good friends. Conversations occur when driving *(eyes on the road!)*, when watching television or at sporting events *(did you see him make that play?)*, when hunting or fishing *(quiet, keep a sharp lookout!)*. They tend to "spar" rather than "share."

How did girls perform in the same research environment? You probably know that answer already. Typically, the girls arranged their chairs so they could sit close and speak with lots of eye contact. Their bond seemed less competitive and more sociable. Now think of the ways women tend to interact. Can you see how their communication styles in youth carry through in adulthood? Can you see what "communication" comes to mean for men and for women?

How does this apply to talking and listening in marriage? The study suggested that since women are accustomed to having more intimate relationships with their women friends, when they view their new husband as a "new best friend," they can be very unsettled by his inability to communicate in the style of their other friends. He seems cold, evasive, distant, preoccupied. Men are more accustomed to meeting other men on impersonal, "neutral turf" and working out a nonthreatening relationship that respects each other's unmarked personal territory. They can feel "put upon" when they perceive their wives' communication style as emotional, invasive, too close, obsessive. The study really heated up when it got to marriage counseling. Researchers found that female counselors often noted that the husband was detached and uninvolved while the wife was responsive and sincere. And male counselors often noted that the same husband was trying as hard as he could and the same wife was domineering and pushy! Do you see that communication styles of male and female therapists influenced the way they viewed male and female clients? Amazing!

All of this simply says neither of you should expect your

spouse to meet you on your terms. Men are not *always* task-oriented and women are not *always* people-oriented. Men are not *always* fast-paced and women are not *always* slower-paced. Just as you have come to see that your personality styles can be very different, understand that your communication styles and preferences can differ — and know that you can adapt and adjust to each other with practice, even if you have been doing it wrong for years! Work toward this goal and do not give in to discouragement. There is a lot at stake in "a longing fulfilled" and seeking "a tree of life." As psychologist William James said, "Act as if what you do makes a difference. It does." And it will!

Start Starting

Dr. Jim Martin and his wife Dinah have become tremendous business leaders in Kentucky and a great example of how husbands and wives can commit to each other without giving up their own, individual identity. Each is a very strong, very self-assured person. In the years that he owned a growing veterinary medicine practice, they fought like cats and dogs! Over time, they learned how to quit *competing* and start *completing* — a teamwork skill they now teach to others and employ at home and in commerce. How did they start to rebuild their personal and business successes from a history of difficulty? Jim told a group of aspiring entrepreneurs, "One of the best things you can do is *begin* — don't let the problem-solving phases interfere with the getting started phase."

Goethe wrote, "If you must tell me your opinions, tell me what you believe in. I have plenty of doubts of my own." You can "start starting" right here. Purpose to give your spouse affirming conversation. Choose to *listen* to the positive, rather than *hearing* the negative. In other words, you must also "quit quitting." Pastor and author Randall Ross says, "Refuse to make idols of your past failures — refuse to kneel at the altar of your past failures." Perhaps the hardest place to work out adapting and adjusting your personality is at home — I know it has been so for me. But having past setbacks should not weaken our desire to "get it right" in the future.

Dexter Yager is mentioned often in these pages, but let me tell you a little about his wife, Birdie. She and he were married as teenagers fresh out of high school. No one expected them to last. They had four children by the time they were 24, and eventually had seven. They "lived on an alley in Rome, New York" as he says and dreamed of better days for themselves and their family. When money was tight and resources scarce, Birdie made choices that were not comfortable or easy for her on many occasions. She has more of a reserved and task-oriented personality style and was proud of her ability to keep an orderly house. But to become a people-centered mother, wife and business owner, she learned to take to heart this motto: *Dust keeps! Live every day like it is going to be a memory.* In other words, housework would not "spoil" if it had to be put off one more day. Other things could be more important than maintaining a strict, inflexible schedule. She learned to "take on faith" many of the principles they were applying in their life, even though she would have preferred understanding them before trying to practice them. Today, she says couples should do what is right confidently, without expecting instant validation: "The principles must be *working* in your life before you see the fruit."

After forty years of marriage, does this couple see eye-to-eye on everything? Of course not, but they have developed a mutual respect for each other's insights and goals. She says, "We all have to learn whom we are married to — and study each other." This is a basis for understanding and respecting our mate. This does not mean we must always agree or even be happy about each other's actions or decisions. He says, "If a husband and wife are *like* each other all the time, one of you is not thinking." Birdie says often that she appreciates the space her husband has given her to grow and pursue her dreams, too, without imposing his designs on her all the time. She says, "There is a big difference between leading and pushing. My husband was never 'pushy.'"

Shopping for Fame and Glory

Happiness and fulfillment in marriage are not attainable when they become our *goals* — but they are available in great abundance as *by-products* of serving others. Leo Tolstoy believed,

"The goal of our life should not be to find joy in marriage, but to bring more love and truth into the world. We marry to assist each other in this task. The most selfish and hateful life of all is that of two beings who unite in order to enjoy life. The highest calling is that of a man who has dedicated his life to serving God and doing good, and who unites with a woman in order to further that purpose." There is wisdom worth pondering in his words, even though he did not find the balance in them for himself.

Are you troubled that Tolstoy seemed to imply that a wife's function is to support her husband's service to God and good? His wife Safya was never pleased with his "doing good" at the expense of his own family. In fact, he created a great rift between them as he gave away all his possessions and attempted to live as a poor, *celibate* peasant under his wife's roof! It would be a much better story if he had truly *united* with his wife rather than imposing himself on her and his children. This great, strong-willed influence of the late 19th Century was so consumed by his own vision that he ignored the counsel of those who loved him, was excommunicated from the Russian Orthodox Church when in his 70s and died alone, alienated from his family, in his 80s. Isn't it interesting how close we can come to the truth and yet miss it when we are unable to honor or understand those we claim to love?

Psychiatrist Thomas Szasz said, "How men hate waiting while their wives shop for clothes and trinkets; how women hate waiting, often for much of their lives, while their husbands shop for fame and glory." We really *are* different in the ways we approach life. As a note to men, especially, let me say that we must not repeat Tolstoy's pattern. We must learn to understand and value the needs of people we have committed to in our relationships. We must find the balance that works in our families.

Our Last, Best Chance

"Only two things are necessary to keep one's wife happy," according to President Lyndon Johnson. "One is to let her think she is having her own way, and the other, to let her have it." In spite of this humorous advice, being sensitive to each other does not mean becoming a door mat for your mate. You *adjust* your personality style — you do not *abdicate* it! Continuing to follow your spouse's immature, impulsive, irresponsible lifestyle has its emotional limits, and it becomes increasingly difficult to continue playing Tinkerbell to your spouse's Peter Pan. According to Joseph Barth, "Marriage is our last, best chance to grow up."

Last year, Chris and his wife Cindy conducted several evening workshops for married couples. The first evening was devoted to explaining the Model of Human Behavior. Over the following evenings, everyone completed a *Style Analysis* and discussed how the information fit into their marriage relationship. When Chris asked one wife what she thought about her report, he was startled by her response. "Nikki" replied, "It makes me angry! Why do I have to be an 'S' with 'C' who supports his decisions and accepts everything he does — yet he never cleans up his messes!? Everybody loves him and everybody thinks he's a great, fun guy — but they don't have to live with him!"

Then Nikki began a numbing litany of her husband "Wayne's" impulsive behaviors. He tore off their roof when he decided to replace the plywood and shingles, alone, without help, in the rainy season. She told him it was not wise, but high "D" with "I" Wayne proceeded on, ignoring her sensible reservations. And for several weeks, she mopped up the water that soaked through her furniture and family heirlooms. Another time, he decided to paint all the doors in their house. He took every door off its hinges to begin the process. Of course, as a great starter and a poor finisher, he did not even replace their bathroom door for several years! He has moved from job to job and lost a great deal of money in impulsive business ventures. Because Nikki is someone who needs order and security, Wayne's inability to meet these needs has virtually wrecked their relationship. She said she could endure it for herself, but when a baby came into their lives, she could not continue in chaos. Clearly, their future hangs in the balance.

Our office received a call from a husband who came home one day and announced to his wife that they were driving to Denver for a weekend of skiing. She didn't have to worry about a ski outfit

— he had bought one on his way home. Where were they going to stay? He said it was ski season — hotels were everywhere! They left with little cash and no reservations. When they arrived in Denver, she found her new ski clothes did not fit. No problem, he said, they would exchange them at an area sporting goods store. But the store said they were made by Obermeyer and suggested the factory in Vail. So, at the height of ski season, they drove to the "Ski Capital of America" with no place to stay. Once in Vail, the husband found the factory and spoke with Mrs. Obermeyer herself. The outfit was exchanged for one that fit. Then they began looking for hotels — all of which were booked solid for months. Finally, at the sixth hotel's registration desk, he poured out his story and asked the manager to rescue him from his impulsive, illogical decisions. A man in line behind him volunteered that a dentist attending their dental convention in the hotel was unable to make it because of an emergency and instructed the manager to give this couple his friend's room! And since the husband was such a charming guy, perhaps they would like to join the dentists in their social activities, receptions and banquet over the weekend! The man told his wife she worried too much — things always have a way of working out!

Can you see this episode from the wife's perspective? She feels she has lived with an "emotional terrorist" for years and sees no hope of his changing behaviors. Because it "always works out," she continues to live on the edge. Can you see why she might have preferred to have been found frozen stiff and starved to death in their car that weekend, rather than see it "all work out" one more time! There comes a time in such a relationship that a wife becomes exhausted. The laughter that attracted her to her husband in the first place can become a flood of tears.

Of course, this can happen when wives are irresponsible in their behavior and decisions, too. How many husbands feel like Ricky Ricardo, saying yet one more time, "Lucy, you got some 'splaining to do!"

A Box of Frustrations

Ron Ball tells about a couple who went to see a marriage

counselor because their relationship had deteriorated to the point that they could not speak without insulting each other or creating a disagreement. They planned to walk away from their marriage vows. The counselor told the couple not to discuss anything over the course of the next week, but to write down on slips of paper each irritating thing the spouse did over that time. They were to drop their complaint slips into separate, sealed shoe boxes and then bring them to the next session. As the counselor watched the following week, the wife opened her box and dumped 98 complaints in front of her husband, who read even the "picky" comments aloud without defending himself. Then he handed her his own box, stuffed with 105 slips of paper. As she opened the first, she read the words "I love you." And they appeared on every piece. A marriage *can* be restored and grow when a husband and wife learn that love "always protects, always trusts, always hopes, always perseveres (I Corinthians 13:7 NIV)."

If there are hurts in your marriage relationship — and it is fair to assume there are — I hope this information is giving you the desire and the tools to make positive changes. Dr. Billy Graham once wrote that "bitterness and resentment are conditions of the heart which develop because a person allows an offense or disappointment to take root and grow until it affects his thoughts, actions and his interpersonal relationships."

We could relate a number of sad and funny stories about married couples whose *blends* have not yet *combined,* but our purpose in this chapter is to give you direction and hope that *your* relationship can grow and improve. So, let's move on to some positive examples of adapting and adjusting to each other, because "Lucy… we got some *loving* to do!"

Thinking Out Loud

Chris and Cindy say they have been happily married for three years — that doesn't count the first nine years they spent misunderstanding themselves and each other. Before their wedding, they did not know each other well enough, even though they felt they did. And, because they were "committed to marriage," they knew they could make it work by sheer effort. But right from the beginning, his "I with S and D" clashed often with her "C with D and I."

After she cooked one of their first meals together, she asked him how he liked it, or how he would have liked it better. And he proceeded to make suggestions — after all, she had asked what he thought! And as his creative "I" spewed out idea and after idea, it became obvious to Cindy that he was going to be impossible ever to satisfy completely. To this day, they have different recollections of the event, but if one expects to receive a particular response in answer to such a question, they have learned to include a not-so-subtle hint: "Just in case you're wondering, your response is supposed to be…" It's amazing how simple it is to meet your mate's expectations when you know the script!

Being an "I," Chris feels like there is so much activity going on in his mind all the time that he can't sort through his thoughts and feelings internally. He has to verbalize them, get them out where he can "hear and see and categorize them," as he says. This can be unnerving to a steadier, more stable, more critical thinker like Cindy. You see, her style "keeps its own counsel" and thinks things through before speaking. So, Chris thinks out loud while Cindy makes thought-out pronouncements.

Can you imagine the friction that was created until they learned about personality styles? They "know their lines" now. He tries to be a little more careful in his words and she knows not to take anything to heart until he has talked his way through and finally says, "This is what I think we should do." And he knows better than to "tinker around" with what she says, because it is past the "tinker" stage and close to a "conviction" when she speaks.

Because their thought process are very different, they arrive even at good decisions by following different paths. He uses more feeling and less logic, while she uses more logic and less feeling. While his solution may be correct, he has more difficulty if he is asked to "show his work" (as his high school math teachers often did). He may not be sure how he arrived at his answer, but it's a good one! On the other hand, Cindy can provide step-by-step insights and principles that have led her to a decision.

"Inquiring minds want to know..." so after Chris made one of his illogical or spontaneous decisions, Cindy often asked him, "Just what were you thinking, what was going on in your mind when you did this?" Of course, what he heard in her questions was, "Have you lost your tiny mind?" To this day, she insists she was not being accusatory — she really wants to know and understand his thought patterns. And he has been amazed to discover how other styles perceive issues. He has discovered that just because he *thinks* something, he doesn't have to *say* it — and he thinks of things that no one else thinks of! Since they have learned about each other's individual personality style, they more carefully phrase their questions and responses to each other. They understand that communication is not just what you *say* but what other people *hear*.

Steam Versus Smog

Because communication is more than what we say, let's look for a minute at the style of our speech. Remember the story about the young Yager boys? Jeff would punch Steve and then want to play checkers? Some of us are as quick to lash out verbally, and when it is over, we expect others to dismiss what we have said. After all, to us it may just be "blowing off steam." Abraham Lincoln said, "Some people are like a boat I know that has a six-foot boiler and a nine-foot whistle. Every time they blow the whistle, it takes so much steam the engine stops."

When you blow off steam, your marriage relationship stops, too. You may be a "D" or an "I" who lives in the sunshine, moving from one mountaintop experience to another. But chances are good that you are married to an "S" or a "C" who tends to live in the shadows, moving about in the valleys more than you. Can you see that when you blow off steam it settles in their valleys, and it becomes smog that they have to breathe all the time? In some ways, you control their supply of fresh air. Even if you are not "dumping smog" on your spouse, consider this analogy Cindy shared with Chris: Because of his personality style, he has a "steep, sloped roof," while she has a "flat roof." When the storms come, everything rolls or slides off him, but with her personality style, it's as if *it has no place to go!*

In the Driver's Seat

We have mentioned Jerry and Cherry Meadows from Nashville, Tennessee. She says he used to be very forgetful when he was driving and often missed the highway turnoff near their home. She always "navigated" for him and he came to depend on her instructions. Then, one day, she realized that she was sending him another message as she continued to "drive" from the passenger seat. She was saying in effect, "Jerry, I trust you for our future, but I don't trust you to get me across town."

If you got to know Jerry and Cherry, you would feel that she has more "bubble" and more "push" in her personality style. So, it was very natural for her to jump in and fill any void she perceived in their life together. After all, "Nature abhors a vacuum." This can result in one person trying to manipulate or change the other person to conform to more "acceptable" behavior. Difficulty occurs when spouses feel they have taken on a "child" to raise rather than a partner to work with. And through her actions, Cherry was concerned that she was portraying this attitude to her husband.

She says, "At one point, Jerry said to me, 'Cherry, it must be awful for someone as *perfect* as you to live with someone as *imperfect* as me. I know… you've died and gone to hell — this is your punishment!'" So, on the way to becoming wealthy in terms of their personal and professional lives, Cherry established some parameters for herself. Here they are in her own words:

"Jerry used to leave dirty clothes on the floor and it made me so angry. I never wanted to pick up his underwear. I just knew if we spent our time fighting over this, we would not be spending our time building our relationship or working on more important things… I read a few books and established a few rules for myself:

WHO DO YOU THINK YOU ARE ANYWAY?

"Accept Jerry totally."

"Find something — anything — about him I could admire."

"Tell him on a regular basis."

"Protect his sensitive pride. (I corrected his driving. How could I say I trusted him to take care of our family if I didn't trust him to take me across town?)"

"When you are doing something wrong, apologize — start over and do it right. (It's so hard when you *learn* something wrong, and it's easier to try to change your spouse than change yourself.)"

"Be the completer — be whatever he needs. (If you don't *complete* your husband, he might never become the man he is supposed to be.)"

"We could succeed or we could fight. We could be 'right' or we could be rich." They couldn't be both.

Peggy Boggus, who owns a very successful Georgia-based international company with her husband Jerry, says we can focus very constructively on our own shortcomings, rather than concentrating on the deficiencies of our spouse. At a critical point in their young business' growth, she did not feel he was doing all he could to assure their success. She tells us, "I asked Jerry, 'What do I have to do to motivate you?' He said, 'Peggy, *you* don't motivate me — *I* motivate me. *You* love me.' He needed love, respect, belief, support, and admiration from me." If this is sounding repetitive, that's because it is. It is important for husbands and wives to learn how to support their spouses.

Looking for Leadership

Once at a conference, Chris stood behind a book table as a woman looked over various titles on marriage relationships. She stopped at Pastor James Walker's excellent book from Bethany House publishers, *Husbands Who Won't Lead and Wives Who Won't Follow.* Chris watched as she picked up the book and read the "teaser" printed on the back cover. Then, just loud enough to be overheard, she said to herself, "My husband really needs to read this book..." She put it down and walked away. A few minutes later, her husband also saw the book and picked it up to glance through it. You have already guessed his comment as he placed it back on the table: "My wife really needs to read this book!"

Most "enrichment" books (like *this* one!) are read by women, some of whom hope to use the information they read to straighten out their husbands. Peggy Boggus has more "D" in her style than Jerry does, and he has more "S" than she. So, it would be second nature for her to "fill a void" in his life. Regarding this tendency and these types of books, Peggy says, "Read and listen for yourself — not to teach your mate. Jerry needed my admiration, respect and belief, not my teaching."

Mark Twain said, "I can live for two months on a good compliment." Many men and women have discovered to their surprise that generous praise is the fuel that powers their spouse's drive. Psychologist William James wrote, "I now perceive one immense omission in my Psychology — the deepest principle of Human Nature is the craving to be appreciated." In doing this for Jerry, Peggy unlocked his tremendous power and potential.

If you are a "D" type, one of your main "drivers" is control. If you are a "C" type, you are driven by compliance. Either way, you tend to want to make things right according to your own definition. And you may have developed a reputation as a meddler when you hoped to be seen as an encourager. "The strongest human instinct is to impart information," according to Kenneth Graham, and "the second strongest is to resist it." Jerry Boggus says, "If they ain't askin' the questions, they don't want to know the answer." But this may be a hard truth for us to accept.

Our culture calls for a strong male as the leader and protector in his home. However, women often have strong leadership traits and very strong instincts for protecting their families. It can put a woman in a difficult situation if she is a "D" and has an "S" husband. She may expect him to lead but he may feel threatened by her strong nature. Or he may view his leadership style as restraining or balancing his wife's more dominating style. One of my dear male friends is a very high "S," married to a very high "D." When I talking with my friend's wife about this exact situation, she told me this story: The school year was getting ready to start and their daughter wanted to enroll in a different school. The mother had been negotiating with the two schools and was very frustrated because nothing seemed to be happening quickly enough. Washing her hands of the situation, she told her husband, "You can make this decision, but I want you to make it *right now!*" My friend told me he made the decision in two seconds to put their child in the new school. He jokingly told me that his wife made all the *minor* decisions but he got to make all the *major* ones. So far, it seemed that everything was a *minor* decision! If a husband and wife understand this scenario, they can work through it. However, it still can be challenging.

Scott and M. J. Michael faced a similar challenge, because her focus was so tight and his was so broad. Scott gets talking and sometimes has trouble completing one story because it reminds him of another one. He jokes that right in the middle of an important idea, a television satellite passes overhead in outer space and he starts "picking up ESPN on the steel plate" in his head! M. J. is much more analytical and decisive than Scott, who struggled for several years to discover dreams and goals that would set his life on fire. Rather than wresting for control in their marriage, she gave him time and encouragement to grow. Today, she says proudly to women who are impatient with their own husbands, "I married a *sail,* not an *anchor!*" Rather than chopping down his mast, her "cool breeze" helped him get under way.

Dare to Believe...

Chris's wife Cindy recently had lunch with a friend who has a lot of "D" and a healthy "I." Her husband is an "S" with a good amount of "C." The wife thinks like Sir Edmund Hillary, who said to Mount Everest, "We can conquer you, mountain, because you are not getting any bigger — we are!" However, the husband thinks more like S. Omar Baker, who said, "They say they climb mountains *because they are there.* I wonder if it would astound them to know that *the very same reason* is why the rest of us go around them."

The husband's employer has decided to relocate the company,

which means either they will have to sell their house and move across town, or he will have to commute an hour and a half to work each way every day, or he will have to make his dream of owning a consulting business finally come true. The wife has felt frustration at her husband's seeming inability to take charge of their lives and family affairs, to simply decide between his options and take action. He used to come home and complain about his work situation, and she offered him understanding and compassion. In the past, she would try to "fix" it, but that was not what he wanted. She has felt he just wanted sympathy, and began agreeing with him that he was stuck in a hopeless, messed up situation. Lately, she told Cindy, she hasn't even been able to fake sympathy. She said, "I don't know what to tell him anymore."

Cindy replied, "Tell him he has provided what the family has needed so far. He is a competent and capable man with a fine mind and that you are sure his skills and abilities are right for fixing the problem himself." Cindy has observed in her marriage and in the lives of other couples that when one spouse says good things about the other, that person starts to believe it… and then act *on* it… and then act *like* it. She told her friend, "When that happens, you'll believe and act, too!" This is the "practical payoff" for following Goethe's advice: "Treat people as if they were what they ought to be and to help them become what they are capable of being."

…The Great Thing Can Happen

Charles Kingsley, chaplain to Queen Victoria, wrote, "Thank God every morning when you get up that you have something to do that day which must be done, whether you like it or not. Being forced to work and forced to do your best will breed in you temperance and self-control; diligence and strength of will; cheerfulness and content; and a hundred other virtues the idle never know."

Comedienne Lucille Ball said, "One of the things I learned the hard way was that it doesn't pay to get discouraged. Keeping busy and making optimism a way of life can restore your faith in yourself."

The cure for fear and discouragement is faith and action — whether in your marriage, your work or your life. My friend Bill

Florence says, "Fear knocked at the door. Faith answered and no one was there." Faith is a big issue for him and his wife Peggy, who see faith as active hope. A major motivator for them in doubtful circumstances is the motto: "Believe the great thing can happen!"

Austrian management consultant and economist Peter Drucker tells us, "You can either take action, or you can hang back and hope for a miracle. Miracles are great, but they are so unpredictable."

The Trappist Monk Thomas Merton wrote, "The truth that many people never understand, until it is too late, is that the more you try to avoid suffering the more you suffer because smaller and more insignificant things begin to torture you in proportion to your fear of being hurt."

Helen Keller rose above disabilities that stagger our imaginations even today. She wrote, "Security is mostly a superstition. It does not exist in nature, nor do the children of men as a whole experience it. Avoiding danger is no safer in the long run than outright exposure. The fearful are caught as often as the bold."

I just quoted six people from very different walks of life on the subject of taking action, overcoming discouragement and learning to lead in the face of fear. Each of us must understand that initiative, courage and leadership do not depend on our personality style or gender. *You* can make decisions and take actions that will improve your life and marriage. *You* can recognize leadership in a husband who is an "S." *You* can learn to control yourself when you wish instead to control the world. No, you can't turn back the clock… but you can reset it and wind it up again! The point I hope you see as I quote so many people and experiences in this book is that people really can learn to *adapt* and *adjust* who they are for great success in their relationships, without *abdicating* their own personality and role in life.

Holy Honkers

Are you ready for a funny story about controlling husbands and wives? Dr. Gary Chapman, who lives in North Carolina, tells how some men on Sunday morning get up, get dressed, go sit in the car and read the paper. After a while, if their wives do not come, they start blowing the horn. He calls them "holy honkers." A man confessed to Dr. Chapman that he had been a "holy honker," but his wife had cured him of doing that. One Sunday he was sitting in his car, waiting for his wife, blowing the horn. In a few minutes, she walked outside and got in the car — completely naked! He said he didn't know what to do. He didn't think he should go on to church at this point, but he didn't want to tell her to get out of the car, either. So they sat in the car and talked about it for a while. She said if he would quit blowing the horn, she would quit coming outside naked. They agreed on that. He gave her his suit coat and she wore it back into the house to finish dressing!

Some couples struggle for control over many issues, rather than looking for ways to help each other. For instance, many husbands have a habit of leaving the toilet seat up. "Dear Abby" probably could have made a career just dealing with this one complaint. Wives have argued for years that it is unsightly, unhygienic and inconsiderate — especially after they have fallen in accidentally, during a middle-of-the-night visit to a darkened bathroom! Husbands who will not admit that it really is a control issue for them say, "It's no big deal! If I have to put it up, why can't she put it down?"

How can a woman communicate why this is important to her? As you know from our story about the two mountain goats at an impasse, "butting heads" is not the solution. Once I heard a man say, "All my life, I'd rather be right than be happy. It was a bad choice!" The secret is in seeking to "help," not to seeking to "win." As Ed Courtney says, "When it becomes more difficult to suffer than to change, you'll change." On par with a women's loathing of a left-up toilet seat is a man's hatred of the driver's seat remaining moved-up in the car. Banging his knees on the steering column as he tries to get behind the wheel establishes a quick connection in his mind: he can "remember" to put the other seat down if his wife "remembers" to slide this seat back! In this way, she can help him and he can help her — *communication*, not *conflict!* Everybody wins!

Sometimes when I am with my four daughters, it seems like we try to outtalk each other. Everyone over-communicates! One day, I was talking with a friend and my children began answering some of the questions my friend was asking me! I began to anticipate which child would have the best answer to which question, so I began a little game. I pointed to one child after each question was asked. After doing this a couple of times, the girls got in on it and began pointing to whichever sister could answer best. It was amazing how much we agreed on who knew the answers to which question. How important it is to understand six things that happen when people try to communicate. They are:

1. What you *mean* to say
2. What you *actually say*
3. What the other person *actually hears*
4. What the other person *thinks he hears*
5. What the other person then *says* about what you said
6. What you *think he is saying* about what you said.

Is it any wonder we sometimes become frustrated when we are trying to speak or listen to another person. Maybe we should all get a "pointer" and think through who knows the best answer — and then listen more closely when that answer is given!

A Word to "D's"

One afternoon I was leading a seminar in Greensboro, North Carolina. After the seminar was over a very tall, well-built black gentleman walked up to me and said in a rather stern voice, "I need to tell you something!" (I thought to myself, "Oh, no, what have I done?!") I looked up into his piercing eyes as he said to me, "I'm a high 'D'!" Then he turned and introduced his wife, who was as tall as he. (I'm 6' 3" and had to look *up* to speak to both of them!) He said, "My wife is a high 'D'!" He continued, "We have three grown sons who are Marines, and they are all high 'D's'! I just wanted to come by to tell you... our home is Guadalcanal!"

Do you get the picture? Five "D" types all living under the same roof! That could be an incredible challenge. Each one wants control, each one loves a challenge and no one is afraid of the other one, nor do any shy away from conflict. To them it is a "lively atmosphere." If you are a "D" you are probably thinking, "Five in one family — that's pretty exciting!" If you are not a "D" type, you are probably thinking, "Five in one family — it makes my stomach hurt just to think about it!"

Most families include a combination of "D," "I," "S," and "C" types. It is unusual indeed to find everyone in the family having the same temperament type. When that does happen, whatever qualities that personality style possesses become the predominate themes of the house. That is why five "D" types produce Guadalcanal!

If you are a "D" type, you cannot know what it is like for the other types in your family to live with you. You and your spouse have only *your own* style as a frame of reference. People "do" what they "know." However, if your high "D" has ever interacted with an even higher "D," you may have seen for the first time what "pushy" or dogmatic people are really like. Could that be how your family sees you when your "D" is out of control?

Likewise, when an "I" interacts with an even higher "I," they may see what "silly" or manipulative people are really like. When an "S" interacts with an even higher "S", they may see what insecure or passive people are really like. And when a "C" interacts with an even higher "C", they may see what fearful or critical people are really like. (This is not to imply that all people with this style have these qualities. No one gets pigeonholed or labeled by me, but these are the most common "blind spots" for each personality type.)

The point I want to make is this: In order to appreciate fully the impact our personality style has on our spouse or family, we should look at others with our style. How do people feel about them? How do they respond to them? (We might call this a "reality check!") Then we can ask ourselves, "What is there about different styles that we admire in our interactions with them? What would we like to emulate? How would we prefer that people treat us? And is it possible to develop similar traits in the way we treat them?"

God has a good sense of humor! Bringing us face-to-face with our behaviors in others may be His way of keeping us balanced as we interact with one another. If anyone is "too big for his britches," someone comes along sooner or later with an "overdose" of those same traits to give him a taste of his own medicine! Eventually, each personality type meets someone who possesses *more* of the same qualities than they do. It is usually at this time your eyes open to what you are really like.

Again, if you are the spouse of a "D" type, you are probably not going to "conquer" this person who thrives on conflict. Your "D" will never be as high as your spouse's. Rather, the goal for both of you is to get your personality styles under control. General Dwight Eisenhower said, "What counts is not necessarily the size of the dog in the fight — it's the size of the fight in the dog." Change the phrase "size of the fight in the dog" to "determination in the dog" and you'll get the point we're after. Your level of hope, optimism, dedication and determination are keys to building a strong relationship where your contributions are valued and respected by yourself and your mate.

A Word to "I's"

Because "I's" have an impetuous or an impulsive nature, they sometimes get carried way by temporary attractions, rather than looking at the long-term effects. It is possible for anyone to get caught up in the excitement of the moment, but we must remember that we can reap a lifetime of results for impetuous actions. I saw a sign once that said, "Don't miss a long-term purpose for a short-term event."

Fast-paced people focus on *short-term events* rather than *long-term commitments,* and they tend to have challenges in relationships and reliability. The very *nature of commitment* carries with it long-term effects. "D's" and "I's" prefer to "quick process" business, people, relationships, and circumstances, often failing to realize they need a long-term purpose to sustain and carry them beyond the short-term event that has created excitement or caught their attention. In contrast, there is much to be said for the great strengths that slower-paced "S's" and "C's" bring into relationships, stabilizing them with an ability to "go the distance" over the long-term. Their staying power and commitment levels are worthy of emulation. Fast-paced people, who find themselves continually bored in their circumstances, tend to be tired of *everything* on a short-term basis. It is their view and outlook on life. Everything tends to lose its fun and exciting appeal after the "new" has worn off.

In his book, *Straight Talk to Men and Their Wives,* Dr. James Dobson develops this thought more fully. He believes that we all *need* what he calls "the straight life" — doing the necessary daily things that make life work: earn a living, pay the bills, honor commitments to your family, cut the grass, pay the taxes, have a two-week vacation devoted to the family, etc. While I don't believe he is saying we need a "settle for" existence, he points out four voices that continually call to us, pulling us like magnets away from the straight life. They are the voices of:

1) ego needs,

2) self-esteem,

3) sex,

4) pleasure, romanticism, and fun.

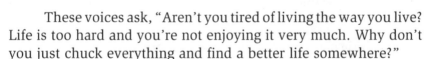

These voices ask, "Aren't you tired of living the way you live? Life is too hard and you're not enjoying it very much. Why don't you just chuck everything and find a better life somewhere?"

Some people "flirt" with leaving the straight life and one day do leave to search for new-found pleasures. But when they leave the straight life, sooner or later they establish another straight life. A life with personal responsibility really is the only life that works! He says that the solution to "boredom" and a desire for "something new" is to bring the voices of pleasure, sex, ego needs, and self-esteem into your current "straight life." This will encourage you to remain responsible, yet provide fun along the way.

If you recognize that this may be true about you, you can also create a sense of accountability for yourself by aligning yourself with people who live by this high standard. You may also find that they also have recognized their own "blind spot" in this area, and they can be a support for you, too. This is not a gender issue —

women and men can be pulled away from the straight life. I am so grateful that Dr. Dobson has articulated this concept, because I have found it to be very helpful.

Even if you are not an "I," you can profit greatly by implementing this scenario into your daily life. If your spouse is a restless, outgoing, fast-paced type and you are not, this may help you to plan more excitement and diversity in your life together. A relationship in which you focus on honoring and understanding each other is more exciting that either of you can imagine!

A Word to "S's"

"Keep doing what is fearful for you until the fear is gone. Action cures fear." These words are from Valorie Haugen in Ogden, Utah. She partnered with her husband, Randy, in forming Freedom Associates, a multimillion dollar, worldwide marketing venture. At the time they began their business together, Valorie was so afraid of contact with people that she did not go to the grocery store unless Randy was home from his job to accompany her. Yet I have seen her speak with confidence and assurance to over 70,000 people at the Georgia Dome in Atlanta. She was dynamic!

Valorie has a lot of "S" in her basic personality style, so it was not just a matter of her learning *how* to speak in front of people. She had to learn that she *could* speak in front of people. As Mark Twain wrote, "Courage is *resistance* to fear, *mastery* of fear — not *absence* of fear." Flying ace and founder of Eastern Airlines Eddie Rickenbacker said, "Courage is doing what you're afraid to do. There can be no courage unless you're scared." Samuel Johnson wrote, "Self-confidence is the first requisite to great undertakings." For Valorie, it was a matter of "becoming." If you are an "S" spouse, you know the challenge that "becoming" presents.

What did Valorie do? Well, the graphs of her *Style Analysis* tell the whole story: She got her "S" under control by reading books that helped her understand herself, listening to tapes that motivated her and helped her to see a bigger picture, associating with women she admired, and absorbing confidence from people who believed in her and encouraged her. She relied more on her "I" to help her make friends and her "C" to evaluate circumstances with less emotion, and she coaxed her "D" up a bit, too. It may not have been easy — change seldom is — but she would tell you it was worth it!

If you are married to someone who has this kind of profile, you can encourage their growth, as Randy did — but it is hard to know what to do if you don't understand personality styles. You have just read what can happen when a husband and wife work together to *complete* each other. Here is what happens when they fail to grasp the idea and *compete* with each other...

I was in the middle of conducting a seminar in Raleigh, North Carolina, when a woman gasped, "Oh, my goodness!" Everyone was staring, so I asked her, "What?" She said, "I see it! I am a 'D!' And my dear husband, God rest his soul, he was a high 'S.' We were married for 38 years. He's gone to be with the Lord. All my life, I tried to make him be like me. When little kids came to our door to sell things, I wouldn't buy anything from them. But my husband was such a big 'sucker' that he would buy something from every one of them. I just fussed at him because I thought he was so naive. And now I see it — we were just different, weren't we?"

The good thing about "D's" and "S's" is that they often find each other and can make a complete team. "D's" are great leaders, but they can push others around — an "S" partner can smooth ruffled feathers. "I's" are great talkers and entertainers, but sometimes can't shut up — an "S" partner is more controlled and diplomatic. And "C's" seem to get everything right and expect perfection — an "S" partner seems practical and shows mercy. Every style has strengths and weaknesses that can benefit from working together.

Justice Darling provided a wise word for "S" types: "A timid question will always receive a confident answer." In other words, if you're not sure of yourself, you embolden someone else to speak authoritatively, even when they are as unsure as you are! Many "experts" seem to claim that title because they go unchallenged. "S" types seem timid and find it easy to be swept along by someone who seems to know where he's going. If you are an "S" and have children with high "D" or "I" traits, you may find discipline challenging. You may have a hard time saying no, and an even harder time making it stick. You will do well to remember these words of Heywood Broun: "Appeasers believe that if you keep throwing steaks to a tiger, the tiger will turn vegetarian." You must not give in just to avoid a confrontation with your children. A big help in this area is a spouse who backs up the "S's" word — children are wonderfully skilled at playing one parent against the other, and they get very good if the game is allowed. So, if you are married to an "S," teamwork in rearing your children is vital.

If you are an "S," you also need to be careful about becoming an *enabler* for your mate's weaknesses. Because "S's" want peace and harmony, they can be quick to make excuses. They cover for alcoholic spouses by making the "sick, can't come in" phone calls. They may absorb physical abuse and rationalize that they somehow "deserve" it because they did not measure up to expectations. They allow their children to dictate menus, bedtimes and behaviors. Rather than allowing the ones they love to learn from the consequences of their misbehavior, they take the load on themselves. There is a circular chart in the next section for "C's" that will help you understand and end this cycle.

"S" spouses are the sweetest people in the world, but they can become "suckers," because they never know how to say "no." Charles Spurgeon told pastors, "Learn to say no; it will be of more use to you than to be able to read Latin." "S's" over-obligate themselves trying to meet everyone's expectations and demands. Herbert W. Swope wrote, "I cannot give you the formula for success, but I can give you the formula for failure, which is: Try to please everybody."

The instinct to help everyone who asks can be tempered when "S's" learn to say, "Let me get back to you. I would rather let you know than let you down." Their mates can help them in two ways: 1) they can make sure they are not abusing their "S" spouse's good nature themselves, and 2) they can "run interference" to protect their "S" spouses from obligating themselves too heavily.

A Word to "C's"

Three hundred and fifty years ago, Thomas Fuller wrote, "Keep thy eyes open wide before marriage, and half shut afterward." This great advice applies equally to "C" type spouses and to their mates. "C's" are very detail-oriented. Orderliness is very important to them. Visual clutter and confusion can literally make them sick. They enjoy quiet time for thinking. They enjoy relationships but have a hard time letting down their guard. They enjoy being right and feel a blow to their pride and self-worth if they are shown to be wrong.

It's a hard thing for "C's" to do, keeping their eyes half-shut to the imperfections in the people around them. They make great organizers and efficiency experts because they are "born improvers." However, as Kin Hubbard noted, "It's pretty hard to be efficient without being obnoxious." Knowing how much they like lists, here is a list of "Twelve Things to Remember" from Marshall Field, founder of the great Chicago department store that bears his name:

1. The value of time
2. The success of perseverance
3. The pleasure of working
4. The dignity of simplicity
5. The worth of character
6. The power of kindness
7. The influence of example
8. The obligation of duty
9. The wisdom of economy
10. The virtue of patience
11. The improvement of talent
12. The joy of origination.

It's a formula for business success, to be sure, but here is a shorter list for happiness. According to Allan K. Chalmers, "The grand essentials for happiness are: something to do, something to love, and something to hope for." These words are meant for the "C" type person perhaps more than any other type. "C's" are task-oriented, so the *do* part comes naturally for them. However, until

they learn always to include the *love* and *hope* part of the prescription, life cannot be grand or happy. A wise friend once said, "Greatness is not the pursuit of perfection, but the pursuit of completion." Completion of your work and completion of your character. Ebeneezer Scrooge exemplified the importance of coming to this completion in *A Christmas Carol.*

"C" type spouses and parents can be endlessly critical of their family members' performance. Most "C's" do not intend to be mean or picky. Again, they notice details, and details count. They love to give advice and become frustrated when it is not followed. They would do well to remember this, from Jonathan Swift: "How is it possible to expect mankind to take advice when they will not so much as take a warning?"

Hannah Whitall Smith, author of such best-sellers as *Hinds Feet On High Places,* wrote: "The true secret of giving advice is, after you have honestly given it, to be perfectly indifferent whether it is taken or not and never persist in trying to set people right." A Japanese proverb says, "Advise and counsel him; if he does not listen, let adversity teach him." There is a reason why "C's" have difficulty listening to *this* advice themselves: it is mostly because they *are* "C's." It is part of their makeup. They are correcting matters *only* for the good of those involved and for the protection of what is right. How could anyone argue with that?

The best argument is that things get very complicated when you step in to "rescue" someone from a problem. It looks like this:

First, you come up with the exact plan you believe the person needs. You are the *Rescuer.* You may even step in to "help" make sure the plan is followed. The person you are trying to rescue is probably in this mess because his thinking is skewed, so to make your plan work, you may have to become its *Enforcer.* Of course, change is never an easy process, so your efforts may not be appreciated. In fact, you may be viewed as the *Persecutor* for all your fine efforts — as in "I was doing just fine until *you* stuck your nose in *my* business!" Ultimately, you will feel abused, mistreated and maligned for trying to help. And that makes you the *Victim*. What a cycle!

Another major issue for "C's" is security. For a "D," it means bases are covered; they are in control. For an "I," it means things are all right; people still like them. For an "S," it means there is no hostility; everyone seems to be getting along. But for a "C," security means the future is predictable with no cause for concern; finances are secured.

Look back at the stories in this chapter about the husband who pulled the roof off the house and the one who took his wife skiing with no advance plans. Their wives had a "C" type outlook, and almost every pattern the husbands had developed was a threat to their wives' need for security. For balance in this area of *your* marriage, both of you will have to communicate what is important to you, what makes both of you feel secure. When you both can agree to work hard at adapting yourself to help your mate, you will be on the way to success.

As a "C," practice warmth. You will be uncomfortable at first, but as you release your smile, wit and friendship to people (including your spouse!), you will find security in your relationships. Bertrand Russell was a very high "C" who offered this tremendous insight on relationships: "A sense of duty is useful in work, but offensive in personal relations. People wish to be liked, not endured with patient resignation." This may be why a number of "C" types admit to loneliness, a lack of close, durable friendships.

The "C" personality usually has a high moral standard and wants you to comply with the rules. I think it was Robert Orben who quipped, "I value people with a conscience. It's like a beeper from God." In pursuit of honesty, they can be blunt. They do not make statements to be hurtful or insulting; they just call 'em as the see 'em. Mignon McLaughlin said, "It's important to our friends to believe that we are unreservedly frank with them, and important to friendship that we are not." Oliver Wendell Holmes advised, "Don't flatter yourself that friendship authorizes you to say disagreeable things to your intimates. The nearer you come into relation with a person, the more necessary do tact and courtesy become." In dealing with a spouse, "C" types should take these words to heart.

Finally, let's look at one more area in which "C's" can learn to relate better to the unpredictability of life in general and marriage in particular. That is, learning to roll with the punches and find humor in life's ups and downs. Henry Ward Beecher led New York's Plymouth Congregational Church through the Civil War, denouncing slavery, promoting temperance and advocating reconciliation with the defeated Confederacy. Yet he managed to keep his perspective. He said, "A person without a sense of humor is like a wagon without springs — jolted by every pebble in the road." Sir Winston Churchill fought clinical depression frequently. It bound him to his house at times, where he could not eat or sleep. Painting in oil was one of his few sources of comfort during the times that "the black dog" was his companion. Yet he surmounted his disability with this philosophy: "In my view, you cannot deal with the most serious things in the world unless you understand the most amusing." More to the point, Malcolm Forbes said, "People who never get carried away should be."

Remember the wonderful quote from Joanne Woodward at the beginning of this chapter. A cheerful attitude is not "natural" to a "C" type, but it is far more attractive to others — and you can adapt! By working on this issue, probably more than any other, you will see a wonderful improvement in your relationship.

An Issue of Forgiveness

Our anger with others is almost always because they have not met our expectations. They have not come up to our standard or done what we feel was appropriate. This is an issue with every personality style. If you tend to "keep score" a little more than others, learning to "forgive and forget" is especially difficult. But it is necessary for your emotional health. Psychiatrist Henry

Maudsley was physician to the Manchester Asylum over 130 years ago. He wrote, "The sorrow which has no vent in tears may make our other organs weep."

In marriage, instant forgiveness is a very important habit to learn. Counselor Jay Adams wrote: "Forgiveness is not a feeling but a promise or commitment to three things:
1.   I will not use it against them in the future.
2.   I will not talk to others about them.
3.   I will not dwell on it myself."

Forgiveness is a matter of choice, a matter of will. It is not an easy way to live, but it is the worthwhile way. Are you willing to persevere in forgiveness, or will you stubbornly cling to the traits of your personality that hold you back from the life and the love you really desire? "The difference between perseverance and obstinacy," said Lord Dundee, "is that perseverance means a strong *will* and obstinacy means a strong *won't.*"

Phyllis Diller used to say her in comedy act, "Never go to bed mad. Stay up and fight!" Well, sometimes that would be better than locking out emotions and feelings. Cherry Meadows has a simpler solution: "Forgive people as the offense occurs." Some people have difficulty doing this; some find it more difficult to admit making a mistake or needing forgiveness themselves. Jonathan Swift wrote, "A man should never be ashamed to own that he has been in the wrong, which is but saying, in other words, that he is wiser today than he was yesterday."

Gary Smalley has written many helpful books on marriage relationships. He says the two reasons for disagreement are offense and misunderstanding — offense requires an apology, while misunderstanding requires an explanation. That's pretty basic, isn't it? Note that he never says disagreement requires self-defense. We needn't "prove" that we are right or vindicate ourselves. One of the first things I remember Dexter Yager saying was, "People of integrity expect to be believed, and when they are not, they let time prove them right." A defensive attitude will never allow you to have this kind of freedom.

It is difficult to insulate children from disagreements their parents may have, even though it can create a great deal of worry and insecurity in young ones. Even worse, many parents also isolate their children from the love, forgiveness and "forgetfulness" that should follow disagreements. After newlywed Dave Roever's face and body were blown apart by a grenade in the Vietnam War, he saw many young wives who could not adjust to their husbands' permanent injuries. He and his wife attribute a good portion of their success in adapting and adjusting to their parents' examples as they grew up. Dave says, "You could have put a Sherman tank in our front yard and you wouldn't have given us (children) more security than knowing our mother and father loved each other."

Trevor Chatham, a very successful Australian business leader, knew that any kind of achievement would require change and struggle, and that success in marriage would be no exception. He says, "I worked out the kind of person I needed to become to deserve the family I wanted." We can learn do that, too!

Jack and Effie Reid are a very lively and unpredictable couple, although Jack would say those qualities are hers and he's just along for the ride. He says: "It's a matter of temperament — we can take the big problems in stride, but the little problems can wipe us out." She says, "Don't sweat the small stuff — and honey, it's all small stuff!" Whether in our personal or business life, it is *communication* and *acceptance* in big and small stuff that can make the difference. Another pair of opposites, Glenn and Pam Shoffler from New York, found a similar key when they began working together at home and in business. They say, "We learned to accommodate each other — as your attitude, so is your action."

My friends Ron and Toby Hale, from Tennessee, are another couple that have found great success in marriage and in business. They are proof of what makes a relationship work: "Make each other feel important. Say, 'I believe in you... I am proud of you... You are special... I love you... I can count on you... You are beautiful...' And always keep the door open after a disagreement."

And with that "open door" advice, we'll close this chapter.

Chapter 10

DISCover Your Work Design

In his seminars, my friend Zig Ziglar quotes a study conducted by the Carnegie Foundation, Harvard University and the Stanford Research Institute. Zig says, "Fifteen percent of the reason you get a job, keep a job, and move ahead in that job is determined by your *technical* skills and knowledge… regardless of your profession. The other 85% has to do with your *people* skills and *people* knowledge." This explains why learning to adjust and adapt your personality style is a key to success and why it is important that you be able to "read" and understand other people.

We may not think this is fair, that *task skills* should be more important in accomplishing *tasks*… but "that's life!" We can protest the rules, but that will not help us win the game. The best thing we can do is learn how the game works and win the prize by playing according to its rules, rather than sitting out the game in protest and letting others win by default. The people without challenges in life are in cemeteries! As columnist Sydney Harris wrote, "When I hear somebody sigh that 'Life is hard,' I am always tempted to ask, 'Compared to what?'"

Actually, developing "people skills" is not a simple matter for any of the personality styles. Each of us has traits that help us in this area, accompanied by traits that hold us back. For instance, a "D" type individual may have a great drive to lead people, but he cannot do it unless he learns how to enlist their cooperation. He may achieve great goals but find them unrewarding, unless he also brings along with him those he loves, with whom to share his prize. An "I" type may have the wonderful ability to reach out to total strangers in friendship, but to reach them *effectively* he must learn to focus himself on them. He may energize others with his intense optimism but "wear them down" because of his excitability. An "S" type may have the desire to support many people but he also must manage the demands this creates on his time. He may be able to cooperate with a variety of people but be unable to act decisively in his own behalf or in their best interests. A "C" type may possess insight to analyze and make recommendations, but he must also possess the ability to persuade and convince others. He may be correct in his facts but misunderstood in his voice tones or motives.

So, our goal in this chapter is not providing ready-made solutions for every work-related issue. Rather, we will try to communicate some principles for building, recognizing and appreciating co-workers' contributions in meaningful ways. We will try to identify some characteristics of leadership and ways they can be emulated by all personality styles. We will try to point you toward methods for building effective teams because we realize: **T**ogether, **E**veryone **A**chieves **M**ore.

Cover All the Bases

Encouraging teamwork requires certain skills because *teams* are made up of personality *combinations.* Let's say you attended a training session or seminar and as the meeting was coming to a close, the leader or host made this request: "Would you please pick up your chair on the way out and stack it with the others near the door? And if any of you can stay for a while, we need to clean up the meeting room. Thanks for your help." How would you react?

If you were a "D" type, your first reaction probably would be to think, "Well, *I* didn't mess it up — why should I clean it up? I've got other things to do. Get real!"

If you were an "I," your immediate mental response might be, "Cool! Maybe we can order a pizza while we work — who knows, this might turn into a party! This could really be fun!"

If you were an "S" type, you probably wouldn't think anything about pitching in. "Sure, I'll help." No reward would be anticipated or expected. In fact, you would probably feel very useful and satisfied with yourself because you were able to meet this need.

If you were a "C," this request would probably generate some questions: "Don't they have people who do this already? Why are we being asked to do this? Didn't we pay a fee to attend? Shouldn't this have been planned as part of that cost?"

How do you learn to lead a group as diverse as this? First, *understand* that to each of these individuals, their viewpoint is at least appropriate, if not correct. Because there are rules for civility, they may conduct themselves differently from their feelings, but it is important for us to understand what may be going on "under the surface" in addition to what we can observe in actual behavior. Second, *acknowledge* that these thoughts may be going on — and offer a rationale along with appropriate motivation for different styles. In effect, take away the excuse that would hold back an individual from participating in the project.

I was speaking in Missouri recently and the young man who met my plane told me he had taken several courses on speaking to an audience. He said every course focused on the speaker instead of the audience. It told him how to project his voice and use gestures and examples, but it didn't tell him how to phrase his ideas according to the listening styles of his audience. However, there are ways to do exactly this.

I served for several years as Minister of Education at a large urban church. During this time, I gave a note to the Senior Pastor, telling him about the four "groups" in his Sunday Morning audience and how to "reach" all four in delivering his sermons: First, "D" types need a cause — they want to know if they are going to charge city hall or overthrow the government! They do not want to leave church thinking, "That was a nice sermon..." They want to *do* something with what they have heard. In seminary, we had one thought drilled into us regarding our sermons: *"So what?"* In other words, "How does it apply to *me?"* Then, "I" types are motivated when they see the "payoff." Messages about "the abundant life" reach them — fun and excitement and acknowledgment and activities are important in communicating with them, as well as strong word pictures and stories that can capture their imaginations. "S" types need assurance. They want to "feel" the arms of God all around them. The "friend who sticks closer than a brother" and the promise that "I will never leave you nor forsake you" are major parts of their theology. "C" types do not want emotion but *exegesis* — a four-dollar word that means digging out the meaning of the Bible's words in their original languages. This type perks up when the pastor says, "In Hebrew, this phrase means..." When he meets the different needs of different people, his congregation feels he is a great teacher and leader because he has spoken to them at their level of interest and understanding.

In any leadership role — project manager, pastor, coordinator, labor boss, classroom teacher, or *whatever* — we must learn to be cautious about saying and doing things only in the manner with which *we* are most comfortable; that is, according to our own style. We miss up to 75% of our audience doing things that way. We can take the attitude that since we are the leaders, people should adjust to us. But who is supposed to be more mature, the leader or the follower? The *leader* has to make the adjustment. This is another "that's life!" situation. I often wish it were not that way, but if I am going to succeed, I must make adjustments along the way... or I can sit back and watch others succeed!

Speaking "Albert"

In the movie *The Dream Team,* four mental hospital patients found themselves alone in a big city. Their psychiatrist had taken them to a baseball game but was mugged in an alley. A character named Albert did not speak; rather, he made gestures with his eyes and funny expressions with his face. Occasionally, a word would slip out but in only an indirect reference to something that had taken place. It was Albert who saw the psychiatrist mugged in the alley. When questioned as to whether or not he knew anything about it, Albert sort of shrugged, looked off and nodded absently. Another patient pronounced this a definite *yes.* When asked how he knew, the patient answered, "You have to learn how to speak 'Albert!'"

This is a great insight for you in working with a team or leading a group. "Speaking Albert" involves understanding how others communicate and getting your message across to them. You will become more effective when you learn how to "Speak D-I-S-C" to different people, those who approach circumstances and situations from different perspectives.

I spoke in Huntsville, Alabama, to the Corps of Engineers, the team that handles many intricate details for the U. S. Army. I was pleased to be speaking to such an elite group. In our morning session, I told a few funny stories and jokes to get the audience awake and alert. I did not even get an occasional smile from anyone. The day wore on, longer and longer. Like "60-Second Manager" Ken Blanchard, I believe "feedback is the breakfast of champions," so it is hard for me to keep my enthusiasm when I don't feel it is being returned by my audience. I escalated my attack — my very best stories, my very best illustrations, my funniest jokes... nothing seemed to work. I felt like a man who has been treading water for a long time and is starting to drown.

Late in the afternoon, I told a real "side-splitter." One man almost grinned. That got me through the day. By the end of the session, I was totally exhausted. I knew I had lost my "magic touch" and thought about getting out of the seminar business. Maybe I should just buy a gun and end it all! At the grueling conclusion of the seminar, no one left. Everyone stayed and wanted to talk with me. One by one, they told me this had been the greatest day of their lives! They said they had never had so much fun or enjoyed anything so much. I thought to myself, "Well, you could have fooled me!"

Finally, on the drive home to Atlanta, it dawned on me. All day long, I had spoken to a roomful of people who were very *task-oriented* and very *reserved*. Hmmmm... what style is that? Of course — almost every person scored very high "C" behaviors in his *Style Analysis*. It made sense to me now. "C's" want quality information they can understand, process and apply. My "fun and games" style is not necessarily their cup of tea, but they can still enjoy it *in their own way*. More amazing is that even when you understand a good deal about personality styles, the practical impact still can "slip through your fingers" while you are in the midst of a situation that is foreign to your own behaviors and thought patterns. Although I already understood "C" types intellectually, I more fully experienced and appreciated their learning style because of this encounter.

The truth is, when you are "speaking Albert" (a communication style that is foreign to you), you will do so with an "accent," so you must be very clear about what you mean. And when you are "hearing Albert," you must make an effort to listen carefully for the true meaning beyond the mere words.

I have lived long enough to believe that every misunderstanding, argument and conflict really goes back to our trying to make another person become and behave like ourselves. In one of his books on relationships, Dr. Wayne W. Dyer wrote about the true nature of conflict:

> Virtually all fights revolve around the absurd thought, "If only you were more like me, then I wouldn't have to be upset." This is an erroneous assumption about the people in your world. People — including your spouse, your children, your parents, or anyone else — will never be the way you want them to be. When you find yourself upset with someone else, you are really saying to yourself, "If only you were thinking the way I am thinking right now, then I wouldn't have to be so upset." Or "Why can't you do things the way I want them to be done?"

The conflict enters in when you cannot accept a person for who he is and appreciate his own, special style. When you attempt to force someone into a mold that does not fit, you create frustration, dissension and lack of teamwork. Becoming upset at someone for functioning in the way he was designed to operate makes no sense at all. If I had thought through the Corps of Engineers situation earlier in that day, I might have realized what was taking place. That would have taken a lot of pressure off me, and it would have made the entire seminar more enjoyable and less strained. I would not have measured their "C" level of interaction with my "I" yardstick.

"Teamwork Makes the Dream Work"

This is a phrase I have heard many times over the past few years from leaders who have built very successful enterprises involving a variety of people and personality styles. What these people have learned is that every individual has a one-of-a-kind contribution he or she can make to the whole. Here again is our "Contributions Chart," first shown on page 28. Our purpose in Chapter 2 was to show how adjacent traits can help support the predominating trait. This time, let's use the same chart to demonstrate how each of the four "DISC" types plays a special role.

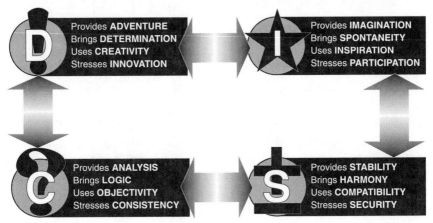

Here are some examples of utilizing these traits as a team to accomplish a project:

In working toward a goal, the "D" welcomes the challenge and provides a sense of *adventure*. He helps others to feel there is a lot at stake, much to gain and much to lose. There is urgency in his actions. The "I" provides *imagination* and keeps fuel flowing to the fire. He is a "dream builder" who can inspire and influence others. His skills can allow people a "taste" of their success even before they achieve it, so they will work harder to reach the goal. The "S" provides *stability* and functions as a "shock absorber" along the way. He will be the calming voice in times of emotion and disagreement. He considers people as part of the equation. The "C" can be counted on to provide *analysis*. He can document the sense and express the sensibility of what you are doing together. His skills provide proof that the plan or project is real.

This same chart shows us that "D's" bring *determination* — they do not like to lose and will "press on" through discouragement. "I's" bring *spontaneity* — they'll find an enjoyable way to do it and can see their way past obstacles. "S's" bring *harmony* — they encourage synergy and cooperation. "C's" bring *logic* — they interpret events using more intellect and less emotion.

This chart also indicates the "D's" ability to use innate *creative* skills — he can figure some way to get the job done. An "I" uses innate *inspiring* skills — he can find a way to make you want it, too. The "S" uses built-in *compatibility* skills — he can find a common cause to hold the group together. The "C" uses his *objectivity* skills — he is not as likely to be swayed by heated arguments or temporary circumstances.

Finally, the chart shows that a "D" stresses *innovation* and is interested in pushing limits to improve. An "I" stresses *participation* and genuinely enjoys involving others in reaching the goal. An "S" stresses *security* and is fulfilled by helping to establish a "safety net." A "C" stresses *consistency* and ensures that things happen according to plan rather than circumstances.

"D's" think it up. "I's" sell it. "S's" enjoy it. "C's" improve it. We each have a role to play and a position to fill — in a way that no one else can. So, in pulling together your team or operating effectively on someone else's team, it is important not to get caught in the comparison trap. C. S. Lewis, Oxford and Cambridge professor of Medieval and Renaissance English as well as author of *The Screwtape Letters, The Chronicles of Narnia, Mere Christianity* and more than 40 books had this to say about comparison: "No man who says, 'I'm as good as you,' believes it. He would not say it if he did. The Saint Bernard never says it to the toy dog, nor the scholar to the dunce, nor the employable to the bum, nor the pretty woman to the plain. The claim to equality is made only by those who feel themselves to be in some way inferior. What it expresses is the itching, smarting awareness of an inferiority which the patient refuses to accept. And therefore resents." Where would either Disney brother have ended up if they had built their relationship on comparison and competition? (Read their story on page 245.) Where will your team go if you mistakenly create a similar environment?

The Right Job, Not the Wrong Person

We have cautioned several times that this information should not be used as a predictor of success — after all, people can be taught how to adapt and adjust their personality styles to achieve great things. You have heard people say, "He's the wrong person for that job..." Aside from being a negative comment, it's a poor perspective. It negates the individual and exalts the task. Now, it might be true that it is the wrong *job* for the *person,* but in building a team or reaching a goal, we must be careful not to eliminate an important factor simply because it is not particularly appealing to us. Sometimes we simply need to help someone change his perspective. Here are two examples:

First, have you heard about the two competing shoe salesmen who sailed to West Africa near the close of the 19th Century? Coming off the boat, both salesmen noticed all the barefoot native people. One man cabled his home office: "Nobody here wears shoes. Coming home by next ship." The other man cabled his office: "Nobody here wears shoes. Send one million pairs on consignment." Can you see how a different perspective on the same event can make a *continent* of difference?

Second, a salesman we know attended a training meeting where information was passed out regarding the benefits of the company's automobile association and its emergency roadside service, legal assistance and fleet repair prices. A very high "D" had been designated to deliver the presentation. He began by asking how many of the sales staff used the auto club and a number of hands went up. Whether he realized it or not, he then sabotaged himself by asking those who had not enrolled in the auto club to raise their hands. He told them they were not going to be as successful as the others because it was obvious they did not believe in their own product. His "natural" instinct was to be confrontational, to "power play," "bully" and "shame" the sales staff into complying with his purpose. What he did next was good, probably not on purpose: He asked several people who enjoyed auto club membership to relate stories about the excellence of its service. However, he never related a single story about his own experience, which must have caused some to wonder if he had actually used the auto club himself. And after the people completed their stories, he returned to his heavy-handed technique.

The basis for his approach was fear and shame: you will not succeed unless you do this; you ought to be embarrassed that you have not done this yet. His thinking may have been along the lines of psychologist Abraham Maslow, that "fear of loss is a stronger motivator than hope of gain." However, a fear-based future limits the present. Most people, regardless of their styles, tend to rebel when pushed. Can you see how the desired result could have been achieved by allowing a "D," an "I," an "S," and a "C" to share, one by one, what the auto service had meant to them? In that manner, everyone in the audience could have been reached. Understanding this concept increases a leader's effectiveness in delegating a job to a team member. And it increases a team member's productivity in doing the job — not to mention his or her level of job satisfaction!

A very interesting article appeared in the January 10, 1995 issue of *The Wall Street Journal,* focusing on the issue of being in a job that fits your personal behavior style. The article cautioned against being "swayed by title or salary if the chemistry or cultural fit isn't right." Even the most prestigious position or most generous compensation package will not fulfill your longing to feel productive and useful. The writer of the article noted that the real key is focusing on your personality and operating style, seeing how it would "mesh with that of the company's chief executive." When even a conservative business newspaper reminds us to consider the importance of how our personality style acts, reacts and interacts with the styles of others, we should take the time to do so. Beyond its obvious potential for making the difference between failure and success, how you *combine* with others in the work place could mean the difference between emptiness and fulfillment.

At a seminar in Knoxville, Tennessee, I was describing some "D" traits. I mentioned that this type of person can make a good police officer, pointing out the ability to be hardnosed and tough in various situations. "Everyone knows" this is the behavior they need to exhibit. After the session, a gentleman told me he was a little concerned about my statement. He was not a "D" but served on the police force of his city. He said his *Style Assessment* revealed a very high "C." As we spoke, I thought, "What kind of police officer would a high 'C' make?" Then I began thinking how good they would be with paperwork and writing tickets and keeping things in order, enforcing the law objectively with everyone. I asked him what his job was on the police force, and he told me he was on the S.W.A.T. team. Again, that didn't fit together in my mind, because I didn't think "C" stood for "commando." Then, with one more question, everything came clearly into focus. I asked him what he did on the S.W.A.T. team, and he smiled. "I'm a sniper." I thought to myself, "Perfect! If I were a hostage, I know he wouldn't shoot me by mistake. But if I were his target, I would hate for him to be aiming at me. High 'C's' don't miss!"

Zig Ziglar understands that he has a strong "D with I" personality style — I have heard him say that with my own ears. Interviewed in the November, 1994 issue of *Success* magazine, he was asked, "Why did you go into business for yourself?" Zig answered, "My personality style prevents me from working for someone else. I like to be creative, implement things quickly — that doesn't work in a corporate setting." Isn't it amazing how people who really understand themselves deliberately put themselves in situations where they can achieve maximum effectiveness and success? Zig did not say his personality prevented him from working *with* people. He said it prevented him from working *for* someone else in a stifling environment. Because he is focused on being productive, he works in harmony with himself rather than frustrating himself.

If you are a "D" type and find it difficult to work for others, there are certain barriers you must pass through and hurdles you must jump over before you can "be your own boss." This process is necessary to protect you from the excesses in your style that can bring you to ruin. Dennis Peacocke has written that "problems are God's barbells to strengthen us for the success that is coming our way." Therefore, we should not try to circumvent or get out of our circumstances too quickly. It may be that you are there for a specific reason — to learn, to grow, to better yourself, and to take those lessons with you when you do become your own boss.

Henry Ford said, "The question, 'Who ought to be boss?' is like asking, 'Who ought to be the tenor in the quartet?' Obviously, the man who can sing tenor." Until you learn the kind of self-control and discipline spoken of in the last paragraph — until you can "sing tenor" — you probably *need* to continue working for someone else who already has achieved mature thinking.

Getting What You Want

Speaking of "C's" and "D's," they seem to have the greatest potential for difficulty in working and relating together because of their style differences and expectations. "C's" generally expect standards and rules to be followed, "coloring inside the lines." "D's," however, tend to have a "the end justifies the means" outlook. Usually, one wants to be right while the other wants to be "more" right. Each needs the other, and if they can resolve their expectation differences, they can become an effective team.

As a leader, the "C" wants everything to be done according to the master plan. But the "D" tends to be more improvisational and is more willing to adopt an entirely new plan if it might have a better chance of succeeding. "C's" have difficulty respecting what they view as the "D's" reckless and impulsive behavior, while "D's" have difficulty respecting "C's," whom they may view as being bullheaded and obstinate.

In my own experience, I have seen that "C's" and "D's" have difficulty getting along when either is subordinated to the other. Instead of understanding and utilizing their differences, they sometimes work against each other. Can you see how frustrating this can be for them? After all, both are task-oriented — they want to get the job done. But the "D" wants to control the project and wants to be right. The "C" wants the project to be under control and wants to be more right. Unless they learn to "Speak Albert," you can predict a short but turbulent association.

Who is in the wrong when such a team fails to come together? Neither person… and both people! Again, the behavioral *style* of one individual is not more "right" than another; it is simply different. So, neither the "D" or "C" is "wrong" for thinking as he does about the task. However, there can be a big difference between your behavioral *style* and your *behavior.* I would say the "wrong" people in such a situation are the ones who do not acknowledge the worth, the value, and the contribution of the other human beings, even if they disagree with their point-of-view. Remember, one of the basic tenets of this book is that everyone wants to be understood and valued — and we "owe" that effort to everyone. We can be like the foolish farmer whose horse drowned when he shoved a hose down its throat trying to make it drink, or we can be like the wise farmer who put salt in his horse's oats and made it thirsty enough to drink on its own.

Zig Ziglar tells his audiences, "You can have anything you want in life if you are willing to help enough other people get what they want in life." In applying this information, our reference point should become other people rather than ourselves. You cannot force other people to see things from your perspective, but you can try to see things through their perspectives. When you do this, you "move" yourself to a better negotiating position — rather than "sitting across the table" from an "opponent," you are sitting on the same side of the table with a partner.

Standing Down

Do you remember the movie *War Games,* in which a high school boy almost sets off a thermonuclear war when he "hacks" into the Department of Defense to play their computer attack simulations? Suddenly he finds he is not involved in a harmless game but has initiated a first strike that the master computer will not abort. The U. S. military escalates quickly to "Defcon 5," as the world moves unknowingly to the brink of annihilation. Finally, with only seconds to spare, the master computer is defeated in playing a simple child's game, and our great military power is ordered to "stand down."

What does this movie have to do with personalities? Just this: it reminds us that our "harmless games" can escalate just as quickly and cause plans to "blow up" in our faces when we fail to understand and use this simple information. We have said before that most people are not *against* you but *for* themselves. Nevertheless, our first instinct is to mount a counter-offensive when we feel attacked by others. This can devastate our business and professional success as others either counterattack or sanction us in response.

Sales people who succeed learn not to "attack" objections but to negotiate from their customer's side of the table. Cavett Robert is legendary in sales training and has produced some wonderful material on "harmonizing objections." His emphasis is not on "defense" but "harmony." Many times, we mistakenly see someone's questions as opposition. Cavett says people want reasons to say *yes* to you — but they want their own reasons, not yours. They want to know that your solution will meet their needs and not just your own. Doesn't this make sense?

In harmonizing people's objections, you are really adjusting your personality style to see their response as a request for more information. You are placing yourself in position to see issues from their perspective. You are listening for what they are really saying, rather than preparing to annihilate them and their arguments when you get a chance to speak.

An excellent example involves two businessmen who lived in the Greater Washington, D.C. area. Tom and Lori Milo own a distribution company and were looking to expand their business to a new area. They met with Ed and Sue Gansor to discuss the profit potential and mechanics. Tom knows that, as John McCormack wrote in *Self-Made in America,* "the majority of Americans have never done anything inconvenient — they have done only what they want to do." So, in explaining his business offering, he knew he had to identify *why* Ed and Sue would want to join him and why he would want to include them. In other words, what did they want and what could he help them get that would empower them to work hard with him for their mutual success. Sue was quick to respond with her goals and dreams. Ed confesses he was not interested in any discussion that was not "bottom-line." In fact, he says he was ready to call the meeting to a close when Tom suddenly switched gears and said, "Tell me, Ed, how do you like commuting to work?" Of course, as a task-oriented person, Ed hated sitting in traffic two hours a day. He started to listen when Tom quoted Will Rogers — "The trouble with the rat race is that, even if you win, you're still a rat!" If Tom could show him how to get out of the rat race, he was willing to listen. A tremendously profitable partnership has grown from that first meeting because Tom and Lori were able to adjust themselves to meet Ed and Sue at their points of need and interest.

One of the best methods for harmonizing objections is called *Feel, Felt, Found.* It requires that you actually listen to what the person is saying. You may even ask a few clarifying questions to make sure you understand what the person means beyond his words. And then you say, "You know, I understand how you feel. In fact, I felt the same way about it at one time… May I share with you what I found?" This approach says, in effect, I have heard and understood your valuable comment; I have been there, too; may I provide you with some helpful information for your consideration? You will be even more effective when you pause quietly after asking, "May I share with you what I found?" The other person *must* say yes and make some effort to listen to you — or else come off as close-minded to everyone else. Again, if your attitude is not negative or confrontational, but rather is "how can I help you get what you want so I will get what I want as a by-product?", you will move yourself to his side of the table.

Identify Excuses

Another excellent approach is to ask the question, "Why do you say that?" This is not the same as asking, "What is going on in your teeny, tiny mind?" It is an effort to either uncover a true obstacle or allow the person to discover for himself that his argument is weak. It is difficult to provide a generic example, but if you keep your cool and ask this question with the attitude that you really do want to understand, you will see how effective it is at establishing rapport and communicating with people. Oftentimes you will see people talk themselves into your point-of-view as they try to explain their own "gut reaction," which they may have viewed previously as a well thought-out response.

Sometimes, you may uncover a real question that simply requires additional information. Often, you will uncover an excuse or smoke screen thrown up to avoid making a change or taking a risk. Have you heard about the man who was always borrowing his neighbor's yard tools? Usually, they were not returned when promised. Often, they were returned in poorer condition. And the man always had an excuse for failing to meet his obligation. One day he knocked on his neighbor's front door and asked if he could borrow the lawn mower. The neighbor said, "Gee, I'd loan it to you but my wife is making lasagna for dinner tonight." The man asked, "But what does your wife making lasagna have to do with you letting me use your lawn mower?" And the neighbor replied, "Well, actually nothing at all. But I've found when people don't want to do something, one excuse is as good as another."

Just as we want others to recognize their excuses, we need to eliminate our own. Motivator Jim Rohn tells his audiences, "You know you are getting ahead in life when your excuses no longer get in the way." In fact, many leaders take the blame when something goes wrong, even when it is not their fault. Their purpose is not relieving others of their responsibility but allowing them to save face in an embarrassing situation. A leader may say, "That's probably my fault. I should have told you something but I didn't…" And then he may repeat something he *has* told them previously that would have prevented the problem in the first place and will fix it now. But he will not tell them that he is repeating himself. He understands that the first time they did not have "ears to hear." If they realize he has said it before, they will appreciate his tact. A great leader explains: "You can be right, or you can be rich. Eating crow once in awhile can make it possible to eat steak more often!"

Three Strikes

"D" types love the competition of business. Unfortunately, many people in business still believe that for them to win, someone else must lose. Denis Waitley's "double-win" concept is foreign to them. They believe in order to "get a bigger piece of the pie," they must supervise the way it is cut and make sure someone else gets a smaller piece. They have never heard economist Paul Zane Pilzer explain that through cooperation it is possible to bake a bigger pie with more for everyone.

An example of such narrow thinking can be observed in many labor negotiations. I am confident numerous business school dissertations have been written about the impasse, strike and collapse at Eastern Airlines. The 1994 baseball season ended in a strike, too — the first time in history that the season was not completed. In a nutshell, what happened was this: High "D" owners would not submit to working under the authority of a strong commissioner. They attempted to work out contract details with many high "D" representatives from the players association. Between these two factions stood regiments of high "D" lawyers, exerting their influence and control. Is it any wonder the situation ended in a stalemate? Owners lost revenue from the games and television broadcasts; players lost income from not playing scheduled games; the industry itself lost fan support. But the lawyers came out ahead. It is very difficult in business or personal relationships for people to compromise or negotiate in a friendly atmosphere if everyone is seeking only to win or to justify his own point-of-view.

We once heard Scott Michael tell about a cartoon t-shirt he had found. It showed Rudolf the Red-Nosed Reindeer sitting in his den, smoking a pipe and reading the newspaper. On the wall behind him were the stuffed heads of other "antlered animals," with name plaques beneath each: Comet, Cupid, Dasher, Donner, Blitzen, Vixen and so on. The cartoon caption read, "All of the other reindeer *used* to laugh and call him names." He liked it so much he showed it to his mentor, our mutual friend Dexter Yager, who pronounced it the most stupid shirt he had ever seen.

Shocked, Scott asked why. He replied, "Now he has to pull the sleigh all by himself!" When you blow up the rest of the team, you sometimes create more work than you can handle on your own.

Administrative boards are another example of conflict. A cartoon in *Alliance Life* magazine showed the church board room ripped apart, several people knocked to the floor, clothing ripped and soiled, eyeglasses broken, coffee cups overturned — and one fellow had a chair smashed over his head and the seat had come past his shoulders to pin down his arms. The caption showed the board chairman recording the final vote: "Then it's settled! We paint the Sunday School room blue!" Why is this more true than humorous? Consider this: most churches and synagogues try to appoint people with business knowledge and success to help in making decisions. So, they elect leaders with a lot of drive and determination. Does this make a team? Usually, it makes a bunch of leaders struggling for control. "Anything with more than one head is a monster!" and that is what a church board becomes when everyone is convinced his way is best. What complicates communication even more is that each person feels he is honestly trying to "do God's will." Everyone's actions and attitudes seem to say, "I'm really not trying to be ugly about this, but God Himself put me on this committee to make sure we get *red* carpet... and His will shall be done!"

Do you know what someone has to go through to become a foreign missionary? In addition to years of college or seminary study, many missionaries are required to have medical training, to learn several languages, to become debt-free, and to travel widely seeking financial support that will underwrite their work for up to four years. They pay a big price in terms of duty and dedication. Yet I have heard that after all this effort, the most frequent reason missionaries give up their assignments and return to their homeland is because they cannot adjust to working with other missionaries who serve with them on the field. Isn't that amazing? Their failure may have less to do with adjusting to tsetse flies and more to do with whether the toilet paper unrolls from the top or from the bottom!

"D" is for Dirty Work

Paul Hornung, former great running back for the Green Bay Packers, faced a major problem back in 1962. The team was going to the playoffs in a couple of weeks, but at that same time he had to report to his Army unit for a weekend Reserve meeting. He went to his head coach, Vince Lombardi, and told him about the situation. Of course, Hornung wanted more than anything to play in the football game, but when military duty calls, nothing gets in its way... unless, of course, you are a high "D." Hornung says he remembers that day so well because Coach Lombardi immediately picked up the telephone, called *directly* to the White House and got President John Kennedy on the line. He explained the situation and was assured by the President that the matter would be taken of. In a few minutes, an Army General called Lombardi back and told him that it would not be necessary for Paul Hornung to report for duty. Hornung just stood there, smiling and shaking his head in disbelief. As he walked out of the room, he said, "Well, there's nothing like going to the top when you need something done!" Then he saw a little grin on Lombardi's face. Without saying a word, his expression spoke volumes.

"D" types frequently charge ahead where others hold back. For Lombardi, I'm sure it seemed calling JFK was not a "shot in the dark" but the only "reasonable" thing to do. He was bold enough to try what Hornung never thought to do — and bold enough to accomplish it. In building an effective team, you will often find that your "D" type team members don't mind doing the "dirty work" if there is a challenge connected to it. They'll go right to the source rather than worrying about protocol. They recognize this truth from J. H. Boetcher: "The individual activity of one man with backbone will do more than a thousand men with a mere wishbone."

As the saying goes, "Sometimes it is easier to ask forgiveness than it is to ask permission." In other words, any number of people along the way can say "no" and hold you back from succeeding. If you go ahead and succeed, you'll find very few who are offended that you didn't get their okay first. Of course, we expect that you will be moral and ethical in doing what you have set out to do.

Righteous Indignation

Simeon Strunsky commented, "Once a man would spend a week patiently waiting if he missed a stage coach, but now he rages if he misses the first section of a revolving door." Temper is a challenge for every personality style, but "D's" seem particularly prone to mismanaging their own. They exhibit little in the way of self-doubt, they love to be in charge, and they are more interested in the "big picture" than in the "little people." So, they can "steamroller" right over others and not even sense a slight "bump" in their road.

A preacher said that he had prayed for years and years that God would remove his hot temper. Finally one day, he felt God say, "Why should I remove something that I gave you?" He said he was puzzled by the thought but came to realize that God had given him his ability to feel strongly about things that were important to him. He said anger can be a wonderful gift when its energy is channeled in the right direction. Whenever he thinks about how sin destroys people's lives, wrecks homes, causes people to ruin relationships and even take their own lives, it makes him so mad he can hardly contain himself. Channeling his anger in the right direction, he has been able to preach and teach effectively, to build a church and focus his efforts on helping as many people as possible.

Anger produces a lot of energy in all of us. When we get angry, it usually leads us to do something about a situation. If we lash out and are destructive, our anger has been released as rage. *Indignation* is different from rage, in that when we are indignant we look to correct the situation that has caused our anger, rather than simply exacting some kind of revenge for our disappointment or discomfort. I have observed that the "size" of our temper often is in *inverse* proportion to our productivity in life. In other words, those who accomplish great things have learned to measure their responses, instead of flying off the handle all the time. Rather than being hurtful or harmful to other people, they allow life's injustices to motivate them, making things right where others have made them wrong.

Lump the Losers Together

It is important in sports, business or family to "know your players." In other words, what are the strengths and weaknesses of each team member? When do they function best and where do they need support? You can understand a lot about this by observing a player's personality style.

At the same time, remember that one player's personality plus another player's personality equals a *combination*. How people combine is a key consideration. For instance, when two "I" types get together, something exciting happens — and they have to be careful that they don't get each other in trouble.

When Casey Stengle retired as manager of the New York Yankees, he turned over the reigns to a young coach, Billy Martin. Martin asked Stengle for some advice, and he was told to "room the losers together." Casey said when you put someone who has a bad attitude with someone who has a good attitude, it is only a matter of time until the first "poisons" the second.

Regardless of the personality style, it is very important that we recognize the importance of seeking the right kind of friends. Temptation usually comes when we seek wrong company. "Birds of a feather usually flock together" …and then feathers fly! If we are careful whom we hang around with and spend time with, and whom we listen to, we will be better off.

We can edify and encourage others, too! We can determine not to be well poisoners. Rather, we can become life enhancers. When we encounter people who tend to be negative, we may be able to turn them around because of our own positive perspective. But we must be careful not to pick up their attitude in the process. Pam Shoffler, in New York, teachers her business associates to *insulate* themselves from a negative attitude but not *isolate* those who lack a positive outlook — and not to expect immediate acceptance. She says, "Positive people intimidate negative people. But don't step down to their level to be a friend." If you put the cages of a singing canary and a crow next to each other, the canary may learn to "caw" but the crow will never learn to sing.

There are people who do not buy into the "positive mental attitude" approach at all. A major reason is that they say motivation doesn't last. Zig Ziglar responds, "Neither does a bath — that's why you have to do it again and again." By positive mental attitude, I do not mean you should become the kind of person who denies reality and sees only silver linings in thunder clouds. I am talking about an attitude of *purposeful cheerfulness.* Thomas Carlyle wrote, "Wondrous is the strength of cheerfulness, and its power of endurance — the cheerful man will do more in the same time, will do it better, will preserve it longer, than the sad or sullen." He should know, because he was "wired" in the opposite pattern and struggled throughout his life to improve in this area. Wilhelm Von Humboldt wrote, "I am more and more convinced that our happiness or unhappiness depends far more on the way we meet the events of life than on the nature of those events themselves."

Incurable Optimism

Over half-a-century ago, prospector Rafael Solano sat discouraged and exhausted on a boulder in a dry river bed. According to writer Morris Mandel, Solano told his three companions, "I'm through. There's no use going on any longer. See this pebble? It makes about 999,999 I've picked up and not a diamond so far. If I pick up another, it will be a million — but what's the use? I'm quitting." The men had spent months searching for diamonds in Venezuela. They had worked, stooping, gathering pebbles, hoping for a single sign of a diamond — but they never thought of giving up until Solano said, "I quit!" One of the other men said, "So... pick up another and make it a million."

"All right," Solano said, and stooped down, reaching his hand into a pile of pebbles. It was almost the size of a hen's egg. "Here it is," he declared, "the last one." For that one-in-a-million pebble, New York jeweler Harry Winston paid Solano $200,000 — named "The Liberator," it was the largest diamond ever found, up to that time.

Does this give you a "kick" to keep going? Or do you feel someone is "yanking your chain" whenever you hear a story like this? "If you don't believe in positive thinking," asks Jerry Meadows, "what kind of thinking *do* you believe in? Negative thinking? No thinking at all?" He has a way of getting to the heart of the matter, doesn't he? You don't have to buy into his prescription — but I have discovered that, regardless of their personality style, this is the way people who are very successful in their personal and business life choose to think.

Jody Victor is an Ohio businessman of middle age and middle size, but he is youthful in his attitude with oversized enthusiasm for living. His optimism is more than contagious — it is incurable. He says, "People ask me, haven't you ever been discouraged? Yeah, I tried it once, but I didn't like it!" People who succeed in their relationships choose to be contagious and incurable. Interestingly, he makes some people nervous — they don't know what to do with *all* his positive attitude! So, he has learned how to scale back when he spots a slower-paced individual who has not yet been vaccinated against SNIOP Syndrome. (That's **S**usceptible to the **N**egative **I**nfluence of **O**ther **P**eople!)

As you work together on a team, it is important to recognize and utilize the contributions of people who have this outgoing, people-loving, fast-paced, enthusiastic style. Appreciate them but help them to understand the importance of "scaling back" when it is appropriate.

A Doubtful Future

As a quick example, let me share briefly the work history of Mark Day, a young man who grew up in Lubbock, Texas. Mark's first job in high school was working for Chick-fil-A®, a wonderful restaurant company founded by my friend Truett Cathy, author of the book *It's Easier to Succeed Than to Fail*. The Corporate Purpose of his company is: *To glorify God by being a faithful steward of all that is entrusted to us; to have a positive influence on all who come in contact with Chick-fil-A*. It would be fair to say that Mark tested the company's resolve...

WHO DO YOU THINK YOU ARE ANYWAY?

Early on in his food service career, Mark learned that an ice cube dropped into the french fry vat would bubble and even shoot up out of the hot cooking oil. One day in the restaurant's mall location, the store was almost empty, he was bored, and his "I" was restless. With nothing better to do, he packed a large drink cup with ice chips and deposited them in the fryer. At the counter was a row of microphones which order-takers used to relay customer requests to food preparers. Mark pulled a microphone close to his lips and in his best NASA announcer voice began the countdown: 10... 9... 8... 7.... Around "5," he noticed everyone in the kitchen area had ducked for cover, and there was a rumbling sound coming from the fryer. At "2" he prepared to take cover himself — just as he saw an old lady walking toward the counter for an iced tea refill! Mark hit the deck — BOOM! The ice exploded from the fryer, shooting grease onto signs, shelves, ceilings, counter space, and even some of the tables. As it stopped raining grease, he peered over the top to see the little old lady had hit the deck, too. Miraculously, no one was hurt. And now, years later, Mark says it was quite a job cleaning everything afterwards, but it was almost worth it!

Mark enjoys telling that story. He enjoys even more what comes after people stop laughing. Then he says, "But that's not what got me fired..." The straw that broke the camel's back was when a woman asked him if the chicken salad was fresh. He replied, "Well, ma'am, I don't know. But you try it and if it gets fresh with you, you bring it back to me and I'll slap the fire out of it!" He says he didn't know she was a close friend of the owner.

Hearing that history, would you believe that within just a few years, Mark Day would form a company that earned millions of dollars in consumer products distribution? If you had been his boss, would you ever have dreamed it? It is easier to dismiss people who behave irresponsibly than it is to help them grow in responsibility. What would you do with someone like Mark on your team? You might put him at the counter to be with people, but not near the fryer. Of course, even at the counter you would have to keep an eye on him — and the chicken salad!

Chris says he was very much like this himself, but he never

understood why until he began to study personality styles. He was recruited out of college to be the business manager for a touring show after one day of "training" — with his very high "I" and no "C" style. His reports were always late and seldom accurate. Everything about the job was a mismatch for his skills. The president of the company visited him on the road to try to salvage the situation. He told Chris he was the most un-together person he had ever met. Chris explained that he was just so busy he couldn't get everything done. Chris was stunned when his boss told him, "You're not busy; you're just not organized." (As Coach Lou Holtz says, "When all is said and done, as a rule, more is said than done.") He went on to say, "I haven't seen your hotel room, but I'll bet if I opened the door it would bump one shoe... and the other one would be under the bed!" Chris finally ran out of excuses and had to admit to himself that he was failing miserably. Walking alone to his hotel room, his eyes were so filled with tears that he couldn't see to get the key in the door lock. Finally he got the door open, and it bumped one of his shoes. And yes, the other shoe was under the bed! Chris says a profound change occurred that night: No matter how disorganized his life is, to this day his shoes are always together. *If* you can find one, you know the other will be next to it.

It would be easy to make excuses for irresponsible or even immoral behavior by saying, "I'm an 'I' and these are my weaknesses." But doing so will not provide an opportunity to grow past this weakness. "I" types, perhaps more than any others, are good at excusing themselves. In fact, to accomplish your task in correcting an "I," you cannot simply "call him on the carpet." When their emotions are shocked, they seem to shut down; they do not process harsh words. They pull into themselves — they may seem panicky. Or, they may seem really glib. "I's" tend to make light of a serious circumstance. They may seem to be saying, "Take it easy. This is no big deal. We're still buddies..." even when they are dying inside. If you are working with an "I" or if you are one, you will benefit by recognizing this pattern. Do not be put off by it. Dealing effectively with this style means that you do not allow them "wiggle room" to escape responsibility while you assure them that they are not alone and that you care enough to help them through the problem.

Years ago, a well-known musician and evangelist told Chris, "You know, you and I are not well-rounded at all. We have flat sides, so we don't 'roll straight' and we probably never will. But the great thing is that people like us are so good at polishing our flat sides that people don't even see them that way. People think they are facets and they say, 'Wow, what a gem!'" Chris gets a chill up his spine as he remembers the comment because he understands that the attitude behind the comment brought disaster and shame on the man years later and eventually worked to do the same in his own life until he learned to get under control.

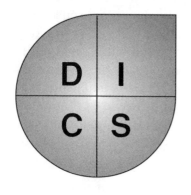

It's impossible to "roll straight" if your behavior is out of control, if you don't manage the ups and downs of your personality style. This illustration shows what the man really meant. For instance, there may be times when it is very appropriate to have your "I" stick out, but you need to make sure it is *serving* you rather than being your *master*. Or if your "C" looks like a flat tire, you may need to "pump it up" so you can stay on course through certain situations in your life. Your own behavioral style is "active" rather than "static" — you are making adjustments all the time, and your goal is to demonstrate appropriate, *well-rounded* behavior. Whether you are a "D," "I," "S," or "C," you will have to "pull yourself back in" or "pump yourself up" at appropriate times so you can roll straight and smooth.

I cannot tell you how many times someone has said to me, "Dr. Rohm, I wish I had your personality!" I always respond the same way: "Well… I wish I didn't!" Being a high "I" may seem fun, but it has so many challenges. I am well aware that "I" types have a lot of potential, but they usually waste it because they are so unfocused. Knowing that constantly encourages me to stay focused.

A Secret Service Story

This little section is not about protecting the President of the United States. It is about a well-kept secret for success in all your business relationships. The secret is: *offer great service.*

We were fast outgrowing our first office, which was in my basement at home. We were adding more work areas and finishing a bathroom. We kept moving things around to create space, but it was often difficult because the existing furniture got in the way of the building materials. One day a carpenter accidentally kicked over the ceramic toilet bowl and broke it into several pieces. I gathered them up, put them in the original box and took it back to the Home Depot store where I had purchased it. I did so make sure I got another one exactly like it.

At the service desk I explained how we had accidentally broken the toilet and I wanted to purchase a new one. The service representative told me I could just trade it out for a new one. I explained again that *we* were the ones who broke the toilet — it was *our* fault, not theirs. He said that was okay and that I could still just trade it out for an even exchange. I explained again that it was our fault. It didn't come broken in the box — we broke it! He said that would be fine; Home Depot would give me an even trade. I loaded the new toilet in my van and brought it home for the workers to install, and I told them what had happened. One worker said, "Yeah, that's typical of Home Depot. They always go way beyond the call of duty. That's why everyone does business with them."

I thought, how true that is. When we raise our "S" and become a Super Servant offering Superior Service, we win in the long run. It may be that Home Depot lost a little money on the toilet bowl deal, but I have told this story so many times that the advertising alone far outweighs any loss on the toilet bowl! One of the most difficult sayings of Jesus is, "Whosoever shall lose his life shall find it." The Bible is filled with examples that show how we live by dying, we gain by giving, and we have by sharing. It is in receiving, understanding and applying this concept that we find great victory in our personal life and business relationships.

As an active man in his mid-40s, Dexter Yager suffered a massive stroke in October of 1986. The doctors told his wife Birdie that if he lived, he would never walk again. She envisioned herself and her seven children lifting this paralyzed and helpless man in and out of a wheelchair for the rest of his life. That was the best they could hope for. But Dexter made a vow: he would walk again. His close friend, billionaire Richard M. DeVos, picks up the story here, as he related it in the book *Compassionate Capitalism*:

> Late in 1988, a coliseum in North Carolina was filled with Dexter and Birdie's friends and co-workers. The plan was simple. Birdie would wheel Dexter onto the stage. He would wave his good arm, share a few words of encouragement, and then be wheeled off the stage again.... Then Dexter appeared. He wasn't in his chair. He was walking. It was more of a step, drag, step, but he was walking. And the gloom lifted like a curtain. People's eyes filled with tears, not of grief but of joy and gratitude. Dexter was walking.

What sustained him in the two years of rehabilitation that brought him to the stage was the love and support from thousands of friends around the world, from the President of the United States to folks no one ever heard of. But what each did was simply repay a kindness that had first been shown to them. What motivated Dexter during those two years and over the past ten was his desire to get out and serve others in new and exciting ways.

In his book *Empire of Freedom*, American Trucking Associations Vice President James Robinson relays this important detail about Dexter's character:

> Dan Williams has known Dexter Yager for over 30 years. "Dexter was born a server," he told me. "It's the little things that you always remember. And I remember the time just a few years ago when Bunny and I were traveling to a meeting in Rio de Janeiro. As we struggled with our luggage at the airport, Dexter spotted us from a distance and rushed over to help us with our bags. Imagine that — after he had suffered a stroke. There were people all around us, but it was Dexter Yager who came over to help us. He is a born server, and the more you serve, the more you get."

Is there a common secret that has made both Atlanta-based Home Depot and Charlotte-based InterNET Services outstanding success stories in American business? Yes, it's *service.* In other words, those who serve... deserve!

Now the question is, in your business team, what style is most naturally concerned about s-s-s-service? Yes, it's the "S" type personality. This person is especially valuable because he will make sure people are not lost in the process. Now here's the real stunner: neither Bernie Marcus, the founder of Home Depot, nor Dexter Yager, the founder of InterNET Services, is an "S" by nature. These "D" types have learned to serve. And s-s-s-serving is the s-s-s-secret of their s-s-s-success!

Pushing the Rope

While every team benefits from having this kind of "S" behavior — and if you don't have it naturally, you should learn how to "synthesize" it — there are work areas in which "S" types can use help and encouragement. Teddy Roosevelt said, "Far better it is to dare mighty things, to win glorious triumphs, even though checkered by failure, than to take rank with those poor spirits who neither enjoy much nor suffer much, because they live in the gray twilight that knows not victory or defeat." Generally, "S's" are twilight people. You will frustrate yourself and irritate them if you try to turn them into "D" or "I" types. It will not work and they will not cooperate.

Georgia businessman Jerry Boggus has an easygoing, people-oriented style. He placed motivational statements everywhere when he was developing the "umphh!" to start his own company because he knew this area was a challenge for him. He knows the frustration of trying to get people to do what frightens them. He says, "There are only a few things that are impossible to do. You can't push a rope. You can't nail Jello to a wall. You can't climb a fence leaning toward you, and you can't kiss a girl leaning away from you. And you can't get people to do consistently what they don't want to do." The key to consistent performance is getting people to *want* to. Appreciating, including, and encouraging are important in motivating an "S" toward consistent performance.

"C" Your Problem Clearly

Whether he originated this saying or not, Benjamin Franklin is credited with it: "For want of a nail the shoe was lost; for want of a shoe the horse was lost; and for want of a horse the rider was lost, being overtaken and slain by the enemy, all for want of care about a horseshoe nail." The person on your team who attends to these details habitually is the "C" type personality. In fact, data and detail are the fuels that drive them. As noted before, they are note-takers and list-keepers.

Within the Quality Control Movement that has swept through American industry, the "C" types get credit for I. C. A. — that stands for Irreversible Corrective Action. The idea behind I. C. A. is that a problem should be fixed only once. Whatever action is taken to correct a problem should truly correct it so that it does not happen again. Of course, this requires unraveling the problem all the way down to the root difficulty and then fixing it at that point so "the fix" will not "reverse" itself and cause the problem again. "C's" are perfect for this kind of work, while other styles may not appreciate its importance or understand its functions.

The follow-through that makes I. C. A. work is a simple stipulation: When the person who is responsible for determining what the I. C. A. *should be* makes his corrective action, he doesn't get to fix it *again* if something goes wrong. Instead, it "escalates" to his superior for added accountability. It has been interesting on several occasions to see this concept at work in corporate America. It really tests whether a company is committed to real service and quality because, in some cases, the root reaches all the way to the foundations of the organization — and fixing it may require the leaders rethinking or restructuring a major part of their operations. Including your "C" team members in the corrective process is a smart move. They see things that others often overlook. If you don't have much "C" yourself, this can be a wonderful discipline to engage in — just back up your thinking by running it past some *real* "C's" before you take action.

Critical Condition

This type is good at critical thinking. Sometimes "C's" are "too good" at critical *comments,* as well. It is easy for them to dismiss ideas presented by others in a team project as unworkable or impractical, instead of offering positive options or solutions. Charles Brower wrote, "A new idea is delicate. It can be killed by a sneer or a yawn; it can be stabbed to death by a quip and worried to death by a frown on the right man's brow."

Did you know the operating plan for Federal Express was originally a class project for college student Fred Smith? He was assigned to design a new business venture but received only a grade of C–. His professor said the idea was impractical. Since FedEx did over a billion dollars in sales last year, C– was probably an unfair grade! Think where document delivery would be if Smith had embraced his broke teacher's evaluation of his idea! Fortunately, he believed more in himself and the practicality of his dream than he did in his business and economics professors. He must have agreed with President Reagan, who once said, "Economists are people who see something work in practice and wonder if it will work in theory."

Actor Channing Pollock once said, "A critic is a legless man who teaches running." A real danger is that critical comments can also "chop the legs" off the person who is trying to find a solution or needs encouragement. For this reason, "C's" can develop a reputation for being negative or "picky," when they think they are being helpful. Any critique should be tempered with optimism and suggestions on how to achieve the goal, being careful not to injure the pride of others who are involved. In short, "C's" need to raise their "I" and "S" whenever they offer criticism. The oft-used phrase of John Cassis is true: "Nobody cares how much you know — until they know how much you care."

Each of us needs to be cautious about criticism, not just "C" types. We all can learn to be more positive and encouraging — this is not a "C" issue alone. This quotation from Theodore Roosevelt has inspired many people to think seriously about this issue:

"It is not the critic who counts; not the man who points out how the strong man stumbled, or where the doer of deeds could have done better. The credit belongs to the man who is actually in the arena; whose face is marred by dust and sweat and blood; who strives valiantly; who errs and comes short again and again; who knows the great enthusiasms, the great devotions and spends himself in a worthy cause; who at the best knows in the end the triumph of high achievement; and who at the worst, if he fails, at least fails while daring greatly; so that his place shall never be with those cold and timid souls who know neither victory nor defeat."

No one has ever erected a statue to honor a critic, and this is why my friend, Dr. Buford Adams, likes to say, "I despise the guys who criticize and minimize the enterprise of other guys whose enterprise has made them rise above the guys who criticize."

'Tis a Gift to Be Simple

"C" types seem to be able to organize themselves with very little effort. It's as if they *think* in flowcharts. Most other people are "organizationally challenged." The drawback a "C" may face with his organizing gift is *detail-itis*. This is a virus that can lead to the "paralysis of analysis" — not being able to do anything at all until all the unknowns are known. But faith, trust, and calculated risks are inevitable in personal growth.

The balance for a "C" is found in *simplification*. Hans Hoffman said, "The ability to simplify means to eliminate the unnecessary so that the necessary may speak." Charles Kettering, cofounder of Delco and benefactor of the Sloan-Kettering Institute for Cancer Research, used this approach in developing his own unique method for solving problems. He would break down each problem into the smallest possible sub-problems. Then he did research to find out which sub-problems had already been solved. He often found that what looked like a huge problem had previously been 98 percent solved by another. Then he tackled what was left. If this seems amazing to you, you are probably not a "C." But it will work for you, too!

Because "C" types love detail, they may tell you how to make a watch when you ask them only what time it is. So, a word to the wise for "C's" from Randall Ross: "Explain *why* you need to do it before you explain *how* you ought to do it." In true "D" fashion, "If you have anything to tell me of importance, for goodness sake begin at the end!"

Admit It — You're Wrong

Precision and excellence are part of the "C's" "detail orientation" — we see it in their speech, writing and work. The rest of us would do well to emulate them in these areas. As Mark Twain said, "The difference between the right word and the almost right work is the difference between lightning and the lightning bug." The rest of us may settle for a "near miss," but for a "C" accuracy is crucial.

"C's" have little trouble recognizing the shortcomings of others, but do not like to have their own pointed out. Rather than telling them, "You made a mistake — you are wrong!", we find greater success in suggesting they check over an area that we "have a question about." In other words, we let them discover their own errors whenever we can, rather than pointing them out as if they are self-evident. Sometimes "C's" seem so self-righteously correct that we may want to "rub it in" when we discover their mistake. This is a major blunder — we will prove nothing using this tactic except that we are unskilled and unwise in dealing with people.

On the other hand, "C" types should recognize they will gain more points by frankly admitting their mistake when they find one, rather than trying to excuse it or rationalize it. One of the hardest things in this world to do is to admit we are wrong. And nothing is more helpful in resolving a situation than its frank admission.

You will remember that we spoke about the importance of phrasing your comments constructively rather than critically. Thomas Dreier bluntly observed, "One thing scientists have discovered is that often-praised children become more intelligent that often-blamed ones. If some of your employees are a bit dumb, perhaps your treatment of them is to blame. There's a creative element in praise." So, whether we are on the giving or receiving end of evaluation or correction, praise is another key in building successful business relationships.

It's hard to avoid giving the impression of a "know-it-all" when you almost do know it all. This is great advice from Jerry Boggus: "Learn to ask questions, rather than just giving answers. And never give answers so quickly that people feel it was a dumb question." Whatever your personality style, it makes good sense, don't you think?

Recognize Team Strengths

At our office, we filled out *Style Assessments* on ourselves and our spouses — and our spouses did the same. We saw an interesting trend: We tend *not* to acknowledge in others the traits that are stronger in ourselves. For instance, Chris's "I" is extremely high, so he did not rate his wife Cindy's "I" as high as it really is. Cindy's "D" is higher than Chris's, and she scored him with very little "D," using herself as the norm. Rick Herceg's wife (also a Cindy) has a lot of "C" and said that he is an "I." However, he is our "token 'C'" in an office of "I's." To us, he is "Mister Detail," our director of customer service and event planning.

This tendency to underrate others seems common in all styles. "D's" are accustomed to being in charge and seem to underestimate others who have the same style. "I's" seem oblivious to differences because they are self-occupied and think everyone sees things as they do. "S's" seem to be less judgmental and condemning because they tend to make more allowances for others. "C" types love consistency and excellence, and they notice when others do not meet the standard. They may "write them off" as lacking these important traits.

We see issues through our own personality lenses and filters. The most *natural* thing in the world is to see them through our own perspective. However, the most *supernatural* thing in the world is to see those issues through the lenses, filters, and perspectives of others.

The reason I mention this is that our "impressions" of people are not necessarily an accurate picture of contributions they can make. For example, a "C" may recognize that, sometimes, an "S" type who can practice "C" type traits might be better equipped to deal with a particular situation than the "C" himself.

An interesting example of how this works in a team can be found in Walt and Roy Disney. Chris has a friend who was an "insider" when Walt was planning his EPCOT and Walt Disney World projects in Florida. You may have guessed that Walt had a lot of "D" and "I." However, he lacked an understanding of finances. His board of directors approximated the cost of his ideas by how excited he got in describing them and how big his gestures were. Chris's friend said, in describing the Florida project, Walt Disney's hands and arms were "making helicopters" in the air! Several board members just buried their heads in their hands, muttering to themselves, *"Billions... billions..."*

I have read that in getting the original Disneyland project off the ground, Walt went to potential investors like Art Linkletter, who turned him down. He applied for financing from over 400 banks who didn't find him credible. And then, his brother Roy became involved in that process. He put together the deal and was a key player in Disney organization, even taking over the Florida project when Walt passed away.

Why was their team so effective? You probably know that Walt Disney was fired from several jobs early in his career because he was "a dreamer." He couldn't apply himself to boring, repetitive tasks for very long and his task-oriented employers dismissed him as someone who would never achieve anything important. When he approached thoughtful, reserved investors, they probably thought, "We have no previous model by which to evaluate him or his theme park ideas. And we don't think he knows a balance sheet from a bed sheet. He would lose our money and then move on to try something else." But when investors listened to Roy, they probably thought, "This man speaks our language. We're not sure he could 'think up fun' anymore than we could, but he could handle the money. He explains his brother's ideas in ways we understand, and he could keep him on target." Walt Disney was a master team builder who learned to appreciate the skills of others and inspire them into becoming members of his team. But without enlisting his brother to make the finances work there would have been no fuel to drive his dreams to reality.

Theoretically Speaking

Robert Frost once commented that "the brain is a wonderful organ; it starts working at the moment you get up in the morning and does not stop until you get to the office." The ability to "shift" their minds into forward-driving "cognitive gear" is a tremendous asset for "C's." The rest of us have experienced moments when our minds have "left" us, and we know we can count of them for clear thinking under pressure. A challenge for "C's" is to remember their thinking has a practical end result: it affects people.

For instance, we have mentioned before how "C' types are compliance-seeking — "here are the rules; let's follow them." According to Bert Masterson, "Someone has tabulated that we have 35,000,000 laws on the books to enforce the Ten Commandments." How many of those laws came about as theoretical, rather than practical, solutions? Of course, any personality type can become controlling and try through its favorite methods to force people into complying with its rules and wishes. I mention it here because "C's" have a propensity for making lists and setting things right.

Regardless of our personality type, when we become overly detail-oriented, we can grant a higher priority to the task than to the people affected by its outcome. Ron Ball told us a true story about a task-oriented, rule-driven city bus driver who was called before his supervisor because of complaints that he was not stopping to pick up passengers on his route. He responded to the official's reprimand by saying, "You can't expect us to stay on schedule if we have to stop and pick up passengers!" A theory is only as good as its application, and a process is only as good as its benefit to people.

Have you heard the great story about a centipede with

arthritis who was told by a wise owl that changing himself into a stork would eliminate 98% of his leg pain. The centipede asked how he should change himself into a stork, and the owl replied, "Oh, I wouldn't know about the details. I only make general policy…" We need to make sure our policies are not just general but applicable, as well. To succeed with others, "C's" can use their great critical thinking skills to identify opportunities within the existing circumstances, rather than pointing out why the circumstances are all wrong for any opportunity.

Kumbaya, My Lord

We could write many more pages about the amazing ways personalities are expressed in relationships without ever worrying about exhausting variables and possibilities. You probably have thought about examples in your own experience as you have read our stories. The major idea we hope you recognize is that these personality principles really can work in all your relationships. You may recognize traits in other personality styles that you wish were more prevalent in your own life, and now you should understand how you can emulate them for greater harmony, versatility and success.

However, you will find that applying this material is a lot like going to church camp when you were a kid — did you ever have a final-night experience like this? Everyone sat around the camp fire, singing folks songs or gospel choruses. One by one, kids approached the fire, tossed in a stick, and told what the week of camping had meant to them — the new friends, the crafts, sports and activities, the devotional studies and personal growth. Oftentimes, kids would feel so impacted that they *promised* things would be *different* when they got back home to their families. They pledged to be nice to their sister, to be more obedient to their parents, and to one day give their lives in "missionary service in foreign lands!" But when they got home, their sister had not been to camp — she didn't know her part in the play. Her response to their efforts at "turning over a new leaf" was to rake it into the pile and set it on fire!

Likewise, you may feel frustrated when people do not respond immediately according to the expectations you have developed in reading and trying to apply this personality information. You may be tempted to give up and say, "This personalities stuff may work for other people, but it doesn't work for me." Remember that Mark Twain said, "One learns people through the heart, not the eyes or the intellect." You are learning the *art* of understanding yourself and others. Your proficiency will improve with practice, not with theory.

You must understand and remember that you cannot control others nor change anyone else. However, you can get yourself and your own personality under control... and that is the good news! By doing so, in time, others will see the change in you and be more open to changing themselves. I remind myself every day that "Rome wasn't built in a day" ...and neither was Rohm!

What you are really working on is "integrity" in all its *Webster's New World Dictionary* definitions:
[1]the quality or state of being complete; unbroken condition; wholeness, entirety
[2]the quality or state of being unimpaired; perfect condition; soundness
[3]the quality or state of being of sound moral principle; uprightness, honesty, and sincerity.

President Dwight D. Eisenhower wrote, "The supreme quality for leadership is unquestionably integrity. Without it, no real success is possible, no matter whether it is on a section gang, a football field, in an army, or in an office."

This information holds out a wonderful promise to you: You needn't be an angry, frustrated spectator, sitting in the stands and "booing" while others take home the trophies. You *can* and *will* win the trophies as you learn to play the game according to the rules... As we said before, *"That's life!"* And what a great life it is!

Appendix

How to Read Graphs

The Seven "D" Blends

The Seven "I" Blends

The Seven "S" Blends

The Seven "C" Blends

The "Even" or "Level" Pattern

Appendix A

How to Read Graphs

Learning to read your *Style Analysis* graphs is not difficult. When you know what to look for, you can gain some very helpful insights, whether from your own graph or from someone else's. As my friend Steve Yager says, "The graphs tell the story!"

First, understand that our questionnaire asks you to select, from four different phrases or word choices, the phrase that you feel *most* accurately describes you. Then it asks you to select, from the remaining three, the one phrase that is *least* accurate in describing you. This is repeated with twenty-four sets of descriptive phrases, until you have selected twenty-four *most* and twenty-four *least* phrases to complete the questionnaire.

Some of these choices are primarily preferences of a "D" type individual, while others are most often chosen by "I's," "S's," or "C's." So, it is a matter of adding up the number of choices for each and entering them at the appropriate plotting points on your first graph, "Graph I – Environment." This graph shows how you believe you need to "behave" in your environment in order to achieve success.

"Graph II – Basic Style" is a measure of "who" and "how" you are at your core. Rather than drawing from your preferences, it draws data from what you have said you are *least* like — the behaviors you tend to avoid. Briefly, the behaviors you are *least* like, you are *least* like most of the time. (For example, if you *avoid* boiled Brussels sprouts, it would be reasonable to expect you to avoid them whether they are on a blue plate or a white plate; whether alone or in a casserole, whether at home or at a restaurant. Perhaps some environment might cause you to eat them — dinner at the White House, for instance — but you would not be comfortable doing so.

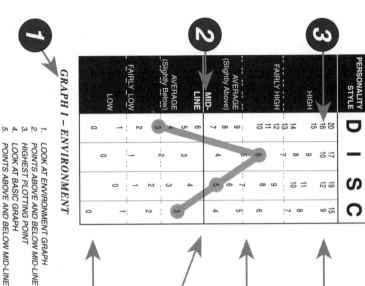

GRAPH I – ENVIRONMENT

1. LOOK AT ENVIRONMENT GRAPH
2. POINTS ABOVE AND BELOW MID-LINE
3. HIGHEST PLOTTING POINT
4. LOOK AT BASIC GRAPH
5. POINTS ABOVE AND BELOW MID-LINE

GRAPH II – BASIC STYLE

6. HIGHEST PLOTTING POINT
7. COMPARE SIMILARITIES AND DIFFERENCES
8. COMPARE HIGHEST PLOTTING POINTS
9. COMPARE LOWEST PLOTTING POINTS
10. COMPARE AVERAGE PLOTTING POINTS

You would adapt somehow, but you probably would not want to have another serving.) Most people are very consistent about the things they avoid, regardless of their environment. So, these selections tend to be very reliable in identifying your Basic Style. The plotting points on "Graph II" are in descending order, and do not show "what you are *least*," rather the term "least" means the graph's plotting points come from your *least* choices.

A more complete explanation of the scoring theory comes with our *Style Analysis* reports. We have provided a brief rationale for the graphs so you will have an idea of how they are created. Our focus in these pages is how to interpret the graphs for practical application.

Ten Steps in Reading Your Graphs

1. *Look at your Environment Graph.* This is Graph I, on the left side of page 252. It has this name because it shows how you believe you should behave for success in your environment.

2. *Observe which plotting points are above and below the midline.* In this example, the points above the midline are "I" and "S"; below the midline are "D" and "C."

3. *Look at the highest plotting point in Graph I.* In this example, it is "I," in the "fairly high" segment. This is the predominate trait in this individual's style. Refer to the "I" type behaviors for a description of this style.

4. *Now, look at the Basic Graph.* This is Graph II, on the right side of page 252. It has this name because it shows how you tend to behave most naturally, the way you are on "autopilot."

5. *Again, identify which plotting points are above and below the midline.* In this example, "I" and "D" are above; "S" and "C" are below.

6. *Look at the highest plotting point in Graph II.* In this example, it is "I," in the "high" segment. This is the predominate trait in this individual's style. Refer to the "I" type behaviors for a description of this style.

7. ***Compare similarities and differences.*** This individual, who is "wired" as an "I with D" in his Basic Style, actually finds in his Environmental behavior that he lowers his "D" and his "I," and raises his "S" to "slightly above average." These are the kinds of differences you are looking for — especially the very pronounced differences.

8. ***Compare highest plotting points.*** It does not always follow that both graphs will show the same predominate trait or even follow a similar pattern. For example, an individual may have a very high trait in his Basic Style that he must "lower" in order to "raise" a *different* trait in his Environment Style — so, while his graph would show a predominance of one style in Graph II, it could show a different predominate style in Graph I.

   Remember that the "highest plotting points" reveal your strongest contributions (and, in Graph II, areas in which you also feel most comfortable). They also reveal whether you are primarily task-oriented or people-oriented, whether you primarily tend to be fast-paced and outgoing, or slower-paced and reserved.

9. ***Compare lowest plotting points.*** Does your Environment cause you to adapt your Basic Style significantly? In each graph, what are the traits which are least familiar or comfortable to you? These are your lowest plotting points.

10. ***Compare average plotting points.*** What falls in the mid-range? These are traits you can raise and lower more easily. Also, they may be areas in which you have little drive or passion.

   As you check each of these ten areas, ask yourself questions like these: *Based on what I know about each trait's characteristics, what does this information tend to indicate? What response can I expect, based on this information? Does this graph tell me this person is task- or people-oriented? Does this person seem comfortable in a fast-paced situation, or better with a slower*

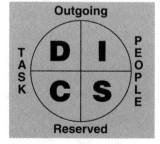

pace? How does it tie in to the DISC Model of Human Behavior (shown again at the bottom of page 254)? If the graph represents me, where can I protect myself from excesses, and where can I strengthen a potential weakness? If this graph represents someone else, where can I work to ensure success as we work together? How does this information help me to understand myself better? How does this information help me to understand this other person? How can I reasonably interpret this information to help myself and others grow in terms of cooperation, productivity and successful relationships? In other words, how can I utilize these insights to become a better observer — not an "analyzer" — of myself and others?

As we have said before, this information can be a valuable key to understanding ourselves and others, but it should not be used to predict success or failure in any relationship. This book is filled with practical ways to adapt and adjust to all types in order to achieve success. To truly understand each other, *communication* is important — talk with each other about perceived strengths and weakness, asking for comments and ideas that can help you understand what the graphs may indicate to you.

Someone once asked, "Is it better to have a lot of one particular style — for instance, a lot of 'D'?" I believe this is like asking, "How does *blue* taste?" It is really not a valid question. If you are looking for a leader, you cannot simply say, "'D' types are good at giving orders, so I'm looking only for a 'D' to do this job!" You may need a leader who can inspire commitment, or one who can support workers, or one who can comply with the job's existing parameters — each of which might be a challenge for a "D" type who has not learned how and when to adjust his style. So, you want to examine *blends* and *combinations* (see Chapters 2 and 3) to find an arrangement that permits maximum success for everyone involved.

With this background information, you will find the following *Appendices* very informative, complete with charts and explanations of all twenty-nine, various behavior style blends.

WHO DO YOU THINK YOU ARE ANYWAY?

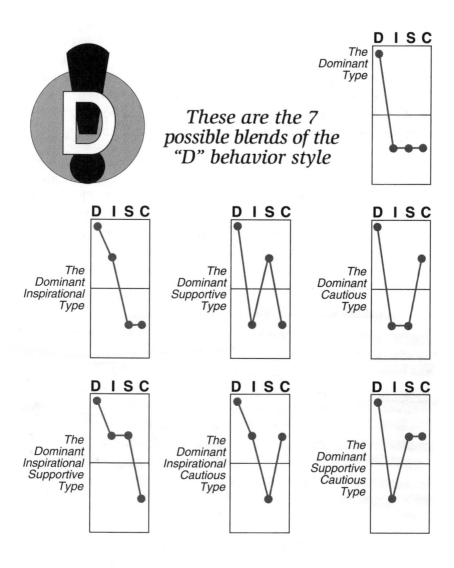

These are the 7 possible blends of the "D" behavior style

The Dominant Type

The Dominant Inspirational Type

The Dominant Supportive Type

The Dominant Cautious Type

The Dominant Inspirational Supportive Type

The Dominant Inspirational Cautious Type

The Dominant Supportive Cautious Type

Appendix B

Understanding the Seven "D" Blends

The seven possible blends involving predominate "D" traits are shown at the left — and in this chapter, two pages are devoted to explaining each of these blends.

Because the goal of this information is to help you understand yourself and others, it makes sense to start by first understanding your own blend. Look at your "educated guess" graph, which you completed on page 24. See whether your "D," your "I," your "S," or your "C" has the highest plotting point. Then you will know which of these four chapters to check for information on your style. Next, look to see if any of the other three plotting points are also above the midline on your "basic" graph. This will tell you which blend to read about.

You may want to complete a Personality Insights *"Style Analysis"* to get an accurate, objective appraisal. An order form with a special discount may be found in the back of this book. Thousands of our readers and customers have completed this assessment. It is not a test — there are no right or wrong answers. It is simply a tool to help you better understand yourself... and others.

Note: When we refer to a "D with I" blend, it is not the same as an "I with D" blend. Similarly, a "C with S" blend is not the same as an "S with C" blend. For the sake of explanation, we will refer to a blend that is primarily "D" with two secondary traits of "I" and "C" as a "D with I and C"— regardless of whether the "I" is higher than the "C," or the "C" is higher than the "I." As you read the description of your own blend, the strength and influence of your secondary traits will probably relate closely to their position on your graph.

The "D" Type Personality

The Dominant type

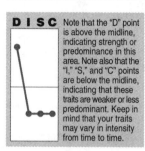

D I S C Note that the "D" point is above the midline, indicating strength or predominance in this area. Note also that the "I," "S," and "C" points are below the midline, indicating that these traits are weaker or less predominant. Keep in mind that your traits may vary in intensity from time to time.

The **Dominant** type personality likes to be in charge. They are task-oriented and enjoy seeing projects completed quickly and efficiently. They are uncomfortable when under someone else's control. They like to be the boss and give directions. They love a challenge — the bigger, the better! They have a desire to "win at any cost." Never tell them "it won't work;" they will prove you wrong. They make things happen. Because of their high-risk, adventurous attitude, they create opportunities (and jobs) for other people. They are great at developing projects, but they need to pay closer attention to the *people* they involve in those projects.

Two character traits they should seek and cultivate are *self-control* and *self-discipline*. When these qualities are in place, "D" types can use their energy to create many good events and projects. They should work on being more friendly and warm toward people. Their insensitivity to their own feelings can make them appear to be too strong with other people at times.

A popular T-shirt shows a basketball player springing from the floor, above the heads and hands of the rival team, getting off a three-point shot. The back of the shirt reads: "You miss 100% of all the shots you do not take!" This may be the high "D" thought for the year!

According to Target Training research, 1.2% of the population has a Dominant-only style.

"D" Action Plan:

1. *Value to Organization:* Thinks big; deadline conscious; competitive; able to handle many varied activities; few dull moments; changes gears and adjusts quickly

2. *Ideal Environment:* Freedom from supervision; new products and ideas to work on; forum to express ideas and viewpoints; non-routine work with opportunity for advancement or expansion

3. *How They See Themselves Under Pressure:* Pioneering; adventurous; upbeat; competitive; fearless leader

4. *How Others See Them Under Pressure:* Nervy; "gutsy"; abrasive; rough; firm; pointed

5. *Keys to Motivating — this behavior style wants:* Opportunity for rapid advancement; unusual assignments; independence; control of their own destiny; new or challenging opportunities

6. *Keys to Managing — this behavior style needs:* Skill in adjusting their intensity appropriately to match the situation; Put rules in writing; an awareness of parameters; respect for other people's personal property; to understand the importance of annual medical evaluation, because of their stressful level of activity

7. *Areas for Improvement:* Learn to be more warm and friendly, more supportive of other people's plans; more careful and cautious; remember that "all that glitters is not gold"; remember to listen

When you work with the "D" type:

DO: Expect acceptance without a lot of questions; take issue with *facts* but not the *person* when you disagree; present your case efficiently; verify that your message was heard; provide alternative choices for making their own decisions

DON'T: Be disorganized or messy; forget or lose things; distract them from the business at hand; let disagreement reflect on them personally; approach them with a ready-made decision that does not allow for their input or choice

The "D with I" Blend

The Dominant / Inspirational type

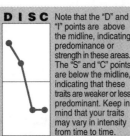

DISC Note that the "D" and "I" points are above the midline, indicating predominance or strength in these areas. The "S" and "C" points are below the midline, indicating that these traits are weaker or less predominant. Keep in mind that your traits may vary in intensity from time to time.

The **Dominant/Inspirational** type is very active and outgoing. These are action-oriented individuals, who enjoy completing *tasks* but also enjoy *people*. Activity excites and energizes them — difficult assignments make their blood flow faster! They are motivated by big opportunities. If pressed between making a hard decision that will impact either the overall organization or just a few people, their "D" will win out and they will decide in favor of the organization. To them, "The show must go on!" They usually have the "start-up" skills required for any job. And they possess the people skills to see that everyone is included in the process. They have a strong need for variety and change, and they can become "overbearing" at times. They need to remember that they do not always have to take the lead; it is all right to help and support others, too.

Overall, "D/I's" tend to have a good balance between task-oriented and people-oriented skills. They usually communicate well, and they are genuinely interested in people. They sometimes have difficulty staying focused. They move through life at a fast pace. Their philosophy is expressed in the currently popular slogan: "If you're not living on the edge, you're taking up too much space!" They would do well to slow down occasionally, to "stop and smell the roses."

According to Target Training research, 12.8% of the population has a blend of Dominant and Inspirational traits.

"D/I" Action Plan:

1. *Value to Organization:* Has the ability to handle many activities; can change gears quickly; initiates activity; bottom line oriented; likes variety

2. *Ideal Environment:* Working with a manager who makes quick decisions; new products and ideas to work on; a support team with a sense of urgency; the opportunity for rapid advancement

3. *How They See Themselves Under Pressure:* Competitive; confident; pioneering; assertive; positive; winner

4. *How Others See Them Under Pressure:* Egotistical; nervy; demanding; controlling; aggressive; opinionated

5. *Keys to Motivating — this behavior style wants:* Authority to take risks to achieve results; no close supervision; excitement and prestige; opportunity to work hard and play hard; a new challenge

6. *Keys to Managing — this behavior style needs:* Ability to adjust personal intensity to match the situation; to be confronted when they break the rules; an appreciation of slower-paced people; periods of reduced activity to preserve health and relieve stress

7. *Areas for Improvement:* Slow down a little; think things through longer; do not force issues too quickly; allow others to voice their views; realize that working with others requires patience

When working with the "D/I" type:

DO: Use their jargon; be open; provide probability of success and effectiveness of options; give "strokes" for involvement; understand their sporadic listening skills; realize they may need to be "freed" at the appropriate time to start their own enterprise or business venture

DON'T: Be redundant; ask useless questions; ramble or waste time; direct or order; assume that they have heard what you said; distract their minds from business when on the job

The "D with S" Blend

The Dominant / Supportive type

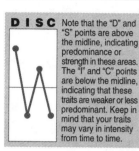

D I S C Note that the "D" and "S" points are above the midline, indicating predominance or strength in these areas. The "I" and "C" points are below the midline, indicating that these traits are weaker or less predominant. Keep in mind that your traits may vary in intensity from time to time.

The **Dominant/Supportive** type is different because their two "above average" traits tend to contradict each other. On one hand, this person likes to be in charge of a situation, but on the other hand, there is a strong desire to offer helpful support. This profile is not as common as other styles. It shows strong task-orientation, but also an enjoyment of people. "D/S" types tend to be somewhat more outgoing than reserved, but they are a little uncomfortable if they are "put in the limelight" too much. A good "D/S" vocational example is a nurse, who must be in control of the patient, while at the same time being supportive and helpful, meeting the patient's needs. While they seem paradoxical, this can be a dynamic coupling of traits.

"D/S" blends are usually stubborn and tenacious. They like to finish what they start and are very thorough in the process. They usually prefer working alongside, or with, just a few people. They also like to operate at their own pace. They would prefer that others not "look over their shoulder," which makes them feel pressured or rushed. They like to rely on their hard work and patience while looking into a situation, rather than going on feelings or intuition. They are tough-minded and do not back down easily from confrontation.

According to Target Training research, 3.1% of the population has a blend of Dominant and Supportive traits.

"D/S" Action Plan:

1. *Value to Organization:* Has a creative approach in solving problems; always looking for logical solutions; presents facts well; handles emotions; objective and realistic

2. *Ideal Environment:* Private office or work area; clear data to interpret and analyze; wants to be part of the team, but does not like catering to office politics; prefers a decisive team; likes people who communicate in a clear manner

3. *How They See Themselves Under Pressure:* Logical; incisive; independent; individualistic; self-reliant; competitive

4. *How Others See Them Under Pressure:* Initiator; dominant; forceful; direct; high risk taker; dislikes losing

5. *Keys to Motivating — this behavior style wants:* Opportunity to demonstrate personal skills; position and titles; control of a project or staff; a leadership position that can produce measurable results; to be seen "in charge"

6. *Keys to Managing — this behavior style needs:* Time to warm up to people; logical answers in logical order; someone to believe in his dreams; to know what is expected; skills in making people feel part of the group; to be warm and close when appropriate

7. *Areas for Improvement:* Be a little more willing to change their minds; be less blunt; show more enthusiasm; work more cooperatively with others in a group setting

When working with the "D/S" type:

DO: Support an environment where they can be efficient; maintain a level of openness to their views; let them decide when they want to talk socially; be supportive of their plans; provide options and choice for their decisions

DON'T: Make statements that intimidate or accuse; be superficial; be too intense in your focus, leaving them little room for input; be insensitive; leave your statements open to interpretation

The "D with C" Blend

The Dominant / Cautious type

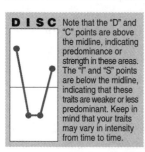

DISC Note that the "D" and "C" points are above the midline, indicating predominance or strength in these areas. The "I" and "S" points are below the midline, indicating that these traits are weaker or less predominant. Keep in mind that your traits may vary in intensity from time to time.

The **Dominant/Cautious** type is *very* task-oriented. People with this blend can accomplish incredible amounts of work in a brief time. Their high focus on task accomplishment is not as common as the other "D" type blends. They sometimes appear to be cold or hard-hearted, but this is because their main focus is on whether quality work is being generated. They are bottom line oriented. Their "D" says, "Get the job done!" Their "C" says, "Don't go broke in the process." They are quick to tell you what *they* think — and also to tell you what *you* should be doing! They do not like to "baby-sit" people. They can be overly critical at times, because they care more about getting the job done than how others feel about it. They *think* their way through life.

They do not feel much sympathy for those who do not do what they were supposed to do. They want you to be responsible and self-disciplined, to expend the necessary energy to accomplish the task. (In other words, if you are sick "don't *call* in… *crawl* in!") They need to work on being a little more friendly with people and warmer in their social relationships. They are pace setters, and they are easily bored with routine, mundane work assignments.

According to Target Training research, 2.6% of the population has a blend of Dominant and Cautious traits.

"D/C" Action Plan:

1. *Value to Organization:* Places high value on time, has a sense of urgency; can be a self-starter; challenges complacency; has few dull moments; initiates activity

2. *Ideal Environment:* New products to create and ideas to work on; working for an efficient manager who is able to make quick

decisions; able to express ideas, viewpoints and expertise, able to be in control; knowing that efforts will be rewarded according to his/her expectations

3. *How They See Themselves Under Pressure:* Likes a challenge; attempts the impossible; tough; a dreamer; competitive; bottom line oriented.

4. *How Others See Them Under Pressure:* Overbearing; caustic; ambitious; dictatorial; unfeeling; pressing

5. *Keys to Motivating — this behavior style wants:* A support staff for detail work; to know the agenda for the meeting; quality work; sound reasoning behind work assignments; freedom from restriction; new territory to conquer

6. *Keys to Managing — this behavior style needs:* To cooperate more with team members; to recognize opinions other than their own; patience with the slower-paced; to recognize other styles' basic needs; to compliment another person's good work; to give people a second chance

7. *Areas for Improvement:* Learn to be more sensitive to the feelings of others, more understanding of other points-of-view; be less critical of the performance of their peers; be able to lighten up and laugh a little more

When working with the "D/C" type:

DO: Come prepared; know your objectives; be isolated from interruption; leave nothing to chance; persuade and motivate by referring to objectives and results; provide systems that work

DON'T: Let them change the topic until you are finished; offer a guarantee when there is risk involved; dwell on details too long; assume anything; let disagreement reflect on them personally; expect them to be very sociable

The "D with I and S" Blend

The Dominant / Inspirational / Supportive type

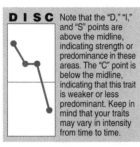

D I S C Note that the "D," "I," and "S" points are above the midline, indicating strength or predominance in these areas. The "C" point is below the midline, indicating that this trait is weaker or less predominant. Keep in mind that your traits may vary in intensity from time to time.

The **Dominant/Inspirational/ Supportive** type is focused on getting a task completed, but in that process demonstrates a high regard for people. They focus more on the overall goal than on the small details that tend to "bog down" the process. They have a high energy level and are constantly on the go. Their strong need for social involvement helps to balance out their dominant nature. So, they are able to "keep an ear to the ground," and they have the ability to move both *tasks* and *people* in a forward, ongoing direction. The one area where they need better focus is in attention to small details.

This style, having a low "C," needs to exhibit more caution, to recognize that their "blind side" is in observing the little things they rush past while focusing on the big picture. They want freedom to run things their own way. They are not afraid of controversy or conflict. They can be very assertive. They like to work at their own pace. They are persuasive and persistent. Once their minds are made up, it is difficult to get them to change. They are steady and stable, displaying lots of self-confidence when working with people.

According to Target Training research, 7.3% of the population has a blend of Dominant, Inspirational and Supportive traits.

"D/I/S" Action Plan:

1. *Value to Organization:* Self-starter; likes to be involved in many projects at once; thinks big; supports or opposes strongly; accomplishes goals through people; pioneering

2. *Ideal Environment:* A team where each member plays a specifically designated role; difficult assignments with

appropriate recognition when complete; lots of activity and lots of people; measurable goals; relaxed supervision; a place to test the limits for growth

3. *How They See Themselves Under Pressure:* Focused; strong; independent; steady; persistent; intent

4. *How Others See Them Under Pressure:* Stubborn, unsystematic; unyielding; bold; tough; arbitrary

5. *Keys to Motivating — this behavior style wants:* To be seen as a leader; opportunity to enjoy their work; exposure to those who can recognize, praise and appreciate their ability; freedom from details and "minutia" work; ability to control their own future; new territory to conquer

6. *Keys to Managing — this behavior style needs:* Supporting helpers with patience for excessively detailed work; "hands on" assignments to guide and direct; identification with winners; prestige and status; to understand that rules and limits do apply

7. *Areas for Improvement:* Be more cautious and calculating in evaluating a situation; realize that it is okay to wait and think things over before beginning a task; learn to be less blunt; be more flexible in positions on issues

When working with the "D/I/S" type:

DO: Provide "Yes" or "No" answers, not "Maybe;" present the facts logically; plan your meetings efficiently; motivate and persuade them by referring to results; define problems in writing; appeal to the benefits which will be received

DON'T: Take credit for their accomplishments; direct or "boss around;" let their outgoing nature overpower you; focus on small details; force them to do repetitive, boring tasks; expect them to be withdrawn — they will be quick to speak

The "D with I and C" Blend

The Dominant / Inspirational / Cautious type

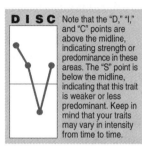

Note that the "D," "I," and "C" points are above the midline, indicating strength or predominance in these areas. The "S" point is below the midline, indicating that this trait is weaker or less predominant. Keep in mind that your traits may vary in intensity from time to time.

The **Dominant/Inspirational/Cautious** type is constantly focused on getting the job done, but likes to have fun in the process. They like to be on the go, but not aimlessly. They enjoy completing a task while mixing business and pleasure. They are quick to speak, especially when giving orders or telling other people what to do. They expect quick results and may speak too hastily; they often neglect the planning that is necessary to see that the job is done well. They may talk others into doing most of the work while they supervise. If their "C" is fairly high, they may complete the final details themselves, to assure correctness.

Their ability to be supportive of others often needs improvement. They need to demonstrate more sensitivity to people with whom they come in contact. They are not focused on the "S" factors of safety, sensitivity, security and stability because they accept that risks occur in completing any task. They want things done correctly, but will usually "go with the flow" if they believe those in-progress decisions or modifications are in the project's best interests.

According to Target Training research, 3.5% of the population has a blend of Dominant, Inspirational and Cautious traits.

"D/I/C" Action Plan:

1. *Value to Organization:* Likes spontaneity; appreciates attention to detail; challenges the status quo; initiates activity rather than waiting for something to happen; is deadline conscious; knows a little about a lot; good mixer

2. *Ideal Environment:* A place where meetings are efficient and bottom-line oriented; orderly, efficient work areas; fast-paced

activity with productive results; opportunity to express viewpoint; tried and proven products to improve upon; a support team with a positive attitude

3. *How They See Themselves Under Pressure:* Flexible; determined and resolute; alert; energetic; smart; quick

4. *How Others See Them Under Pressure:* Restless; hasty and impatient; unapproachable; impulsive; intense; detached

5. *Keys to Motivating — this behavior style wants:* New challenges to resolve; more efficient use of time; other outside involvements; wide scope of activity; opportunity to demonstrate skills

6. *Keys to Managing — this behavior style needs:* Project deadlines; a better appreciation for slower-moving people; honest feedback about their priorities; not to take on too many challenges at once; to be careful about "off-the-cuff" remarks that can be too personal

7. *Areas for Improvement:* Learn to thank others involved in their success; support ideas of team members; listen *more* and talk *less;* be flexible when people have unexpected, special needs

When working with the "D/I/C" type:

DO: Stick to business; give strokes for their commitment and involvement; be open and honest; allow opportunity to "double check" detailed work; support an efficiency-based environment; leave nothing to chance

DON'T: Expect them to "baby-sit" anyone; think their outgoing nature means they are your best friends; be shocked if they change plans or allegiances halfway into a project; ask useless or rhetorical questions; make recommendations without first asking for their input

The "D with S and C" Blend

The Dominant / Supportive / Cautious type

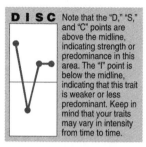

D I S C Note that the "D," "S," and "C" points are above the midline, indicating strength or predominance in this area. The "I" point is below the midline, indicating that this trait is weaker or less predominant. Keep in mind that your traits may vary in intensity from time to time.

The **Dominant/Supportive/ Cautious** type, while having active and outgoing traits, also tends to maintain a conservative viewpoint. They are very concerned about getting their tasks accomplished, while having warm hearts for the needs and feelings of others. Although they want to take risks, they weigh the benefits and consequences a little longer before jumping into things. They tend to be worrisome. They enjoy people, but do not enjoy being the center of attention. They seem hard to please, because of their "overachiever" nature.

This type knows how to be diplomatic and includes people in their plans. They are intellectually curious and enjoy difficult tasks, sometimes wrestling with perfectionism. They think things through and approach their work logically. This type, having a low "I," may be distant or aloof. They may be slow to speak and, when they do, may seem a little blunt.

Sometimes this style is seen as stubborn or opinionated. However, they see it simply as part of the price one pays for success. They love to win and hate to lose. Because their people skills are somewhat lacking, they tend to display anger openly and quickly when they feel others are taking advantage of them. They are goal driven and are focused on getting results.

According to Target Training research, 6.4% of the population has a blend of Dominant, Supportive and Cautious traits.

"D/S/C" Action Plan:

1. *Value to Organization:* Self-starter; thinks big; tough-minded; tenacious; places a high value on time; future-oriented

2. *Ideal Environment:* Projects that produce tangible results;

private office or work area; non-routine work with challenge and opportunity; chance to lead the team; evaluation based on results

3. *How They See Themselves Under Pressure:* Logical; analytical; factual; clear cut; penetrating; crisp

4. *How Others See Them Under Pressure:* Pessimistic; skeptical; superior; critical; blunt

5. *Keys to Motivating — this behavior style wants:* To be seen as a leader; prestige and position; to control the destiny of others; limited socializing; opportunity to demonstrate skills; new challenges

6. *Keys to Managing — this behavior style needs:* An awareness of how their attitudes and actions impact other people; standardized operating procedures in writing; to display empathy for people who approach life differently from their own viewpoint; to understand their role on the team; to know what is expected and how evaluation occurs

7. *Areas for Improvement:* Learn to be more positive; be willing to laugh at themselves; stop worrying and "be happy"; to go out of their way to speak warmly to people

When working with the "D/S/C" type:

DO: Be clear, specific, to the point; use facts and figures; give pros and cons on ideas; stick to business; be patient and persistent; recognize their ability to be both a good leader and a loyal supporter

DON'T: Ramble on or waste their time; be disorganized; make statements you cannot prove; pretend to be an expert when you are not; give orders; be superficial

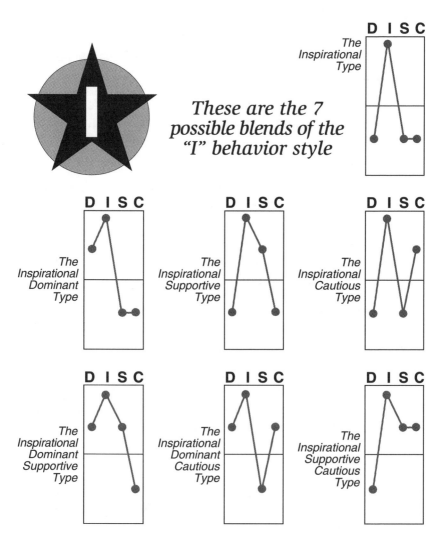

These are the 7 possible blends of the "I" behavior style

D I S C
The
Inspirational
Type

D I S C
The
Inspirational
Dominant
Type

D I S C
The
Inspirational
Supportive
Type

D I S C
The
Inspirational
Cautious
Type

D I S C
The
Inspirational
Dominant
Supportive
Type

D I S C
The
Inspirational
Dominant
Cautious
Type

D I S C
The
Inspirational
Supportive
Cautious
Type

Appendix C

Understanding the Seven "I" Blends

The seven possible blends involving predominate "I" traits are shown at the left — and in this chapter, two pages are devoted to explaining each of these blends.

Because the goal of this information is to help you understand yourself and others, it makes sense to start by first understanding your own blend. Look at your "educated guess" graph, which you completed on page 24. See whether your "D," your "I," your "S," or your "C" has the highest plotting point. Then you will know which of these four chapters to check for information on your style. Next, look to see if any of the other three plotting points are also above the midline on your "basic" graph. This will tell you which blend to read about.

You may want to complete a Personality Insights *"Style Analysis"* to get an accurate, objective appraisal. An order form with a special discount may be found in the back of this book. Thousands of our readers and customers have completed this assessment. It is not a test — there are no right or wrong answers. It is simply a tool to help you better understand yourself... and others.

Note: When we refer to a "I with D" blend, it is not the same as a "D with I" blend. Similarly, a "C with S" blend is not the same as an "S with C" blend. For the sake of explanation, we will refer to a blend that is primarily "I" with two secondary traits of "D" and "S" as an "I with D and S"— regardless of whether the "D" is higher than the "S," or the "S" is higher than the "D." As you read the description of your own blend, the strength and influence of your secondary traits will probably relate closely to their position on your graph.

The "I" Type Personality

The Inspirational type

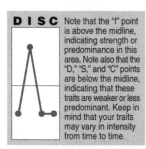

D I S C Note that the "I" point is above the midline, indicating strength or predominance in this area. Note also that the "D," "S," and "C" points are below the midline, indicating that these traits are weaker or less predominant. Keep in mind that your traits may vary in intensity from time to time.

The **Inspirational** type enjoys people — almost too much! They are born entertainers. To them, all the world's a stage… and "there's no business like show business!" They do not have to *look* for a "party;" they *take their own* with them wherever they go! This type does not like feeling isolated. If they must work on a project alone, they will lose interest quickly. "I's" have a short attention span and have difficulty completing long-range projects. They would rather work on short-term goals with immediate results and rewards. They *can* complete long-term projects; it is just much more *difficult* for them to stay focused. They enjoy being around their friends. They usually have lots of stories to tell because every event is an exciting adventure.

Recognition and approval are very important to these people. They want — no, *need* — others to like them. They have an extremely high level of trust in others and want the same in return. Because they are unable to maintain focus over a long period of time, they need personal accountability. They must work on *task-completion* skills and *listening* while others talk, rather than simply thinking about what they want to say next.

According to Target Training research, 1% of the population has an Inspirational-only style.

"I" Action Plan:

1. *Value to Organization:* People-oriented; team player; verbalizes feelings; optimistic; enthusiastic; accomplishes goals through influencing others

2. *Ideal Environment:* Warm and friendly; freedom to move around a lot; a supervisor with whom he can associate;

freedom from lengthy, detailed reports; assignments with many people contacts; lots of activity

3. *How They See Themselves Under Pressure:* Upbeat; fun; enthusiastic; optimistic; persuasive; spontaneous

4. *How Others See Them Under Pressure:* Overly confident; unrealistic; talkative; poor listener; self-promoting; exaggerative; unpredictable

5. *Keys to Motivating — this behavior style wants:* To be part of a team; recognition for achieved results; freedom from details; minimal oversight; participation in meetings focusing on future planning; to be trusted

6. *Keys to Managing — this behavior style needs:* More logic, less emotion; space to mix business and pleasure; consistency; help with time management; to learn setting and sticking with priorities; participatory management

7. *Areas for Improvement:* Be less excitable; control or lessen their need for approval and external validation; let others receive attention and recognition; research the facts before telling others about the situation

When working with the "I" type:

DO: Be informed and friendly; provide examples from people they view as important; give strokes for their involvement; support their big ideas; expect acceptance without a lot of questions; remember they are short term oriented

DON'T: Expect to put them in positions with no accountability requirements; take credit for their ideas; assume they have heard what you said; let them change the topic if you are not finished; talk down to them; be cold or tight-lipped

The "I with D" Blend

The Inspirational / Dominant type

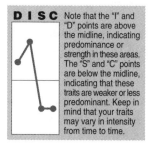

Note that the "I" and "D" points are above the midline, indicating predominance or strength in these areas. The "S" and "C" points are below the midline, indicating that these traits are weaker or less predominant. Keep in mind that your traits may vary in intensity from time to time.

The **Inspirational/Dominant** type is very outgoing and enjoys being with people. This type has a driving need to accomplish tasks — to do great exploits. They have lots of "nervous energy" and are constantly on-the-go. Their need for activity often causes others to misunderstand them, and some people feel nervous just being around them. But "I/D" type people feel guilty when they relax. They often appear restless or unfocused. They may have a dozen projects going at once, with none of them producing any tangible results — but just give them a little more time and one of their risky ventures will pay off! This personality type could benefit from being more cautious before jumping into a situation. They need to remember the carpenter's maxim: "Measure twice — cut once!" Their optimism is contagious, but without accountability and personal responsibility, it can lead to wasted potential and personal emptiness.

Often, their *talking* will inspire others' *doing*. So, the "I/D" person needs to remember to share the limelight with others. They are incurably optimistic and know how to make things happen.

According to Target Training research, 12.8% of the population has a blend of Inspirational and Dominant traits.

"I/D" Action Plan:

1. *Value to Organization:* Pioneering; builds confidence in others; positive; sense of urgency; sense of accountability; can support or oppose strongly

2. *Ideal Environment:* A very tolerant manager; freedom to "come and go"; difficult assignments in areas they find challenging; varied work activities; opportunity to try new ideas or

approaches; a support staff for details

3. *How They See Themselves Under Pressure:* A motivator; good communicator; charming; winsome; delightful; attracting others

4. *How Others See Them Under Pressure:* Self-advancing; self-serving; "pushy"; unrealistic; driven; a poor listener

5. *Keys to Motivating — this behavior style wants:* Public praise and recognition; excitement; active participation on the team; feedback on performance; opportunity to develop people and organizations; optimistic co-workers

6. *Keys to Managing — this behavior style needs:* To focus on results and productivity; people to associate and work with; to handle routine paperwork more efficiently; to concentrate on tasks rather than socializing; to understand that they cannot make everyone happy

7. *Areas for Improvement:* Remember the difference between talking and doing; don't expect everyone to see things as they do — and don't have hurt feelings about it; have a "quiet moment" each day; remember, optimism is great, but "realism" doesn't hurt either

When working with the "I/D" type:

DO: Provide solutions, not opinions; include time for socializing; understand that this person hears "No!" as "Maybe..."; understand that this person hears "Maybe..." as "Yes!"; be bright and cheerful; double check their work for oversights

DON'T: Leave decisions hanging in the air; be negative or pessimistic; talk down to them; think they will run out of something to say; be too talk-oriented; deal with the abstract

The "I with S" Blend

The Inspirational / Supportive type

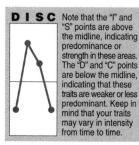

D I S C Note that the "I" and "S" points are above the midline, indicating predominance or strength in these areas. The "D" and "C" points are below the midline, indicating that these traits are weaker or less predominant. Keep in mind that your traits may vary in intensity from time to time.

The **Inspirational/Supportive** type really enjoys being around people. Perhaps more than any other type, they have the capacity to love, enjoy and desire the friendship of everyone they meet. They sometimes have trouble keeping their thoughts and emotions to themselves. They are very expressive and transparent. They may have a difficult time keeping a secret. It is not that they cannot be trusted — it is just that they enjoy talking so much, and sometimes words accidentally slip out of their mouths before they think. They also have vivid imaginations. They can daydream too much if they are not careful.

The key to this type's success is personal responsibility. Because their task-orientation ('D" and "C" traits) is lower, they can have a very difficult time staying focused on a job until completion. They need to remember the difference between "talking" and "doing." Just because they have talked about doing something doesn't mean they actually plan to do it! Their happiness and enthusiasm about life is a worthy example from which we all can profit.

According to Target Training research, 12.1% of the population has a blend of Inspirational and Supportive traits.

"I/S" Action Plan:

1. *Value to Organization:* Enthusiastic; people-oriented; a "peace keeper;" optimistic; builds up others; big thinker; creative problem-solver

2. *Ideal Environment:* Regular meetings for recognition; a place where their ideas can be heard; assignments with high people contact; opportunity to tell some favorite stories; job with

incentives; office with name on the door

3. *How They See Themselves Under Pressure:* Alert; gregarious; fun-loving; unassuming; inspiring; optimistic

4. *How Others See Them Under Pressure:* Talkative; moody; poor listener; overselling; self-promoting; quick to jump to conclusions

5. *Keys to Motivating — this behavior style wants:* Activities that include the whole team; feeling of security; to be trusted; activities that don't infringe on family time; "strokes"

6. *Keys to Managing — this behavior style needs:* To be realistic; not to overestimate/exaggerate outcomes; help in organizational skills; documentation of expected results; a rational approach for getting from point "A" to point "B"; good record keeping systems

7. *Areas for Improvement:* Learn to listen more; repeat back what someone has said when and where appropriate; don't assume people are thinking along the same wavelength; accept the fact that good attitudes do not replace hard work; remember to let others talk

When working with the "I/S" type:

DO: Appeal to the "people" aspect of any project; expect their emotions to show; use objective, not subjective, criteria; include socializing time; set appropriate deadlines for goals; read their body language for approval or disapproval

DON'T: Expect this person to "double check" work; overcontrol the conversation; get sidetracked by "dreaming" with this person during working hours (rather, dream over lunchtime); ramble; focus on the abstract; legislate or talk down to this person

The "I with C" Blend

The Inspirational / Cautious type

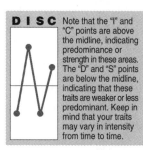

D I S C Note that the "I" and "C" points are above the midline, indicating predominance or strength in these areas. The "D" and "S" points are below the midline, indicating that these traits are weaker or less predominant. Keep in mind that your traits may vary in intensity from time to time.

The **Inspirational/Cautious** type has an unusual pattern consisting of two "opposite" sets of traits. Outgoing, people-oriented skills come across as warm and friendly, yet reserved, task-oriented skills create a built-in need to be productive and efficient. Their "I" says, "Let's look good," while their "C" says, "I don't want to be embarrassed." In other words, they not only have the ability to *talk* about getting the job done, they actually are not satisfied until they *see* it done. Their perfectionist tendencies often cause them to work on a project themselves, rather than designate someone else to do it. They want to be sure things are done in a correct manner. They would rather work with a group of people than by themselves, alone. However, they understand how to isolate themselves — for short periods of time — in order to accomplish the task at hand. Sometimes they feel guilty when they are "playing" because they worry their work isn't getting done. When they are working, they wish they could be having a little more fun.

This type has the people skills to make others feel accepted and the task ability to do any job.

According to Target Training research, 2.1% of the population has a blend of Inspirational and Cautious traits.

"I/C" Action Plan:

1. *Value to Organization:* Concerned about quality; positive sense of humor; turns problems into opportunities; builds confidence in others; adaptable; will gather data before making final decisions

2. *Ideal Environment:* A place where they can both hear and see a picture of the goal; prefers diplomatic relations; prefers a

more casual approach to a direct one

3. *How They See Themselves Under Pressure:* Optimistic; realistic; agreeable; charming; upbeat; dislikes being firm

4. *How Others See Them Under Pressure:* Glib; "wishy-washy"; obstinate; unrealistic; self-serving; poor listener

5. *Keys to Motivating — this behavior style wants:* A title; quality work with a "flair;" a manager who is a friend, rather than a taskmaster; a team approach to problem-solving; flexibility; participatory management practices; work assignments leading to tangible results

6. *Keys to Managing — this behavior style needs:* Help in controlling time; a priorities list; people to associate with; a way to *say* no when they *feel* no; to maintain focus on results; a way to avoid sacrificing productivity just to keep everyone happy

7. *Areas for Improvement:* Concentrate on meeting deadlines; develop ideas into reality, rather than just talking about them; use accurate data in reporting facts and figures; "stop and smell the roses" more often; don't scare people off by being too friendly too quickly

When working with the "I/C" type:

DO: Allow time for asking questions; understand their need for clarification — they want you to like them; provide practical evidence; use a timetable when implementing a new program; communicate details in writing; ask for their opinions

DON'T: Talk to them while you are upset or angry; make promises you cannot keep; use unreliable sources; use words that convey doom and gloom; rush their decision-making processes; be dictatorial

The "I with D and S" Blend

The Inspirational / Dominant / Supportive type

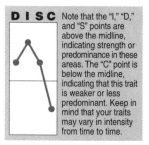

Note that the "I," "D," and "S" points are above the midline, indicating strength or predominance in these areas. The "C" point is below the midline, indicating that this trait is weaker or less predominant. Keep in mind that your traits may vary in intensity from time to time.

The **Inspirational/Dominant/Supportive** type is predominantly outgoing and friendly but also has a desire to lead and see that tasks are accomplished. "People skills" carry them through life. They are warm and accepting of others. They have the ability to stay focused on a job until it is completed. They may get help from as many outside sources as possible in order to complete a task. They know how to "borrow brains" by asking others for assistance — their friendly and persuasive nature allows them to *make* you *want* to help them! They like the team approach, and they don't mind sharing the credit — but they surely don't want the blame if things go wrong.

This type enjoys leading and being out in front on any project. They delegate fairly well. If they recognize their lack of caution, they can "cover their backs" by having someone double-check important details they may have overlooked or should overhaul. They need to slow down a little and think things through more thoroughly.

According to Target Training research, 7.3% of the population has a blend of Inspirational, Dominant and Supportive traits.

"I/D/S" Action Plan:

1. *Value to Organization:* Confident; accomplishes goals through people; creative problem-solver; warm and friendly; can do difficult assignments; produces lots of activity

2. *Ideal Environment:* People and activity; results-oriented team; opportunity to look good publicly; freedom from technicalities; place of importance (their own parking space)

3. *How They See Themselves Under Pressure:* Independent; fun;

pioneering; free-spirited; dedicated; inspiring

4. *How Others See Them Under Pressure:* Driven; stubborn; unsystematic; authoritative; resistant; disorderly

5. *Keys to Motivating — this behavior style wants:* A cheerful work environment; participation in group meetings; exposure to those who appreciate results; public praise; a support team for details and follow-up; independence

6. *Keys to Managing — this behavior style needs:* A tolerant boss who understands their style; freedom for a two-hour lunch provided results can be shown; an environment with lots of people; participatory management; accountability for responsibilities

7. *Areas for Improvement:* Remember the difference between giving real praise and mere flattery simply to get their own way; be more discreet in what they say casually; recognize their own shortcomings, rather than seeing them in others; validate and substantiate information rather than simply taking it at face value

When working with the "I/D/S" type:

DO: Understand that they may push the limits sometimes; remember that they "feel" their way through a situation, rather than "thinking" through it; seek their counsel regarding decisions; offer incentives for work completed correctly and on time; define the problem in writing

DON'T: Ramble on or be vague; simply give verbal instructions — this type needs examples or word pictures; be curt or short with them; leave decisions hanging in the air; be overbearing or "bossy"

The "I with D and C" Blend

The Inspirational / Dominant / Cautious type

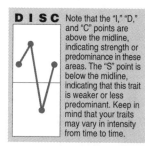

D I S C Note that the "I," "D," and "C" points are above the midline, indicating strength or predominance in these areas. The "S" point is below the midline, indicating that this trait is weaker or less predominant. Keep in mind that your traits may vary in intensity from time to time.

The **Inspirational/Dominant/ Cautious** type really enjoys people, but more so wants to see a job done well. These people could possibly be the best at recruiting others into an organization in order to become part of an effective team. Their *people* skills are high, helping them to have friendly, personal relationships. Their *task* skills are high, helping them to focus on a job through completion. Sometimes, they can seem a little too pushy or cold, and may be viewed as trying to manipulate others. It is not that they want to manipulate; it is just that they get so carried away with the potential they see that they want others to be a part of their dream. Because their supportive ("S") style is lower, they may lack follow-through in making you feel you can count on them in times of difficulty. If they can remember to be a little more reserved at times — and listen better — they will profit immensely.

These individuals are not afraid to tell others what they think needs to be done in order to succeed, but they may lack the patience required to help complete that project or goal.

According to Target Training research, 3.5% of the population has a blend of Inspirational, Dominant and Cautious traits.

"I/D/C" Action Plan:

1. *Value to Organization:* Builds confidence in others; may keep a project moving when others quit; knows when to speak and when to be quiet; exhibits a sense of urgency; is a good mixer; ability to handle many varied activities

2. *Ideal Environment:* A place where there is a sense of accomplishment; a leadership role; support staff for follow-up or thoughtfulness; new ideas or products to work on; contact

with people; being part of task completion

3. *How They See Themselves Under Pressure:* Positive; sociable; systematic; active; quick-witted; efficient

4. *How Others See Them Under Pressure:* Hyperactive; impatient; demanding; biased; restless; discontent

5. *Keys to Motivating — this behavior style wants:* More time in the day; several interrelated projects to work on at once; fast-paced assignments; energetic co-workers; to see the pros and cons of an issue; few dull moments

6. *Keys to Managing — this behavior style needs:* To be a little more reliable while "on the move"; a wide range of operation; many problems to solve; a "forced" vacation, if necessary; to be more appreciative of slower-moving people; to realize one can be "so right" as to be wrong

7. *Areas for Improvement:* Not try to do everything at once; learn to pace themselves better, not spread themselves too thin; not let perfectionism degenerate into indecisiveness

When working with the "I/D/C" type:

DO: Ask for their ideas and thoughts regarding a situation; include socializing time; be isolated from interruption when working; verify that your message has been heard, allowing them time to repeat what they think your message was all about; be open to their new ideas

DON'T: "Butt in" while they are talking; talk too slowly; ramble while telling a story; take credit for their work; monopolize the conversation; be dictatorial

The "I with S and C" Blend

The Inspirational / Supportive / Cautious type

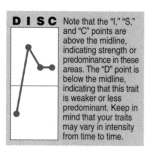

D I S C Note that the "I," "S," and "C" points are above the midline, indicating strength or predominance in these areas. The "D" point is below the midline, indicating that this trait is weaker or less predominant. Keep in mind that your traits may vary in intensity from time to time.

The **Inspirational/Supportive/ Cautious** type is outgoing and friendly, but not overly so. Although they enjoy crowds very much, at times they also enjoy the company of just a few close friends. Because of their warm people skills, others "attach" to them emotionally almost at once. This type goes out of their way to help because they want to be liked. They tend to be fairly "street-smart" and enjoy negotiating a good deal. Their task skills help them to complete a job, but they are not satisfied if people are excluded or "stepped on" in the process — their issue is not simply getting the job done, but accommodating people's needs in the process.

Because they do not like confrontation, they sometimes let people "run over" them. They would rather "take flight" than fight! They do not like to argue and prefer peaceful relationships to adversarial ones. They want success for their co-workers and encourage them to stay focused. Usually, they are steadfast, lifelong friends. They need to be more discerning about whom they trust.

According to Target Training research, 28.5% of the population has a blend of Inspirational, Supportive and Cautious traits.

"I/S/C" Action Plan:

1. *Value to Organization:* Excellent in solving human relations problems; puts strangers at ease quickly; negotiates conflicts; a confidence builder; good team player; works respectfully within organizational structure

2. *Ideal Environment:* A manager who gives positive feedback; an informal setting where people feel relaxed and at home; opportunities to mix business and pleasure; practical procedures;

amiable, even-tempered co-workers

3. *How They See Themselves Under Pressure:* Flexible; diplomatic; warm; optimistic; predictable; cooperative

4. *How Others See Them Under Pressure:* Traditional; fearful; wary; hesitant; intimidated; overly compliant

5. *Keys to Motivating — this behavior style wants:* To be liked by everyone; to create "life and enthusiasm" in their environment; to plan their work and then work their plan; to understand expectations in order to please; a boss who is available to discuss key moves; a secure future

6. *Keys to Managing — this behavior style needs:* Positive, rather than negative, statements; a manager who makes thoughtful decisions; unstressed surroundings; depth and specialization in a project; help in time management; to stick to commitments

7. *Areas for Improvement:* Remember that criticism does not indicate personal rejection; emotions can overrule sound judgment; be quicker to think and slower to speak

When working with the "I/S/C" type:

DO: Remember they are "peacekeepers;" insist they go the "second mile" when working on a project; avoid lecturing, keep conversation at the "discussion" level; use varied tones that communicate sincerity; let them ask questions; be persistent

DON'T: Put them in disciplinarian positions; make them take uncalculated risks; hurry or rush them; think they will "stick with it" if the going gets too tough; make them do cold-calling; think their outward appearance or manner reveals their true inward thoughts

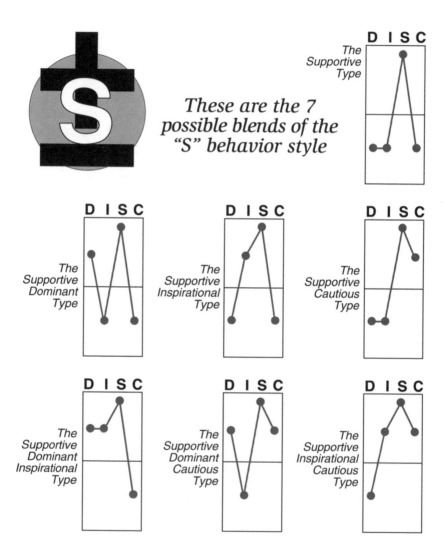

These are the 7 possible blends of the "S" behavior style

The Supportive Type

The Supportive Dominant Type

The Supportive Inspirational Type

The Supportive Cautious Type

The Supportive Dominant Inspirational Type

The Supportive Dominant Cautious Type

The Supportive Inspirational Cautious Type

Appendix D

Understanding the Seven "S" Blends

The seven possible blends involving predominate "S" traits are shown at the left — and in this chapter, two pages are devoted to explaining each of these blends.

Because the goal of this information is to help you understand yourself and others, it makes sense to start by first understanding your own blend. Look at your "educated guess" graph, which you completed on page 24. See whether your "D," your "I," your "S," or your "C" has the highest plotting point. Then you will know which of these four chapters to check for information on your style. Next, look to see if any of the other three plotting points are also above the midline on your "basic" graph. This will tell you which blend to read about.

You may want to complete a Personality Insights *"Style Analysis"* to get an accurate, objective appraisal. An order form with a special discount may be found in the back of this book. Thousands of our readers and customers have completed this assessment. It is not a test — there are no right or wrong answers. It is simply a tool to help you better understand yourself... and others.

Note: When we refer to an "S with C" blend, it is not the same as a "C with S" blend. Similarly, a "D with I" blend is not the same as an "I with D" blend. For the sake of explanation, we will refer to a blend that is primarily "S" with two secondary traits of "C" and "I" as an "S with C and I"— regardless of whether the "C" is higher than the "I," or the "I" is higher than the "C." As you read the description of your own blend, the strength and influence of your secondary traits will probably relate closely to their position on your graph.

The "S" Type Personality

The Supportive type

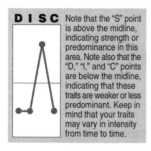

D I S C Note that the "S" point is above the midline, indicating strength or predominance in this area. Note also that the "D," "I," and "C" points are below the midline, indicating that these traits are weaker or less predominant. Keep in mind that your traits may vary in intensity from time to time.

The **Supportive** type is "home" to the sweetest people you will ever meet. They are always helping people and putting others' needs ahead of their own. They mainly function on emotions, rather than logic. They have an extremely difficult time saying no to anyone. They would rather have you like them than to get their own way in an issue. Their view of life can be summarized as "peace at any price." While they may seem shy, they really enjoy people. But because of their reserved nature, they would rather be approached than have to approach someone and initiate a conversation. They prefer to stay with the same steady, stable environment, rather than launch out into a risk-taking adventure.

They do not like surprises and get physically uncomfortable when an argument or conflict suddenly arises. They are chameleon-like: adapting and adjusting to their environment inconspicuously. They need to be a little more bold, and willing to say "no" more often. In a supporting role, they will stay, even when the rest of the team desserts you! They mix well with every other personality style and are "true blue" to the end.

According to Target Training research, 0.9% of the population has a Supportive-only style.

"S" Action Plan:

1. *Value to Organization:* Excellent team player; steady worker; very consistent; shows respect for authority; sticks with projects through completion; receptive to new ideas

2. *Ideal Environment:* Knows exact expectations; practical work procedures; minimal co-worker conflict; very little anger; "stable and predictable" environment; one-at-a-time

assignments

3. *How They See Themselves Under Pressure:* Considerate; a good listener; calm; easygoing; a team player; kind

4. *How Others See Them Under Pressure:* Hesitant; detached; unconcerned; inflexible; indecisive; "wishy-washy"

5. *Keys to Motivating — this behavior style wants:* Advance warning before any change; to be a team player; activities to complete or bring to closure; specialized assignments; security within a situation; logical rationale for change

6. *Keys to Managing — this behavior style needs:* Constant inspiration from leader; conditioning and adjustment time prior to any change; warm and friendly work environment; a feeling of belonging; extra support when taking decision-making risks

7. *Areas for Improvement:* Better prioritizing of assignments; learn to take more risks without becoming defensive; recognize tendencies toward passive–aggressive behavior; vocalize inward feelings; keep up their guard since they are "easy marks"

When working with the "S" type:

DO: Take your time; allow them to ask questions; move in a casual, informal manner; start with a brief, personal comment; provide personal assurances; watch out for areas of disagreement

DON'T: Be "pushy" or "hard-nosed"; threaten with position or power; dominate or demand; rush through issues without giving them time to share their thoughts and feelings; suddenly change rules, context or setting; place them in an unpredictable environment

The "S with D" Blend

The Supportive / Dominant type

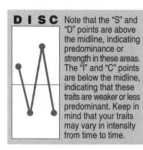

D I S C Note that the "S" and "D" points are above the midline, indicating predominance or strength in these areas. The "I" and "C" points are below the midline, indicating that these traits are weaker or less predominant. Keep in mind that your traits may vary in intensity from time to time.

The **Supportive/Dominant** type tends to be a contradiction in terms. At once, they love people and want to be supportive, yet they are also task-oriented and desire to direct and dominate a project. While they appear reserved, if they are faced with a difficult assignment, they can rise forcefully to the occasion. Although people-oriented, this trait is restrained by their reserved nature. They prefer to be team players, but if forced, they can "go it alone." They are also less likely to doubt or mistrust people, so others sometimes "leave them hanging." They look for the good in life and want you to appreciate them. They tend to analyze problems objectively. Their attitude is one of helpfulness. Rather than being in charge, they prefer to support the out-front leaders. This can actually be its own style of leadership.

As mentioned in the "D/S" blend, people of this type are able to blend dominance with patience and support. For numerous professions, including nursing, this is a valuable characteristic, and no other style does this better than the Supportive/Dominant blend.

According to Target Training research, 3.1% of the population has a blend of Supportive and Dominant traits.

"S/D" Action Plan:

1. *Value to Organization:* A good team member, but under pressure can "got it alone"; objective when challenged; service-oriented; excellent troubleshooter; warm and friendly while remaining job-focused; will follow another person's leadership

2. *Ideal Environment:* A place where performance occurs from hard work rather than from "bursts of energy" or inspiration;

results-oriented atmosphere; opportunity to operate in their own way at their own pace; limited or prepared change in routine; as little conflict as possible

3. *How They See Themselves Under Pressure:* Amiable; deliberate; objective; reflective; analytical; patient

4. *How Others See Them Under Pressure:* Suspicious; unhurried; stubborn; dogged; insensitive; possessive

5. *Keys to Motivating — this behavior style wants:* To be around people who understand how to get the job done; working with ideas that have purpose and meaning, rather than abstract ideas; appreciation; sense of teamwork; feeling of security; activities that don't infringe on family time

6. *Keys to Managing — this behavior style needs:* A manager who is direct yet very sincere; clear instructions followed by freedom to work; a quality product they can believe in; tangible rewards; a "sentimental" environment with family pictures, inspiring quotes, etc.; oversight opportunities

7. *Areas for Improvement:* Frustration over change; suspicion of motives; confront grievances rather than holding them in; fear of new challenges; underestimating their own abilities

When working with the "S/D" type:

DO: Use nonthreatening tone-of-voice; respect their quiet demeanor; provide the facts in logical sequence; use examples to "paint the picture"; know they have a lot of "staying power"

DON'T: Crowd or "invade" their space; interrupt their explanations (i.e., let them finish); talk down to or intimidate them; think that emotion will persuade them; pretend to be an expert if you are not; rush through the agenda

The "S with I" Type Personality

The Supportive / Inspirational type

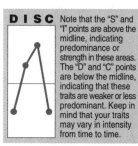

D I S C Note that the "S" and "I" points are above the midline, indicating predominance or strength in these areas. The "D" and "C" points are below the midline, indicating that these traits are weaker or less predominant. Keep in mind that your traits may vary in intensity from time to time.

The **Supportive/Inspirational** type is very warm and friendly. These people can communicate genuine concern for others better than any other personality type. Sometimes their emotions get ahead of their reason, so they are led by their hearts more than their heads. They often allow people to take advantage of them and their good nature. They have a very difficult time saying no, because they generally like everyone they meet and want to please people. Because their task-orientation and task skills are weak, they can find it difficult to focus on a project for lengthy periods.

They do not like conflict at all. So, they must work constantly at being more demanding of themselves, or others will take advantage of them. If facing a "flight or fight" situation, expect them to choose "flight" every time. When painted into a corner, they must not allow themselves to be manipulated by others. They must consciously focus on what is right and wrong, rather than what is popular or what will appease the most people. Their friendly ways and sweet attitude usually enable them to be well-liked (but not necessarily respected) by everyone.

According to Target Training research, 12.1% of the population has a blend of Supportive and Inspirational traits.

"S/I" Action Plan:

1. *Value to Organization:* Likes working for a leader who has a cause; patient, empathic; creative; builds long lasting relationships; good people skills; lighthearted and fun; usually is creative

2. *Ideal Environment:* Little conflict with people; dealing with people on a close, personal basis; stable and predictable

surroundings; participation with a team; an active role in "what's going on"; knowing they are pleasing others

3. *How They See Themselves Under Pressure:* Flexible; good natured; thoughtful; lighthearted; considerate; a team player

4. *How Others See Them Under Pressure:* Hesitant; non-demonstrative; "airheaded" at times; flighty; aloof; distant

5. *Keys to Motivating — this behavior style wants:* Acceptance; co-workers to rely on and trust; appreciation for loyalty and long service; a predictable work environment; projects and plans that come to completion and closure; a feeling of security

6. *Keys to Managing — this behavior style needs:* To know what is expected, and then be allowed to do it; quality product and program to believe in; shortcut methods that don't affect quality; reassurance that they are doing a good job; to be part of a cooperative team effort

7. *Areas for Improvement:* Less frustration over changed plans; see necessary steps to completion when beginning a project; ability to see the bigger picture in their day-to-day work; don't take criticism so personally; realize everyone makes mistakes; view surprises as growth opportunities

When working with the "S/I" type:

DO: Ask "how" questions; show sincere interest in them personally; look for and evaluate areas of frustration; use nonthreatening voice tones; present your case softly; provide personal reassurance

DON'T: Be abrupt or too quick; leave them without backup support; keep deciding for them, or they will lose initiative; let them ramble or get off track; offer guarantees you cannot fulfill; be sarcastic or "blunt" — it hurts their feelings

The "S with C" Blend

The Supportive / Cautious type

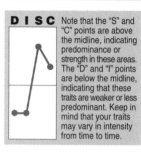

D I S C Note that the "S" and "C" points are above the midline, indicating predominance or strength in these areas. The "D" and "I" points are below the midline, indicating that these traits are weaker or less predominant. Keep in mind that your traits may vary in intensity from time to time.

The **Supportive/Cautious** type is basically reserved in nature. They tend to be more cautious in everything they do. Rather than "jumping right in," they want to make sure everything is safe and correct before they move. They do not like to be put on the spot — they prefer a "wait and see" approach. They can exhibit fear at times, especially if they feel themselves abandoned to make final decisions on major projects by themselves. Others enjoy their company and their kind nature. They can be overly cautious at times, especially when they feel someone is trying to take advantage of them. However, they are usually willing to go a second, third, or fourth mile before they begin to react.

Although they do not make "great starters" when taking on new, unknown projects with additional risks, they do make "great finishers." For an administrator or leader carrying a heavy load, they are the best support personnel that can be found. They are very careful and meticulous in their work.

According to Target Training research, 17.2% of the population has a blend of Supportive and Cautious traits.

"S/C" Action Plan:

1. *Value to Organization:* Service-oriented; enjoys seeing things done correctly; dependable; excellent team player; tends to be consistent; can find agreement between opposing views

2. *Ideal Environment:* Even-tempered workplace with as little conflict and anger as possible; stability, predictability, few surprises; a schedule and practical procedures; assignments completed one at a time; while enjoying tasks, prefers to keep "people needs" ahead of simply getting the job done

3. *How They See Themselves Under Pressure:* Dependable; easygoing; kindhearted; thoughtful; warm; team player

4. *How Others See Them Under Pressure:* Detached; inflexible; insensitive; stubborn; hesitant; holds grudges

5. *Keys to Motivating — this behavior style wants:* Time to adjust to change; written procedures; clear instructions in order to do their job right the first time; reassurance their work is being done correctly; predictable work environment with few surprises; appreciation for loyalty and long service

6. *Keys to Managing — this behavior style needs:* A feeling of belonging to a team; understanding tasks in logical sequence; detailed instructions for complex assignments; support in high risk decisions; ways to avoid feeling pressure when saying no; extra support when pressured for quick results

7. *Areas for Improvement:* Be willing to start projects before having "all the facts"; be more competitive; don't take personal confrontation as personal rejection; take the lead more and make things happen; stop underestimating your own abilities; focus on deadlines to increase productivity

When working with the "S/C" type:

DO: Look for areas of early disagreement or dissatisfaction; show sincere interest in them — be open and honest; use nonthreatening voice tones; be sincere and have an agreeable spirit; provide personal reassurances with clear, specific solutions; take the time to be sure they understood what you said

DON'T: Threaten from your position of power; be domineering or demanding; use personal confrontation or a loud voice; offer guarantees you can't fulfill or promises you cannot keep; be "pushy" with unrealistic deadlines; get into a debate over details concerning facts and figures

The "S with D and I" Blend

The Supportive / Dominant / Inspirational type

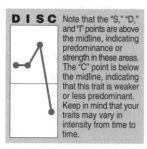

Note that the "S," "D," and "I" points are above the midline, indicating predominance or strength in these areas. The "C" point is below the midline, indicating that this trait is weaker or less predominant. Keep in mind that your traits may vary in intensity from time to time.

The **Supportive/Dominant/ Inspirational** type is mostly people-oriented, with a somewhat reserved demeanor. Although they like being in control of a task, they often feel better in a helper or enabler role. When they must be "out in front," they listen closely, checking to see if their leadership is agreeable to those who are "the led." In other words, the opinions of others play an important role in their point-of-view. While they tend to be mild-mannered and soft-spoken, they can exhibit dynamic skills when called to action. Remember that Superman was a "mild-mannered reporter" as Clark Kent, but when the occasion demanded response, he could "leap tall buildings in a single bound!"

This personality blend may be rare, but it makes for a very effective people. Their ability to stay balanced and keep a good head on their shoulders under stress is an example for all of us.

According to Target Training research, 7.3% of the population has a blend of Supportive, Dominant and Inspirational traits.

"S/D/I" Action Plan:

1. *Value to Organization:* Good with people; can find a "shortcut" or better way; dependable, service-oriented team player; fresh problem-solving ideas and thoughts; possesses a "sixth sense" for making people feel comfortable

2. *Ideal Environment:* A place to create close friendships; does not like a lot of rules; prefers own space (work area and schedule); little conflict with people; prefers others not to be domineering or demanding toward them; a place to think through things without having to respond quickly to objections

3. *How They See Themselves Under Pressure:* Stable; free-spirited;

team player; thoughtful; supportive of others; friendly

4. *How Others See Them Under Pressure:* Opinionated; stubborn; holds feelings within; hides feelings; arbitrary; uninhibited

5. *Keys to Motivating — this behavior style wants:* Opportunities for fun on the job; constant appreciation for good work; "loose" supervision; to be a key player on the team; a stable, nonthreatening work environment; the ability to keep work and family time separated

6. *Keys to Managing — this behavior style needs:* A leader they can respect; clear job parameters; perception of importance and belonging to a team; a little "shove" in taking calculated risks; to relax and pace themselves in stressful situations

7. *Areas for Improvement:* Stop underestimating abilities; write down and stick to priorities; more boldness on issues they care about; speak up when feeling overpowered or intimidated; don't freeze up or become passive or resistant when forced to act quickly; don't hold grudges

When working with the "S/D/I" type:

DO: Use a short-term motivation approach, rather than long term; seek to provide a friendly, cheerful environment; remember that "yes" or "no" answers are better than "maybe"; be prepared to double-check their oversights; seek to be *solution*-conscious, rather than *problem*-conscious

DON'T: Let them paint themselves into a corner; take credit for their accomplishments; let them get sidetracked with their personal problems; do their work for them; put them in a place where there is no backup support; extend yourself by making promises you cannot keep

The "S with D and C" Blend

The Supportive / Dominant / Cautious type

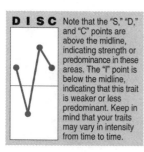

D I S C Note that the "S," "D," and "C" points are above the midline, indicating strength or predominance in these areas. The "I" point is below the midline, indicating that this trait is weaker or less predominant. Keep in mind that your traits may vary in intensity from time to time.

The **Supportive/Dominant/Cautious** type is somewhat reserved and very task-oriented. They strongly consider the needs of people in each project but realize the imperative of completing a job according to plan and schedule. They want things done — and done right! — yet they do not want people to feel "run over" in the process. Their reserved people skills (the "S" traits) dominate, followed by their task-oriented traits ("D" and "C"), while their outgoing people skills (the "I" traits) are inhibited. So, they enjoy people but they are cautious about "invading your space."

This type cannot rest until accomplishing the major project entrusted to them. They want everyone involved to be fully informed of every detail, so no one will feel neglected. Even when this is not possible, people tend to feel that "S/D/C's" really do have their best interests in mind.

According to Target Training research, 6.4% of the population has a blend of Supportive, Dominant and Cautious traits.

"S/D/C" Action Plan:

1. *Value to Organization:* Service oriented; is a dependable team player; tends to be extremely conscientious; adds a sense of stability to the organization; is an excellent troubleshooter; likes to be an active participant, feeling that what they do matters

2. *Ideal Environment:* Prefers to deal with people in a long-standing relationship; needs personal attention from the boss or manager; prefers an environment where they can be part of a team; dislikes conflict between people; needs to be involved in projects that produce tangible results

3. *How They See Themselves Under Pressure:* Logical; good listener; persistent; practical; objective; persevering

4. *How Others See Them Under Pressure:* Superior; moody; resistant to change; possessive; stubborn; introverted

5. *Keys to Motivating — this behavior style wants:* Identification with fellow workers; an environment where they can ask specific questions; facts for making decisions; a feeling of stability and security as a team member; to be a member of a smaller team, rather than a larger one

6. *Keys to Managing — this behavior style needs:* A little more time to warm up to people; a program to encourage self-worth and creativity; a supervisor who will delegate in detail; capable associates with whom they can work; a sense of belonging; time to adjust prior to actual change

7. *Areas for Improvement:* Don't take criticism of work as a personal attack; has a tendency to underestimate their own abilities; needs help in prioritizing new assignments; don't be resistive or indecisive when forced to act quickly; work harder and stay more focused on meeting deadlines

When working with the "S/D/C" type:

DO: Provide a friendly environment; be patient yet persistent when deadlines are required; respect their quiet demeanor; when possible, provide guarantees that their decisions will minimize risks; present your case softly; use sincere, nonthreatening voice tones

DON'T: Be superficial in your professional relationship; talk down to them in a condescending manner; rush through your agenda too quickly; be abrupt or make decisions too quickly without explanation; think that quantity is more important to them than quality

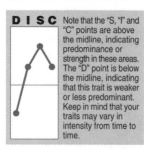
The "S with I and C" Blend

The Supportive / Inspirational / Cautious type

D I S C Note that the "S, "I" and "C" points are above the midline, indicating predominance or strength in these areas. The "D" point is below the midline, indicating that this trait is weaker or less predominant. Keep in mind that your traits may vary in intensity from time to time.

The **Supportive/Inspirational/ Cautious** type is primarily focused on people, but they also like to complete tasks. They want to ensure an orderly environment. People take priority in their undertakings, however they keep the task and goal in sharp focus. They usually make others feel included when working on a group project, and their team approach is advantageous since every part working together produces the best results. A good motto for them would be: "Working together... we can do it!" Their "I" strengths help them to inspire, while their "C" traits appreciate attention to detail.

Because their dominance ("D") factor is low, they can sometimes be talked into doing things they don't want to do. This is not because they are weak-willed, but because they do not like conflict. Rather than create conflict or stress in a group, they will let others have their own way. But when pushed to their limit, their "C" trait of self-preservation can assert itself boldly and firmly.

According to Target Training research, 28.5% of the population has a blend of Supportive, Inspirational and Cautious traits.

"S/I/C" Action Plan:

1. *Value to Organization:* Knows how to turn confrontation into a positive situation; has respect for the organization structure; is concerned about quality; is service-oriented; shows respect for authority; is willing to gather data for decision-making process

2. *Ideal Environment:* A friendly workplace where people seldom get angry with each other; an environment that allows time to make adjustments and changes; jobs that have established

standards and methods; a stable and predictable environment; procedures that make sense

3. *How They See Themselves Under Pressure:* Accepting; compassionate; considerate, likable; cooperative; modest

4. *How Others See Them Under Pressure:* Hesitant; unsure; cautious; haphazard; fearful; stubborn

5. *Keys to Motivating — this behavior style wants:* A leader who sets a good example; complete, clear direction for work to be completed; to be persuaded by both logic and emotion; a team that understands their reasons for not wanting to argue (i.e., personality style); freedom from confrontation

6. *Keys to Managing — this behavior style needs:* To be more objective and less subjective, more direct and less indirect; a quality product in which they can believe; simplified methods that won't affect the quality of their work; to be on a friendly basis with other employees; tangible rewards for good work

7. *Areas for Improvement:* Take action to make things happen; be willing to jump into a new project rather than remaining with only that which is known; exert a little more independence; be less defensive and more proactive; give up passive-aggressive behavior

When working with the "S/I/C" type:

DO: Use voice tones that show sincerity; present your case softly; take the time to be sure they are in agreement in order to have clear communication; expect them to have hurt feelings if you disagree; ask for a commitment of cooperation when establishing new procedures

DON'T: Try to intimidate them by means of loud personal confrontation; threaten them with your position of power; be domineering or demanding; speak down to them in a condescending manner; make their decisions for them, or they will lose initiative

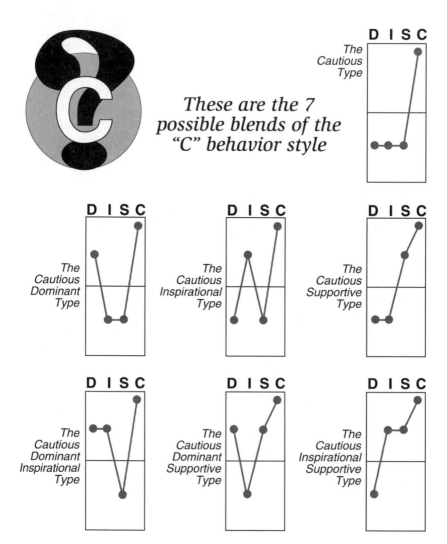

These are the 7 possible blends of the "C" behavior style

D I S C
The
Cautious
Type

D I S C
The
Cautious
Dominant
Type

D I S C
The
Cautious
Inspirational
Type

D I S C
The
Cautious
Supportive
Type

D I S C
The
Cautious
Dominant
Inspirational
Type

D I S C
The
Cautious
Dominant
Supportive
Type

D I S C
The
Cautious
Inspirational
Supportive
Type

Appendix E

Understanding the Seven "C" Blends

The seven possible blends involving predominate "C" traits are shown at the left — and in this chapter, two pages are devoted to explaining each of these blends.

Because the goal of this information is to help you understand yourself and others, it makes sense to start by first understanding your own blend. Look at your "educated guess" graph, which you completed on page 24. See whether your "D," your "I," your "S," or your "C" has the highest plotting point. Then you will know which of these four chapters to check for information on your style. Next, look to see if any of the other three plotting points are also above the midline on your "basic" graph. This will tell you which blend to read about.

You may want to complete a Personality Insights *"Style Analysis"* to get an accurate, objective appraisal. An order form with a special discount may be found in the back of this book. Thousands of our readers and customers have completed this assessment. It is not a test — there are no right or wrong answers. It is simply a tool to help you better understand yourself... and others.

Note: When we refer to an "C with S" blend, it is not the same as an "S with C" blend. Similarly, a "D with I" blend is not the same as an "I with D" blend. For the sake of explanation, we will refer to a blend that is primarily "C" with two secondary traits of "S" and "D" as a "C with D and S"— regardless of whether the "D" is higher than the "S," or the "S" is higher than the "D." As you read the description of your own blend, the strength and influence of your secondary traits will probably relate closely to their position on your graph.

The "C" Type Personality

The Cautious type

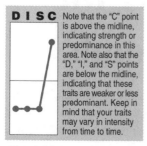

D I S C Note that the "C" point is above the midline, indicating strength or predominance in this area. Note also that the "D," "I," and "S" points are below the midline, indicating that these traits are weaker or less predominant. Keep in mind that your traits may vary in intensity from time to time.

The **Cautious** type is reserved and task-oriented. They are extremely focused people, usually possessing a high degree of intelligence, capable of doing almost anything. They are very analytical in nature and exacting in performance. It has been humorously noted that they "proofread Xerox® copies!" Their precise nature demands that they do everything in their power to achieve perfection. They have a strong desire for quality work. Their standards are incredibly high, and they fully expect everyone to embrace and meet this level of performance. They get frustrated with those who do not follow directions or do not do what they are supposed to do.

In growing up, they always tried to color "inside the lines." They like knowing exactly what rules and guidelines are to be followed at all times. Because they are very logical, they are motivated most by projects that allow them to use their best thinking skills.

According to Target Training research, 0.3% of the population has a Cautious-only style.

"C" Action Plan:

1. *Value to Organization:* Very comprehensive problem-solver; conscientious and steady; always concerned about quality work; deadline conscious; tends to be "an anchor of reality"

2. *Ideal Environment:* New products to work on or improve; a familiar work environment with a predictable pattern; close relationships with a small group of associates; an environment dedicated to logic rather than emotion; predictable patterns of routine work

3. *How They See Themselves Under Pressure:* Conservative; logical; alert; conscientious; precise; thorough

4. *How Others See Them Under Pressure:* Pessimistic; picky; fussy; hard to please; defensive; strict

5. *Keys to Motivating — this behavior style wants:* Explicitly written procedures; reassurances that they are doing the job correctly; a manager who follows rules and policies; to be part of a quality-oriented work group; precise planning that requires few organizational changes; logical arguments

6. *Keys to Managing — this behavior style needs:* To know exactly what is expected; to be involved in projects requiring precision planning and organization; to work for a boss who will be available to discuss key motives; to be given helpful suggestions in time of stress

7. *Areas for Improvement:* May tend to be negative or pessimistic about a new project until it is clear in their own minds; prefers "things" to people — needs to "warm up" more toward people; sometimes should be more willing to yield their position in order to avoid controversy; demands full explanations before any changes are made; can be defensive when errors or work mistakes are pointed out

When working with the "C" type:

DO: Stick to business; be specific — leave nothing to chance; provide solid evidence; support their principles using a thought-out approach; build your credibility by listing pros and cons to any suggestions you make; give them time to be thorough

DON'T: Be disorganized or messy; use someone's opinion as evidence; rush the decision-making process; let them bog you down in too much detail for too long; let them change your topic or focus of concern until you are sure they understand your view; waste their time

The "C with D" Blend

The Cautious / Dominant type

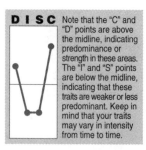

D I S C Note that the "C" and "D" points are above the midline, indicating predominance or strength in these areas. The "I" and "S" points are below the midline, indicating that these traits are weaker or less predominant. Keep in mind that your traits may vary in intensity from time to time.

The **Cautious/Dominant** type personality style is very task-oriented. For these people, the most important thing in life is completing a job with accuracy and precision. They sometimes care more about completing a task that what any one person might think or feel about it. And since their people-oriented skills are below the midline, these skills need purposeful attention and development. They tend to pay more attention to "things" than to people. They are not antisocial — they really do like people — but it is more difficult for them to express those feelings.

They do not realize it, but because of these frailties, they often come across to others as cold and uncaring. Even though they may have the right solution, others may overlook them, perceiving them as a "know-it-all." Simply "warming up" a little would bring them more positive feedback.

According to Target Training research, 2.6% of the population has a blend of Cautious and Dominant traits.

"C/D" Action Plan:

1. *Value to Organization:* Is very tough-minded — knows how to make decisions based on facts, not feelings; is objective and realistic; knows how to present facts without emotions; always looking for logical solutions; has an intuitive nature, sensing what is wrong and needs to be corrected

2. *Ideal Environment:* Projects producing tangible results; a place with very little clutter and standardized operating procedures; where they can use their intuitive thinking skills; data to analyze; their own workspace or office

3. *How They See Themselves Under Pressure:* Diplomatic;

knowledgeable; analytical; accurate; systematic; neat

4. *How Others See Them Under Pressure:* Unfriendly; obstinate; stubborn; strong-willed; independent; self-righteous

5. *Keys to Motivating — this behavior style wants:* Information in some type of logical order; to prove they can get the job done without a lot of supervision; time to perform up to their high standards of perfection; specific answers to specific questions; objectivity, not subjectivity

6. *Keys to Managing — this behavior style needs:* To "soften their edge" and not be so blunt; a manager who prefers quality over quantity; to appreciate the feelings of others; to be able to "sell" their ideas, not just "tell" them; to be a little more flexible when plans change suddenly

7. *Areas for Improvement:* May have a low level of trust in other people; be willing to explain instructions more than once to others without expressing frustration; sometimes thinks their own work is all that matters — but other people matter, too; sometimes hesitant to act without precedent

When working with the "C/D" type:

DO: Show them a sincere demeanor when you listen to them; pay careful attention to their point-of-view; be prepared with your facts and figures; approach them in a straightforward, direct manner; present your viewpoint in a friendly, nonthreatening manner; stick to business

DON'T: Make statements you cannot prove; talk down to them or be redundant; use "slick" gimmicks or quick manipulation techniques; fail to follow through on any commitments expected; expect them to be warm or friendly — they are task-oriented, not people-oriented

The "C with I" Blend

The Cautious / Inspirational type

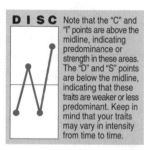

D I S C Note that the "C" and "I" points are above the midline, indicating predominance or strength in these areas. The "D" and "S" points are below the midline, indicating that these traits are weaker or less predominant. Keep in mind that your traits may vary in intensity from time to time.

The **Cautious/Inspirational** type is cautious by nature, but also has moments of inspiration and support for others. They usually try to find better procedures for the projects they are working on. They can be critical or impatient when things are disorganized. They enjoy being with other people, but generally prefer a predictable environment. They maintain a "distance" by sharing an activity, rather than sharing themselves. Their mental acuity allows them to succeed in a variety of endeavors, and their people skills help them build bridges in the process. They think before they speak, then can say it with clarity and inspiring enthusiasm.

Like the "D/S" blend, this style is composed of opposite traits. It can be a dynamic style when it is understood and mastered. For example, a "C/I" physician is able to display strong diagnostic skills while understanding the value of personal attention and concern.

According to Target Training research, 2.1% of the population has a blend of Cautious and Inspirational traits.

"C/I" Action Plan:

1. *Value to Organization:* Has the ability to handle many activities; likes accomplishment, but can handle spontaneity in the midst of getting a job done; is a good problem-solver; is a good thinker and usually communicates well

2. *Ideal Environment:* Opportunities to use their intuitive thinking skills; new products or new ideas to work on; a familiar work environment; freedom from long, detailed reports

3. *How They See Themselves Under Pressure:* Moderate; diplomatic; tactful; conventional; balanced; open-minded

4. *How Others See Them Under Pressure:* Independent; unsystematic; perfectionist; worrisome; hard to please; defensive

5. *Keys to Motivating — this behavior style wants:* Reassurance that they are doing the job correctly; advancement when they are ready; a leader to follow who sets a good example; to be part of a quality-oriented work group; time to perform up to their own high standards

6. *Keys to Managing — this behavior style needs:* Performance appraisals on a regular basis; encouragement to be more of a risk taker; time to test the plan to see if it will work; complete instructions on their work assignments; deadlines for completion of work

7. *Areas for Improvement:* Sometimes bound by procedures and methods if they have followed them for some time; may get in a rut to protect their position; prefers not to verbalize emotions and feelings; does not like to be in a competitive environment; may lean on supervisor too much for help; if the direction is not clear, may feel defeated and quit

When working with the "C/I" type:

DO: Be open and honest, yet informal; understand their sporadic listening skills; provide time for fun; use a thoughtful approach to enhance your credibility; give them time to verify your actions — be accurate and realistic; provide systems to follow

DON'T: Leave things to chance or to luck; forget to follow through — accountability is important; fail to give them recognition for work well done; put them on the spot — give them notice when something different is about to occur; embarrass them or confront them publicly

The "C with S" Blend

The Cautious / Supportive type

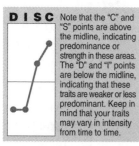

D I S C Note that the "C" and "S" points are above the midline, indicating predominance or strength in these areas. The "D" and "I" points are below the midline, indicating that these traits are weaker or less predominant. Keep in mind that your traits may vary in intensity from time to time.

The **Cautious/Supportive** type is reserved and careful. They enjoy working on projects one-at-a-time. They believe in doing things right the first time, that if they keep working on things every day, their lives will improve. They want the world to be a better place because they have lived here. They like people, but prefer a few close friends to a crowd. They do not like taking risks or trying new things — they prefer experience to initiative! They rely heavily on their own strong, cognitive processes, so they often see through a situation faster than anyone else.

Because their "C" predominates, they are correct much of the time. They do not handle criticism well, because they expect to be on target all of the time. Their strong "S" makes them even more sensitive to self-criticism or feelings of rejection when they don't meet their own high standards. They would rather work behind the scenes than stand before the crowd, where imperfection might bring disrepute. They enjoy opportunities to revere others and especially enjoy doing things correctly.

According to Target Training research, 17.2% of the population has a blend of Cautious and Supportive traits.

"C/S" Action Plan:

1. *Value to Organization:* Takes the time to gather data when a decision must be made; able to define and clarify objectives; adaptable to different situations; always concerned about the quality of their work; constantly seeks to avoid errors

2. *Ideal Environment:* Where assignments can be followed through to completion; where they can use intuitive thinking skills; a job with established standards; where they do not have to show

emotions; prefers to specialize in one area

3. *How They See Themselves Under Pressure:* Knowledgeable; patient; consistent; stable; diplomatic

4. *How Others See Them Under Pressure:* Perfectionist; strict; defensive; worrisome; arbitrary; unbending

5. *Keys to Motivating — this behavior style wants:* Time to adjust when changes occur; possible operational procedures or plans to be put in writing; to be part of a quality-oriented work team; better planning with fewer changes in the organization; quality work with the perception of value

6. *Keys to Managing — this behavior style needs:* To be able to speak up when they know they are right; alternative methods that won't affect the quality of their work; a way to say "no" when necessary; to be encouraged to be more independent; an exact job description and title

7. *Areas for Improvement:* May be overly sensitive to criticism of their work; sometimes too intense for their own good; self-deprecating when it is not necessary; doesn't project self-confidence; can be so objective that they leave no room for subjective thoughts or ideas

When working with the "C/S" type:

DO: Give them time to review the reliability of your actions; use voice tones that show sincerity and appreciation; reassure them with clear communication concerning facts and data; use a timetable when implementing new actions; avoid surprises; provide unhurried time to ask questions

DON'T: Talk or discuss issues when you are angry; confront them over an issue in front of others; say "trust me" without giving them one or two reasons why; threaten or belittle them; let their lack of confidence lead you to believe they are incapable of good work

The "C with D and I" Blend

The Cautious / Dominant / Inspirational type

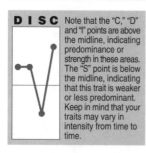

D I S C Note that the "C," "D" and "I" points are above the midline, indicating predominance or strength in these areas. The "S" point is below the midline, indicating that this trait is weaker or less predominant. Keep in mind that your traits may vary in intensity from time to time.

The **Cautious/Dominant/ Inspirational** type is composed of people who are competent to complete almost any task. Their desire and drive for excellence makes their work consistently outstanding. They are sociable, and tend to be quick, positive, and systematic in most endeavors. They usually have good verbal skills and can sell an idea with clarity if their presentation doesn't get hung up in details. They desire achievement with quality. They are not overly concerned with security, but with getting the job done correctly and looking good in the process.

If projects are not moving along in a proper, timely manner, they may become annoyed and irritable. Lack of control frustrates them. Because of their blended style, they have perfectionist tendencies, using persuasion and optimism as key methods to see their projects through to completion.

According to Target Training research, 3.5% of the population has a blend of Cautious, Dominant and Inspirational traits.

"C/D/I" Action Plan:

1. *Value to Organization:* Creates a sense of urgency; able to handle many activities; always concerned about quality work; proficient and skilled in their technical specialty; able to get results and complete the task with high quality standards; competent — can understand all the facts

2. *Ideal Environment:* Where efficiency is of utmost importance; where actions are more important than words; opportunities to develop better ways of doing things; freedom from reports that have no point or value; a team approach with strong support; where people are judged by the quality of their work

3. *How They See Themselves Under Pressure:* Active; pressure-oriented; alert; energetic; dependable; witty

4. *How Others See Them Under Pressure:* Intense; hasty; restless; hyperactive; disinterested; impulsive

5. *Keys to Motivating — this behavior style wants:* A time frame, in order to perform up to their own high standards; a lot of activity so there are no dull moments; more time in their day; recognition for quality work; an environment where quality control can be achieved

6. *Keys to Managing — this behavior style needs:* To be more tolerant of slower-thinking people; regular performance-evaluation approach to measure their work; deadlines to help in the completion of work; reduced activity levels; to work with other task-oriented people who are results-oriented

7. *Areas for Improvement:* Improve on sensitivity, softness; be more approachable; demonstrate willingness to let others share their thoughts and opinions; develop more flexibility

When working with the "C/D/I" type:

DO: Give them time to be thorough; provide solid, tangible evidence; be specific and clear — do not assume things; show them that you want to make a contribution to their efforts; follow through and do what you say you will do; give them the opportunity to solve a company problem

DON'T: Make conflicting statements to them; make belittling statements regarding the quality of their work; force them to make a quick decision with no backup plan; frustrate them with established rules no one keeps; expect them to be creative — they prefer an established system

The "C with D and S" Blend

The Cautious / Dominant / Supportive type

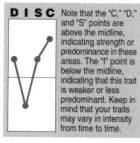

DISC Note that the "C," "D," and "S" points are above the midline, indicating strength or predominance in these areas. The "I" point is below the midline, indicating that this trait is weaker or less predominant. Keep in mind that your traits may vary in intensity from time to time.

The **Cautious/Dominant/ Supportive** type is factual and reliable, completing work with precision and accuracy. They are extremely well-focused — if they are working on a job, check it off your list! "Detail-itis" can get in their way because they know "there is always room for improvement." They generally avoid unnecessary risk or trouble. They know that shortcuts are costly in the long run, so they stick to their high standards. Their reward is threefold: their "C" traits thrive in knowing that they were correct regarding a project, responsibility or activity; their "S" traits flourish on appreciation; and their "D" traits value the achievement of desired results.

These people prefer to work through small groups rather than before large crowds. When they appear to be insensitive, it is because they are focusing completely on the task at hand. They are careful and consistent, but sometimes their analytical nature turns others off.

According to Target Training research, 6.4% of the population has a blend of Cautious, Dominant and Supportive traits.

"C/D/S" Action Plan:

1. *Value to Organization:* Extremely comprehensive when it comes to solving problems; always looking for a better way to do things; logical and objective, yet realistic; knows how to maintain high standards; aggressive for the job, yet sensitive to those with whom they work

2. *Ideal Environment:* Performing technical work; specializing in one area; opportunities to make decisions that produce long lasting results; likes to analyze data; seeks job security

3. *How They See Themselves Under Pressure:* Factual; accurate; incisive; a good listener; correct

4. *How Others See Them Under Pressure:* A know-it-all; superior; pessimistic; blunt; harsh; critical

5. *Keys to Motivating — this behavior style wants:* Limited exposure to new, untested procedures; clearly thought-out objectives; information presented in logical order; clear reasons for doing what they are doing; to have a title and job description that explains what they do

6. *Keys to Managing — this behavior style needs:* To remember that just because they "see" it doesn't mean that everyone else does; a workspace in which they can accomplish their duties; logical answers; clear feedback that provides direction; time to reflect and plan new strategies

7. *Areas for Improvement:* Needs to smile a little more; should be willing to take a public speaking course; should read *How to Win Friends and Influence People;* lighten up and not be overly intense; be more willing to let people show emotions without feeling defensive

When working with the "C/D/S" type:

DO: Use facts and figures when making plans; quote experts in the field who can provide solid data; develop a timetable on which you both can agree for completing projects; use appropriate words that do not carry sarcastic overtones; provide details in writing; provide practical evidence based on accurate documentation

DON'T: Push too hard with unrealistic deadlines; leave things open-ended that could cause misunderstanding; be shallow or superficial; talk to them in an immature manner; expect them to be overly outgoing or very friendly; put them in a "public relations" role with a large group — they will be better one-on-one

The "C with I and S" Blend

The Cautious / Inspirational / Supportive type

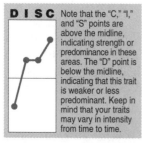

D I S C Note that the "C," "I," and "S" points are above the midline, indicating strength or predominance in these areas. The "D" point is below the midline, indicating that this trait is weaker or less predominant. Keep in mind that your traits may vary in intensity from time to time.

The **Cautious/Inspirational/Supportive** type enjoys other people a lot. They like to do things *correctly* (a "C" trait), but part of their motivation is the opportunity to *impress* others in the process (an "I" trait). They know how to *stabilize* a situation (an "S" trait). They prefer one project at a time, their work reflecting their dedication to quality. They do not like hostility or antagonism, preferring harmony and goodwill among co-workers. They try to be cooperative and modest. They are sociable and will modify their position to achieve their goals. They prefer not to have their environment changed too suddenly. They can be very sensitive to what others think about them personally, as well as what people think about the quality of their work.

Their strong traits cause them to seek many patient, logical explanations and sincere approval. In a crisis, they will try to figure their safest way out without conflict. They are responsible, cordial, and sincere, making excellent team members.

According to Target Training research, 28.5% of the population has a blend of Cautious, Inspirational and Supportive traits.

"C/I/S" Action Plan:

1. *Value to Organization:* Knows how to turn negative confrontations into positive benefits; has a keen ability to solve problems; is flexible and adaptable; has a respect for co-workers as well as the overall organization; likes to work *through* people rather than *around* them

2. *Ideal Environment:* Where friends can be together; opportunities to complete one project at a time; practical work procedures that have predictable outcomes; where creative thinking can be

implemented; jobs with established methods that produce practical results

3. *How They See Themselves Under Pressure:* Cooperative; modest; congenial; adaptable; likeable

4. *How Others See Them Under Pressure:* Hesitant; fearful; intimidated; compliant; unsure; wary

5. *Keys to Motivating — this behavior style wants:* A workplace where there is peace and harmony; to set a good example others can admire; to be accepted as an important part of the team; to be in a support role that helps things go more smoothly; people who understand their reasons for not wanting to argue; freedom from conflict and confrontation

6. *Keys to Managing — this behavior style needs:* To be given assistance with new or difficult assignments; to have more confidence in their ability to perform new activities; support when making high-risk decisions; little pressure to perform quickly; tangible work with tangible results

7. *Areas for Improvement:* To learn to see the end of a project before beginning; to tell how they feel without showing frustration; more flexibility in their work patterns; to pace themselves better when deadlines are included; not to blame others for their lack of self-control

When working with the "C/I/S" type:

DO: Look at both sides of an issue to show them your concern; be accurate and realistic; give them time to "chew" on your suggestions; if you disagree, help them to see that it is with a specific point — not with the whole plan; give them support for their principles

DON'T: Talk down to or belittle them; promise one thing and do another; embarrass or confront them in front of others; let them "dig a hole" for themselves with unrealistic deadlines; cut their budget without showing them why

These are the 3 possible blends of the "Level" behavior style

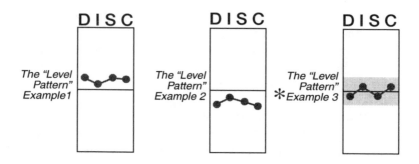

*In the level pattern (example 3) all four of the plotting points are located close to the midline. The graph looks like the example shown above or some variation of that type. In other words, all four plotting points are located close to the midline or fall within the "average" range (gray area shown in sample 3)

Appendix F

Understanding the "Even" or "Level" Pattern

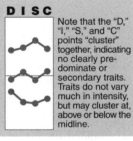

D I S C

Note that the "D," "I," "S," and "C" points "cluster" together, indicating no clearly pre-dominate or secondary traits. Traits do not vary much in intensity, but may cluster at, above or below the midline.

It is not "wrong" to have a graph that shows *all four* D-I-S-C plotting points falling fairly close to the midline. We have met many people who demonstrate this style. Such a style would be similar in appearance to one of three graphs, as illustrated on page 320, opposite.

First, all four plotting points could be slightly *above* the midline, in the "average" area. There are no "spikes" in such a graph that indicate one clearly predominating trait. The D-I-S-C plotting points are grouped closely together, so there are no clearly identifiable secondary or supporting traits, either.

Second, all four plotting points could be slightly *below* the midline, again in the average area. There are no "spikes" to indicate one clearly predominating behavior style. The D-I-S-C plotting points are grouped closely together, so no secondary or supporting traits are clearly identified.

Third, the plotting points could gather near the midline, *above* and *below*, but still within the average range. Again, there are no plotting points that stand out above or below the midline, indicating a particular abundance or lack in any style.

WHO DO YOU THINK YOU ARE ANYWAY?

This simply indicates that the individual who completed the *Style Analysis* questionnaire did not express a particular tendency either way regarding any of the four traits.

For example, if the "D" (dominant) trait plots close to the midline, then you can understand that the person is neither "strong" nor "weak" in the "D" traits — but simply "average." (Of course, this would be true of *any* "D," "I," "S," or "C" traits with plotting points falling close to the midline on *anyone's* graph!)

The "good news" is that people who have such profiles are very flexible — they can adjust and go in either direction in almost any set of circumstances. It may be easier to "raise" or "lower" a particular trait from the midline area than from an "extreme" position of high or low.

The "bad news" is that people who have this type of profile may not have much "zeal" or passion for any one particular behavior style. Of all the personality types, they are the most difficult to motivate. They may feel a little "vanilla" at times. Taking a proactive role in "adjusting" our behaviors requires more than just "fitting in" or not "sticking out." It requires actively *"adapting"* — and that may require additional desire or effort.

By not having a predominate ("strong") trait, nor any supporting traits, nor any less predominate ("weak") traits, such individuals may be seen as a unique "average" of all traits. As our little circle symbol suggests at the top of the page, their behaviors tend to move away from "making a statement" about them — they move toward the center. Without a "leading" trait to guide their course through life, they can lack direction.

In our seminars we say that our "strengths" *carry* us and our "weaknesses" *concern* us. How can we identify strengths and weaknesses in a graph that expresses little in the way of *performance* (your Environment style) or *preference* (your Basic style)? We can gather clues as we consider a few factors:

We may be trying too hard to be "all things to all people"
We might seem "steady" in life but lack focus or zeal in a particular area, or in life in general

We may want too many people to like us, and so we may have "given up ground" in our own behavioral style in our attempt to please others
We may have experienced life-changing stresses and simply need time to refocus, re-energize and adjust.

In statistical validity studies conducted by Wheaton College, Target Training reported that of almost 3,000 participants, only 36 people had all four plotting points *above the midline* in Graph I, their *Environment Style;* and 24 people had all four plotting points *above the midline* in Graph II, their *Basic Style.* No participants in that study had all four plotting points *below* the midline on either graph.

Statistics can be manipulated to "prove" almost anything, but it is interesting to note that fifty percent *more* people identified their *Environmental* behaviors as fitting into this pattern than those who said their *Basic* behaviors fit this pattern. In other words, our own behaviors can be heavily influenced by the roles we play at home, at work, or in our social interactions. Again, however, the percentages within the general population are very small.

Here are several suggestions that can help you to confirm your behavior style if your graphs indicate this "level pattern" of behavior:

1. To determine if this pattern is due to a temporary situation in your life, wait for several days and then complete another assessment questionnaire

2. Ask one or two close friends to complete an assessment questionnaire on your behalf, making selections as if they were you — this will assist you in seeing how others perceive your behavioral style

3. Complete another questionnaire, this time with a specific focus in mind, such as your occupation, married life, parental role, etc. — you may see a more defined style in that particular area of your life.

One woman we know completed a *Style Analysis* that revealed a very level pattern, while those who had observed her in the previous year, she and her husband had lost their home and their family business, they had moved in with her parents, she had taken care of her father as he died of cancer and was responsible for a household that included four generations. She had become "lost" amid the demands on her time and limited resources — and her own identity had taken a back seat to everyone else. Several months later, after a period of adjustment and gaining understanding, her "true" graphs revealed considerably higher "D," "I," and "C" traits. Her "S" did not remain at the same plotting point, either — it plummeted to the bottom! A good part of her stress in trying to please and serve everyone was caused by her straining to deny her own behaviors and meet everyone else's needs and demands. She had "buried" her strong "D," "I," and "C" traits and "manufactured" her nonexistent "S" traits for a period of time — she had adopted such a pattern of behavior for her own emotional survival.

At any rate, please understand that there is nothing "wrong" with an "Even" or "Level" style that *truly* represents who you are. It is not "good" or "bad" — it is just different. It is simply how things are perceived for the 1% of our population that has this particular style.

Perhaps people who make up this group are able to see life with fewer of the biases and prejudices that come from being "wired" with more predominate, identifiable patterns.

You may be wondering if this style is more perfectly balanced — is it the ideal style? Our view is that this is a "category mistake" type of question. It is like asking, "How does blue *taste?*" This style has no "dips" or peaks, and it may fit in comfortably with a large variety of people. But it is not a style you "strive" for — no style is preferred if it does not utilize the strengths of your personal character and integrity traits while encouraging you to gain a greater vision in your "blind spots."

As it is with any of the other behavioral styles, people with this style can adapt and adjust in order to achieve any level of success they desire. They must be careful not to accept mediocrity but seek to become everything they can be.

MORE HELP FROM PERSONALITY INSIGHTS

This is Dr. Rohm's introductory book on personality styles! Filled with anecdotes, practical examples and motivational techniques for parents, teachers and counselors. Featured on the Cornerstone Television Network and The 700 Club. Includes a biblical rationale for the question, "Is D-I-S-C Scriptural?" Almost 100,000 copies of *Positive Personality Profiles* in print.

Price **$12.95**

Dr. Rohm collaborated on this book with Charles F. Boyd and David Boehi. Its theme is "the Art of Adjustable Parenting and Teaching," demonstrating how to discover each child's motivations and how to tailor your parenting style to meet each child's needs, using the D-I-S-C system.

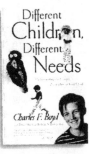

Price **$12.95**

Discover why 200 teachers say, "My students are my best teachers!" Real-life classroom events in short story form, seen through an understanding of personality styles. Compiled by Dr. Rohm from essays of school teachers and administrators who use the D-I-S-C system in the classroom. Excellent for case studies and in-service training.

Price **$12.95**

Self-scoring **Style Assessment** booklets contain the Questionnaire, Basic and Environmental charts and background information. Child and Teen profiles include a companion cassette tape.
Price **$10.00**

 *Adult Profile*    *Teen Profile*

Child Profile

Dr. Rohm presents this three-hour **Video Seminar** with energy and excitement before a "live" studio audience of business owners. Audience involvement makes you feel like you're there! Three hours of fast-paced, fun instruction. (Produced in association with InterNET Services Corporation. 2-tape video album available in VHS format only.)
Price **$30.00**

Dr. Rohm's three-hour *Video Seminar (above)* sound track on three quality audio cassettes! Includes an "Introduction to the Model of Human Behavior," the "D," "I," "S," and "C" types, and "Understanding Personality Blends." Great stories supplement the technical material. Now includes a pocket-size version of the **Funbook** so you can follow along. Listen while you drive, jog, work out, or rake the yard so your neighbors will like you (if you don't "get it," you haven't heard the seminar yet!).
Price **$20.00**

This is like attending the complete "Understanding Yourself and Others" Seminar again and again. You receive two video tapes (above), six cassette tapes (the seminar soundtrack) for use in your car, plus four FUNBOOKS (which Dr. Rohm uses with the studio audience), one Case Studies booklet, and four Self-Scoring Questionnaires. Ideal for small groups. Additional supplies are available in our catalog.
Price **$89.00**

Please call or write to request our complete catalog.
PERSONALITY INSIGHTS, INC.
P.O. Box 28592 • Atlanta, GA 30358 USA • (770) 509-7113

ORDER FORM • ORDER FORM • ORDER FORM

your name — **please print legibly!**   company name

your mailing address — street or post office box

your city, state, zip code   telephone number

credit card number (if charging purchase)   expiration date   name on card

Quantity	Description	Unit Price	Total
		(Prices subject to changes)	
BOOKS			
_____	Positive Personality Profiles	12.95	_____
_____	Different Children Different Needs	12.95	_____
_____	Tales Out of School	12.95	_____
_____	Who Do You Think You Are Anyway?	14.95	_____
SELF-SCORING PROFILES			
_____	Self-Scoring Adult Profile	10.00	_____
_____	Self-Scoring Teen Profile	10.00	_____
_____	Self-Scoring Child Profile	10.00	_____
AUDIO-VISUAL HELPS			
_____	3-Hour Video Series (2 video tapes)	30.00	_____
_____	3-Hour Audio Seminar (3 cassette tapes)	20.00	_____
_____	Complete Video Seminar Album	89.00	_____
	(with 2 videos, 6 cassette tapes, 4 Funbooks,		
	1 Case Studies booklet, 4 Self-Score Questionnaires)		
		SUBTOTAL $ _____	

GEORGIA RESIDENTS ADD 5% .... $ _____
ADD 10% OF SUBTOTAL FOR SHIPPING AND HANDLING .... $ _____

TOTAL BY CHECK OR CREDIT CARD .... *$* _____

If you are paying by check, please make payable in U.S. funds to:
PERSONALITY INSIGHTS
P.O. Box 28592 • Atlanta, GA 30358 • 770-509-7113 • Fax 770-509-1484
or visit our website at http://personality-insights.com
PLEASE REQUEST OUR LATEST CATALOG OF HELPFUL PRODUCTS